the new age of
innovation

the new age of
innovation

DRIVING COCREATED VALUE
THROUGH GLOBAL NETWORKS

C.K. PRAHALAD
M.S. KRISHNAN

McGraw Hill

New York   Chicago   San Francisco
Lisbon   London   Madrid   Mexico City   Milan
New Delhi   San Juan   Seoul   Singapore
Sydney   Toronto

2 3 4 5 6 7 8 9 0   DOC/DOC   0 9 8

MHID   0-07-159828-6
ISBN 978-0-07-159828-6

Design by Lee Fukui and Mauna Eichner

CONTENTS

ACKNOWLEDGMENTS

No research of this magnitude is possible without the active support of a wide variety of scholars and practitioners. They shared with us their insights and allowed us to explore the operations of their firms. As we started to consolidate our findings, we were fortunate to have more than our fair share of academics and practitioners who were willing to review early drafts of the chapters and the book and offer very constructive criticism for improvement.

The following people gave us detailed feedback: Ron Bendersky (Ross School of Business, The University of Michigan); P. V. Kannan (24/7 Customer); Mel Walter (NCR Corporation, formerly National Cash Register Company); Professor Venkat Ramaswamy (Ross School of Business, University of Michigan); Professor Dennis Severance (Ross School of Business, University of Michigan); M. R. Rangaswami (Sand Hill Group); Rajan Nagarajan (CIO, JBS Swift & Company); Ram Shriram (Sherpalo Ventures); Ralph Szygenda (CIO, General Motors); Fred Dillman (Unisys); P. V. Puvvada (Unisys); Dave Barnes (UPS); Laura Asiala (Dow Corning); Janet Botz (Dow Corning); Abbe Mulders (Dow Corning); S. Ramakrishnan (Marketics); K. Ramkumar (ICICI Bank); PRV Rajah (Ramco Systems); Sunil Prabhune (ICICI);

K. V. Kamath (ICICI); S. Sivakumar (ITC); Brian Gillooly (New Paradigm); Jeb Brugmann; and Stephanie Stahl (*InformationWeek*). We sincerely thank them for their valuable feedback on earlier drafts of this book. Our Ph.D. students at the Ross School of Business—Sanjeev Kumar, Vivek Tandon, Ali Tafti, and Jonathan Whitaker—also provided us feedback with very early drafts of the book. Susan Slavin and Diana Jhin from the Ross School of Business helped a great deal in editing and proofing several versions of the manuscript.

We must specially mention three people—Bob Evans (CMP Media), Praveen Suthrum (NextServices), and our colleague Gautam Ahuja (Ross School of Business)—for their ongoing help in improving the drafts of the book. We owe them our gratitude.

Herb Schaffner, our editor at McGraw-Hill, was a unique source of help. He was thorough, demanding, and supportive. That combination helped us get through the editorial process in record time. Our deep thanks to him and his team. Ruth Mannino and her talented team made the production process easy and enjoyable.

This effort would have been impossible without the active support of our wives—Gayatri and Vydehi. Their unstinting support and willingness to take on the burdens of parenting and managing our complex lifestyles made all this possible. To them goes our biggest and most heartfelt thanks.

C. K. Prahalad
M. S. Krishnan

INTRODUCTION

This book is a result of an interesting personal journey. C. K. Prahalad had authored two books: *The Future of Competition* (with Professor Venkat Ramaswamy) and *The Fortune at the Bottom of the Pyramid* in 2004. While at a superficial level they appeared to be unrelated, they presented a unified message. They touched on three critical aspects of innovation and value creation. First, value will increasingly be cocreated with consumers—be they rich consumers in the West or very poor consumers in Bangladesh and India. Second, no single firm has the knowledge, skills, and resources it needs to cocreate value with consumers. Every firm has to learn to access resources from multiple sources. Third, the emerging markets can be a source of innovation.

While researching these issues, it became obvious that there is yet another major change in the focus and processes of innovation afoot. It was the rapid acceleration in "outsourcing" of information technology–related work. C. K. Prahalad's experience in cutting-edge software start-ups, including Praja, Inc., sensitized him to the implications of this trend. Does this mean that the patterns of innovation will morph further? It was an obvious question.

At this juncture, Professor Krishnan joined the research effort. The two of us had worked before on developing a point of view about the role of information technology in strategy. We noticed the emergence of newer business models, fragmentation of traditional organizational structures, centrality of information technology that enabled business processes, collaboration between then-unknown small, specialized Indian firms and considerably larger global firms, and increasingly complex demands on the managerial systems of established firms. These patterns were intriguing. We also recognized through our consulting and research engagements the significant gap that exists between strategic intent and "capacity to act" in organizations.

Four years of concerted effort by both of us to understand the phenomena resulted in this book. Needless to say, it builds on our previous work but presents a new and we believe a unique perspective on the essence of innovation. This book represents the critical operational link in the evolving approach to innovation and value creation. The focus is on *building organizational capabilities* that allow a firm to create the capacity for continuous innovation.

This book is about the nature of innovation—the locus, sources, and processes of innovation and strategy in the new competitive context. More important, we focus on the often hidden links—business processes and analytics—that mediate between innovations, business models, and day-to-day operations. Successful innovations seamlessly connect concepts and ideas to their operational manifestations. We do not present a "charismatic leader" approach to innovation. Neither do we focus on big breakthroughs. We believe that the changing dynamic of markets driven by ubiquitous connectivity, technology, industry convergence (as in computing, communications, consumer electronics, and content), and consumer activism and involvement will create a need for continuous change—not just episodic big breakthroughs.

Development of new features and functionality, new channels, new levels of ease of use, new businesses, and new pricing models is as critical as the hope for a big breakthrough. Given this focus, we will discuss the technology and social infrastructure requirements to deliver an ongoing innovation advantage. The unifying theme of this book is that for successful management of innovations, managers must think differently about innovation and act differently to mobilize the organization. The new game is about more efficiency and more innovation. The managerial agenda in this book is about building this new strategic capital—a new approach to innovation and creating value.

We start with the nature of the transformation of business. We recognize that the nature of the relationships between consumers and the firm has changed radically. Starting over a hundred years ago, firms assumed undifferentiated consumers (for example, the consumers who bought the Ford company's Model T). Since then, we have moved through various levels of marketplace segmentation of consumer groups. We have finally reached the point where the confluence of connectivity, digitization, and the convergence of industry and technology boundaries are creating a new dynamic between consumers and the firm. Traditionally, we have assumed that the firm creates value and exchanges it with its consumers. This firm- and product-centric view of value is being rapidly replaced by a personalized experience and a cocreation view of value.

iGoogle, for example, is about cocreation of value and personalization of experience. Google provides the platform. Individual consumers decide how to use it (personalize it) to suit their particular needs—that is, for fun or learning. So too is skin care personalized by the Ponds Institute at Unilever. The Ponds Institute measures your skin conditions and seeks your views about how you want to look and feel. The company allows you to suggest your personal skin-care budget, to which the company responds by developing a recipe of products for you. It is your personal portfolio. You cocreated it.

As we will argue in this book, these are not isolated examples. This focus on unique personal experiences is increasingly permeating industries as diverse as toys, financial services, travel and hospitality, retailing, and entertainment. The message ought to be clear: Even if a company is dealing with a hundred million consumers, each manager must focus on one consumer experience at a time. The firm can provide the platform around which customers can cocreate their own experiences. Consider Starbucks. You decide whether you want to pick up your favorite coffee and run, stay and read the newspaper, have a meeting, or do your homework. A Starbucks storefront, in this sense, is a platform for experience. We are moving to a world in which value is determined by one consumer-cocreated experience at a time. We will call this phenomenon $N = 1$. This phenomenon extends beyond Google or Starbucks, as we will show in this book. It is one of the two emerging pillars of innovation in all businesses.

Similarly, during the industrial revolution many a large firm was vertically integrated (for example, IBM, Ford, Kodak, Philips, and Siemens). It was only around the mid-1980s that firms started to source critical components from suppliers. Now, most have moved to global supply chains, accessing specialist and low-cost producers. As a result, access to resources is increasingly becoming multivendor and global. This trend toward access to resources from multiple sources (either local or global), and not just from the firm and its subsidiaries, we designate $R = G$. This is the second pillar of innovation in all businesses.

The key is that the supply of products, services, and competencies is multi-institutional. The firms should build capacities to access the global network of resources to cocreate unique experiences with customers. It is not necessary for firms to own all the resource bases they need. Capacity to access these networks of resources is sufficient. The world defined by $N = 1$ and $R = G$ is the exact opposite of where we started a hundred years ago. Our approaches to managing have undergone significant change over the years. Yet the legacy of our past still lingers. In this book, we will start with the two pillars of the next generation of innovations—

$N = 1$ and $R = G$—and develop the nature of the changes that are critical to win in that competitive space.

The intellectual underpinnings of the $N = 1$ and $R = G$ concepts were established in the book *The Future of Competition*, which outlined clearly the new concept of value creation and the rationale for cocreating personalized experiences with customers. Even in emerging markets and among very poor consumers, the need for differentiated and personalized experiences is quite pronounced. Many of the solutions to poverty that treat the poor as one undifferentiated mass have failed, while approaches that recognize their unique circumstances and needs by creating locally responsive and personalized solutions have worked.

For example, in India, self-help groups (SHGs), which are voluntary organizations consisting of about 12 to 15 women in a village, are able to obtain loans from large banks that are developing microfinancing mechanisms to make such loans possible. The loans are given to the groups, not to individuals. The group then decides, based on discussion among its members, who among them and what projects need to be financed on a priority basis. Because the self-help groups have intimate knowledge of the local circumstances—of individuals (their financial standings, their behaviors, and their character) as well as the community—their decisions are as local as they can get. The groups cocreate their own experiences. They also implicitly supervise how the money is being spent. It is no surprise that the repayment rates tend to be extremely high—as high as 99.5 percent.

The ICICI Bank, as the microfinance institution, provides global standards. Global standards and local responsiveness are increasingly seen as the solutions to building inclusive markets and adding the *next 4 billion consumers*. This was the substance of the book *The Fortune at the Bottom of the Pyramid: Eradicating Poverty through Profits*.

We view innovation as shaping consumer expectations as well as responding continually to the changing demands, behaviors, and

FIGURE I.1
The New House of Innovation

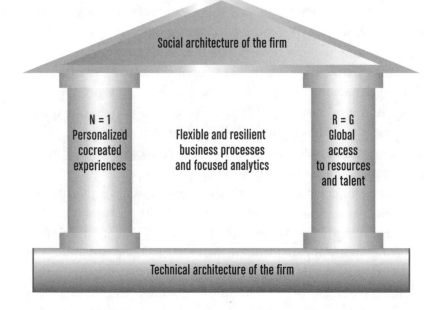

experiences of consumers. We must do this by accessing the best talent and the resources available anywhere in the world. These two ideas must be connected—the resources of many to satisfy the needs of one. We suggest that this is possible only if we pay attention to the glue that enables ideas to be transformed into operations. We will focus on business processes and analytics as the glue.

However, business processes must be connected to the skills, attitudes, and orientations of managers. The social architecture—organization structure, performance measurement, training, skills, and values of the organization—must reflect the new competitive imperatives. So must the technical architecture of the firm—its information technology backbone. We may describe this view of innovation as the *New Age of Innovation*. The relationships between the various aspects of innovation described in the book can be captured in the form of a "House of Innovation," as shown in Figure I.1.

THE STRUCTURE OF THE BOOK

The first four chapters of the book focus primarily on the "what" and "why" of the morphing of the competitive landscape and therefore the value creation (and innovation) space. Chapters 5 through 8 focus on an approach to taking stock of where a firm is in its transformation. We believe that most firms, whether consciously or by happenstance, are moving in this direction; certainly most firms are moving toward $R = G$ in search of cost reductions. We develop a methodology for an orderly and systematic migration from where a firm is to where it needs to be. This transformation need not be traumatic. Small steps, taken one at a time, can lead to significant new capabilities over a very short period of a few years. But these changes must be directionally consistent.

In Chapter 1, we start with demonstrating the trend toward $N = 1$ and $R = G$ in a wide variety of industries. We then develop the managerial demands that this approach to value creation imposes on a firm.

In Chapter 2, we identify the new sources of competitive advantage in a world where the traditional sources of advantage—access to technology, labor, and capital—are no longer unique differentiators for most firms. We suggest that the new source of competitive differentiation may lie in the internal capacity to reconfigure resources in real time. This chapter focuses on business processes— the link between strategy, business models, and operations. We argue that clearly documented, transparent, and resilient processes are a must.

But the $N = 1$ and $R = G$ world demands more than transparency. Managers must develop a deep sense of consumer behavior, consumers' needs and skills (to enable cocreation), and the capabilities of their large network of suppliers to make $R = G$ a reality. Focused analytics that can identify trends and reveal unique opportunities for managerial intervention is an integral part of the capability we need. Chapter 3 focuses on analytics.

In Chapter 4, we describe the specifications for the technical architecture for the firm that will enable it to develop resilient business processes and focused analytics and to anticipate competitive trends and opportunities. First, we describe the new value creation space and identify the new sources of advantage—business processes and analytics. We then specify the nature of the technical architecture that can enable these new capabilities.

We then move to the "how." We recognize that each organization is unique, with its own history. Each has followed its own evolutionary path, often with a large number of acquisitions and mergers. So every large organization represents not just one culture or technical capability, but often multiple subcultures and often a patchwork of technical capabilities consisting of "legacy skills, managerial mindsets, and technical systems."

In Chapter 5, we start with this perspective as a point of departure. We identify the typical legacy issues and the problems of migrating from where a firm is to where it needs to be to compete effectively in an $N = 1$ and $R = G$ world. This migration is a staged process, and we need to ask how an organization can take small steps that lead to big changes over time.

In Chapter 6, we identify the linkages between managerial skills, mindsets, and authority and decision structures and the technical architecture of the firm. We discuss an approach to managing the tension between flexibility and efficiency in business processes in this transformation. For effective competition, both systems—social and technical—must be managed.

In Chapter 7, we identify the need for accessing new skills from around the world to stay competitive.

Finally, in Chapter 8, we build an agenda for managers to move forward in the $N = 1$ and $R = G$ world of competition and value creation.

The transformation of large firms is neither hard nor easy, but it does take a lot of effort. That effort must start with a deep conviction about the nature of the changes required. Change must start with a point of view about the emerging competitive environment. Guiding the organization toward that future in small but directionally consistent steps is the substance of "how." We believe that strategy is about your knowing "what" and "why," and "how."

CHAPTER

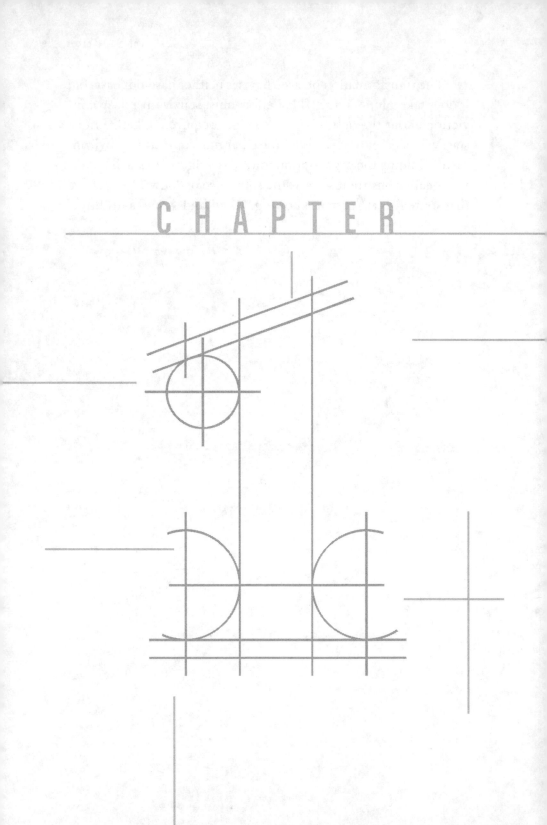

There is a fundamental transformation of business underway. Forged by digitization, ubiquitous connectivity, and globalization, this transformation will radically alter the very nature of the firm and how it creates value. No industry is immune to this trend. It will impact traditional industries such as education, insurance, health care,

THE TRANSFORMATION OF BUSINESS

automobiles, and footwear, as well as emerging industries such as video games, search engines, and social networks. Coming to terms with the implications of this change is critical for survival and growth.

This transformation, as we will examine in this book, is built on two basic pillars:

1. Value is based on unique, personalized experiences of consumers. Firms have to learn to focus on one consumer and her experience at a time, even if they serve 100 million consumers. *The focus is on the centrality of the individual.* We will designate this pillar as $N = 1$ (one consumer experience at a time).

2. No firm is big enough in scope and size to satisfy the experiences of one consumer at a time. All firms will access resources from a wide variety of other big and small firms—a global ecosystem. *The focus is on access to resources, not ownership of resources.* We will designate this pillar as $R = G$ (resources from multiple vendors and often from around the globe).

This view of value creation is 180 degrees different from the model that started the industrial revolution. The Model T from Ford, the icon of the industrial revolution, was built on two premises that are the opposites of $N = 1$ and $R = G$. Consumers were treated as an undifferentiated group, and hence the famous dictum "Any color is OK as long as it is black." All resources had to be within the firm to capture value. Ford was one of the most vertically integrated firms, and its River Rouge plant in Dearborn, Michigan, was the model. While no business today operates along the lines of the original Ford model, we must recognize that model as the precursor of modern business models. Most businesses today are variants of that model. That model served us well. It will not as we move forward.

Let us consider a very traditional business: specialized tutoring of children in high school.

Little has changed in this relationship for decades. Students attend classes at predetermined times. Typical lessons are broken into periods of one hour, each devoted to a particular subject, such as language, mathematics, and history.

Students around the world get homework assignments, which they do on their own, with their parents, with study groups, or with their girlfriend or boyfriend, if they're lucky. Periodic tests and quizzes provide feedback to the teachers and the students about how well they are doing. This system assumes that one learning process will suit all students. Any debate about individualized attention rapidly turns into a discussion of class size and cost.

Now, consider an alternative called TutorVista, a small startup. Here, each student chooses the time when he wants to be tutored. He also chooses the subjects in which he will receive help. He prioritizes his needs. He can also determine how many hours and how intense the tutoring has to be on any topic. He can also choose his teacher! His tutor may be geographically located in India or some other remote location. The tutor will begin the orientation with specific tests to evaluate the student's understanding of the subject and then develop a specific course of study oriented for that student. The lessons are personalized for that student.

All the tutors are independent, well-educated men and women who do this as a part-time activity. To qualify as TutorVista tutors, all potential candidates have to go through a training program briefing them in effective practices in providing remote personalized education. This process, including accent training for teachers, can take from 60 to 100 hours.

Initial results show that U.S. students participating in this system have dramatically improved their understanding of the subjects and their performance in them. It is also not expensive. Students can take as much tutoring as they want for $99 per month.

The affordability is only one reason for the success of the approach so far. More important, TutorVista provides personalized instruction that meets the unique study needs of individual students in online formats that suit the always-on mindset of today's student generation ($N = 1$). Tutors cocreate a "learning plan" with each of their students, and by executing that plan, they cocreate value through improved grades and better retention.

TutorVista had access to 600 tutors at the time of this writing. These tutors are geographically dispersed, and each one is an independent contractor but is bound by the common standards of behavior, ethics, and quality imposed by TutorVista. The tutors can choose to work as much as they want. Resources are accessed as needed from a global resource pool ($R = G$). TutorVista focuses on screening tutors for credentials and providing them with basic training, developing scheduling algorithms, and creating instructional methods. Digitization of the platform for a student and tutor to interact and ubiquitous connectivity ensures that remote tutoring is a reality. TutorVista currently has over 10,000 paying students, and it is expanding its tutor base of over 5,000 tutors to countries outside India, including the United States.

We acknowledge that TutorVista is a start-up with a short history and its programs have yet to be be rigorously evaluated.

However, this experiment represents how even in a tradition-bound field such as secondary education, the power of technology and analytics can be focused on the needs of single individuals through global resources ($N = 1$ and $R = G$). If a tradition-bound institution such as secondary education can be transformed, what about other industries? Is there a TutorVista inside your corporation that fundamentally challenges the current business model?

This megatrend holds massive implications for the creation of value and profit in any business. It challenges established managerial practices in talent management, product development, manufacturing, pricing, logistics, marketing, and brand management. More important, it will lead to radical changes in the technical architecture of the firm—that is, its information technology backbone—and how it is designed. It will also challenge the managerial processes, skills, and attitudes of managers.

Coming to terms with the implications of this transformation is both urgent and inevitable for the survival of business. This book raises the awareness of the underlying transformation and develops a blueprint for companies to transform themselves toward the $N = 1$ and $R = G$ model of value creation. This book is for CEOs, senior executives, and managers at every level who face an imperative to understand that to form strategy and execute it, they must focus on their knowledge of business processes, information technology, and data analysis. To win in the competitive landscape defined by creating one consumer experience at a time, decision makers must develop a whole new mindset for understanding their global supply, logistics, and communications networks. These are the competitive battlefields of twenty-first-century business. We explore these enormous opportunities in the pages ahead, and we also develop a point of view on how to build the social (skills and attitudes of managers) and the technical (information technology) capabilities needed to compete in this emerging value creation space.

To illustrate the thrust of our arguments, consider yet another traditional industry, such as truck tires. Vendors sell their products competing largely on the basis of price, durability, and brand awareness. The dealer and distributor structure is well known. The industry practice is to sell the product to original equipment manufacturers (OEMs) and hope that owners will use the same type of tires when they are ready to replace them. The business model has remained the same in the industry for decades. This is a traditional business model that is firm-centric and product focused. Should this industry remain this way, or can it become a "high-tech–high-touch business"?

Consider an alternative in which the manufacturers do not sell tires but charge for services. They contract with fleet owners to charge per mile of usage. The pricing contract will be based on the type of use, influenced by general factors such as the type of loads (for example, heavy loads), typical route structures (for example, through cities or across long distances), and individual characteristics of fleet owners, such as the training of drivers and therefore the quality of driving, the maintenance of correct tire pressure, and the quality of servicing, such as tire rotation. The tire as a product still exists and is at the core of the business. However, the revenue is based on tire usage, not on a one-time tire sale.

The retail business shifts from a *transaction base* (selling a tire) to an *ongoing relationship* (continuous and ongoing measurements of usage and ability to provide feedback on better usage specific to a user) *with the consumer*. The revenue model now depends on accurate measurements of tire usage on a periodic basis and on parameters of wear and tear that are transparent to the fleet owner and the company, resulting in the ability of the tire company to offer specific advice.

This model has other advantages. The firm gets detailed data on how individual drivers actually drive their vehicles—from the size and weight of their loads, the speeds at which they drive, and the patterns of braking they follow to a host of other characteristics that can help in the product development process.

The company need not focus solely on tire usage. It can focus on driver safety as well. It can help a specific driver improve her skills. Say, for instance, a particular driver has driven only 20,000 miles on a set of tires, but the tires show rough usage. Now assume that we have installed sensors that measure tire performance in real time and relay the data to a central data center. The company can, in real time, alert drivers to be careful, slow down, or check the tire pressure, or in some cases go to the next service station and change the tire. Is this a commodity business with few opportunities for differentiation, or is this a highly differentiated, service-oriented business that cocreates a unique driving experience for a specific driver and improves her skills as well? Will this radically change the meaning of *value* in this business? Will this approach change the nature of relationships between the firm and its consumers?

Well, Goodyear already has a mileage-based service for its fleet customers. Bridgestone is piloting an early version of this model in Europe where the physical measurements are still taken manually and sent via the Internet to the data center. Moving from this phase to remote measurement via well-placed sensors is just a step away. Note the three distinct transformations taking place:

1. The firm is moving from selling a product to selling a service. The product is an integral part of the service. But the value is based on service.

2. The firm is moving from a transactional relationship with a customer to a service relationship with a customer. When strategy focuses on better fleet management—including lower costs, improved safety and skills of drivers, and improved understanding of truck dynamics—the core value proposition shifts from the physical product (tire) to services and solutions (better overall costs) to superior experiences (for individual drivers).

3. When the manufacturer is selling a tire (just the physical product) to the fleet owners, this type of business would be described as a *business-to-business* (B2B) organization. However, when that company is providing feedback that improves individual driver safety and skills, it looks more like a *business-to-consumer* (B2C)

organization. In the new competitive arena of one customer at a time and global networks of resources, B2B and B2C definitions converge.

Does the $N = 1$ and $R = G$ framework apply to other business-to-business firms? Consider NCR (formerly the National Cash Register Company)—a leader in selling automatic teller machines (ATMs) to large global banks such as Bank of America and Wells Fargo. NCR also sells point-of-sale (POS) systems to large retailers such as Tesco and Home Depot, and it is learning that in order to provide value to its B2B customers, it needs to understand the changing expectations, skills, and behaviors of the end consumer. NCR is focused on the consumer's experience, which allows it to develop systems and solutions that make Wells Fargo or Home Depot more successful. NCR believes that it must take the following steps:

> ≥ Learn deeply about retail consumers and their experiences to design systems that become experience platforms.

> ≥ Help its OEM customers such as Home Depot to facilitate value cocreation by them with their consumers.

> ≥ Focus on competitors to be one step ahead of their offerings.

The chain of competitiveness for NCR starts from a deep understanding of the retail consumers who use the ATM (looks like B2C) and cocreating solutions with their corporate customers such as Bank of America (looks like B2B). NCR also focuses on each corporate customer as $N = 1$ with whom it can cocreate solutions. The B2B versus B2C distinction is becoming increasingly less meaningful.

Consider shoes. How many of us are frustrated by not being able to find the right fit? Ever since mass production of shoes became the norm, we have been trying to fit into one of the sizes and shapes that are determined by the manufacturers. But that tradition is also changing.

Imagine a situation in which you go to a shoe store and your feet are measured precisely using a digital camera or scanner. The store sends this information to its company's processing center, which then sends the information to one of its factories. In 10 days you get a pair of shoes that has been custom made for you—not just its color and shape, but its precise fit as well. From then on, your preferences and requirements are part of the database, and you can order any number of shoes till you know that you need new measurements. For this system to work, you must be willing to share the precise measurements of your feet and participate in choosing the style of your shoes. If you are willing to do so, the shoe store's processing center can then send that information to one of its factories anywhere in the world.

Pomarfin, a small Finnish family-owned firm, has been experimenting with this concept. It uses an Italian design group, Mazzucato, to remain at the cutting edge of design, and it uses Estonian factories to cut manufacturing costs. It uses its own dealers for customer interface—that is, for working with customers directly and taking their measurements. The dealers also sell standard shoes from the company. Pomarfin uses software developers in Finland to develop the appropriate scanning technology.

While Pomarfin's service is at an early stage of development, it exemplifies the modern trend of considering one unique customer experience at a time. In order to do it, the company had to develop collaborative relationships with a wide variety of partners—from shoe designers to software developers and digital scanner experts. Imagine what would happen if Pomarfin could also add the capability that Nike has developed whereby customers can not only choose the color but also design the look of their shoes over the Web and add a personal message. In this model, are Nike and Pomarfin in the business of selling shoes or enabling a personalized experience with consumers?

Consider the insurance industry. Most insurance companies

are currently facing multiple challenges simultaneously. Their policy processing costs are getting higher as the competition for customers is heating up. In addition, the turnaround time from the initiation of a policy request to its completion can take, given the level of customization, a significant amount of time.

ING, a global financial services company, was facing these problems. Its 5,000 agents worldwide had to wait 10 days for a policy to be processed and approved. In some exceptional cases, it took as long as 30 to 60 days. ING's internal business processes were embedded in legacy IT systems that were not integrated, and it was difficult to change these processes. To address the problem, the company worked with Unisys, a large IT services firm, to build a system that has allowed ING to bring down the processing time from 10 days to 30 seconds. The new system provides the agent with the flexibility needed to serve the concerns of customers. He can now sit with the customer to develop the combination of features that meets that specific customer's needs.

The newly developed rules-based engine can identify the risks, price the product, and send back the information in real time. In order to do this, ING has had to develop capabilities in its new IT platform to change the internal "rules tables" of policies as frequently as needed. This change has given the company new flexibility: 80 percent of its policies are now automatically generated on this technical platform. The number of policies written has increased by 500 percent since the system was first introduced.

We will discuss this case in greater detail in Chapter 4. The case of ING allows us to pause and ponder. It is often assumed that one cocreated, personalized consumer experience at a time must lead to an increase in costs. However, in the case of ING, it has resulted in reduced costs. Revenues per agent and per call have also increased (better yield-to-call ratio).

Given the enormous potential for improvements in cost savings and increasing revenues generated as a result of adopting a new system, we must also reflect on the hidden costs of the inflexible and archaic internal systems that exist in most firms.

The prevalence of chronic disabilities such as diabetes is a major problem in both developed countries such as the United States and developing countries such as India. Insurance firms are wary of diabetics because the nature of the disease is such that the risk represented by any one individual is almost impossible to determine. The actuarial data are of some help in pricing, but predictions are still unreliable because the progress of this disease and its containment depend on the compliance of an individual to a lifestyle regimen over a long period.

What if insurers could develop an approach whereby the behavior and lifestyle of an individual became the basis for deciding the insurance premium? This could be achieved (and the technology is already in use) via remote monitoring of blood sugar and other vital statistics, once a day at random, based on sensors attached to that person's watch or cell phone.

Through this data, the insurer, doctor, and patient—based on the patient's full consent—could assess the level of compliance of that person to a recommended regimen of medication, diet, and exercise. The insurance firms and the doctors could also advise the patients on course corrections periodically, helping with compliance and lifestyle management. If, however, the person refused to change her lifestyle and did not comply, the risk would increase both for her and for the insurance firm. The premium would then go up. In that scenario, the premiums could be raised every fortnight or every month. Should her compliance with the physician-prescribed regimen continue to decline and reach a level at which she became uninsurable, then there would be a different problem to solve. But most patients would respond well to the initial lifestyle corrections suggested by the physician and not become uninsurable.

In the proposed insurance solution for diabetes, the management of risk is a joint responsibility of the doctor, the insurance firm, and the patient. Consequently, for a patient-monitoring system to succeed, all of those involved have to work from the same database generated through the collection of vital statistics of specific individuals on a predetermined basis through remote sensing. This suggests that the databases would be very large (imagine 10 million customers). Further, this system would require new analytical models that could isolate cases in which the risk levels were increasing (or decreasing through better compliance) and a communication system that can send out alerts to the patients and their doctor and insurance company. In many cases there may be a need for a dialogue between the three groups involved in determining both the compliance levels and the premiums. These event-triggered alerts need to be dealt with in real time. The patients need to get the information and advice when they need it and when they are likely to be most receptive to it and to act on it. There may be a need for support groups that could help patients become more compliant and reduce their risk of heart disease or kidney failure. The system must be able to pull together patients with similar conditions and enable them to support each other as a thematic community. This requires a technology platform for patient-patient dialogue, not just doctor-patient dialogue. Furthermore, we can make it easy for patients to comply by making medicines available inexpensively. We can improve adherence to a healthy lifestyle by, for example, making it convenient and affordable for patients to exercise regularly.

The health-care program just described is feasible today. The ICICI Prudential company in India has introduced an early version of this model of insurance. ICICI Prudential's system offers variable pricing based on compliance, routine testing, and frequent support for patients to help them comply with a regimen personalized to improve their health and reduce risks to them and to the firm. ICICI Prudential does not offer remote diagnostics yet; instead, such tests are conducted at periodic intervals in designated diagnostic clinics. The patients can then go to a designated Web site and, with a password, check their risk status. Testing is part of setting the insurance premium. ICICI Prudential has also built a network of providers—pharmaceutical firms that specialize in diabetes medication such as insulin, diagnostic firms, testing firms, and a wide variety of gyms and fitness clubs.

Is ICICI Prudential providing an insurance product or a health product? Is this insurance based on actuarial data, or is it based on the actual behavioral data for a specific patient? Should premiums reflect the ever-changing nature of risk? Can premiums be a basis for feedback to diabetic consumers? Should insurers be concerned about helping consumers improve the quality of their life?

This transformation of the health insurance industry is feasible today. For it to work, the insurance firms, the doctors (and the hospitals), and the patients must build relationships based on the *transparency* (the same data are accessible to all) of and *access* to data that are reported in a format understandable to ordinary consumers (unlike most legal documents, such as those used in mortgages or product labeling). This transparency of and access to the necessary data would lead to a *dialogue* and a shared understanding of the *risks and benefits* of a particular course of action. We will use the acronym DART (dialogue, access, risks, and transparency benefits) to describe these prerequisites. Similarly, Norwich Union, an auto insurance firm in the United Kingdom, now charges insurance based on individual driving habits and the location where the vehicle is used based on a GPS device installed in the vehicle. This initiative, known as "pay as you drive," has reduced the costs for the Norwich Union company and reduced the number of accidents involving young drivers.

Apple is closer to the $N = 1$ and $R = G$ model of business. Let us consider its entry into the digital music space with iPod and iTunes software. The iPod allows individual users to personalize their experiences with their music selection one song at a time. The iPod's capacity to store thousands of songs allows individual users to personalize specific playlists depending on the time of the day and their mood irrespective of where they are—in a park, at the gym, at home, or in their cars while driving to work. Individual users can also intermix music with a podcast of news and other useful information of the user's choice. In essence, it allows each one of us to cocreate our own experience ($N = 1$). Apple controls over 80 percent of the $4 billion digital music market, which is expected to grow by nearly 100 percent in 2008.

Let us consider the resource base of Apple. The music content is both from large and small firms in the music industry and several independent artists. The podcast content of news and other information is both from traditional media and from individuals and firms. The iPod, as a device, is manufactured with partners across the globe. Let us consider the 30-gigabyte Fifth Generation iPod. The disk drives are made by Toshiba, display modules by Matsushita and Toshiba in Japan, SDRAM memory by Samsung in Korea, and video processors by Broadcom, a U.S. firm. The final assembly of the product is by a Taiwanese firm, Inventec, at its facilities in China. Apple proudly says in its iPod that it is "designed in California." Apple neither manufactures the device nor creates the content, that is, the music it sells. Apple plans to bring this success in creating personalized user experience to the world of movies and videos through new products such as video iPods, iPhone, and AppleTV. Apple is indeed an $N = 1$ and $R = G$ model that leverages a global resource network to cocreate a unique experience with each of its customers. Is this a product or a process innovation?

We will explore numerous other firms and industries at various levels of experimentation throughout the book. We will also learn from some of the obvious brands so well known to the world—from Google to Facebook, eBay, Amazon, and Starbucks. These brands are well known for serving one consumer at a time and allowing customers to personalize their own experiences with the platform that the companies provide. These brands are creating new benchmarks for leveraging business processes.

A seller on eBay can now use the logistics support of Amazon.com. Products sold at eBay can be delivered to buyers at their convenience through the physical logistics infrastructure of Amazon. This way, both eBay and Amazon get more capabilities to serve one consumer at a time. In order to serve that one consumer better, they constantly search for resources from a wider range of firms. Amazon.com has also started to commercially lease capacity in its IT infrastructure to small firms who can use it to make their individual products and services available to consumers.

If only new businesses were moving toward personalized co-created experiences and the building of supplier networks to help create those experiences, then we could dismiss the trend as irrelevant to traditional businesses. Instead, it is well recognized that this movement in online media is leading to customer knowledge and targeting that leaves traditional advertising models behind. The traditional models were based on aggregate targets. In contrast, Facebook and Google have introduced to organizations the capacity to understand individual consumers ($N = 1$) based on their profiles of interest and communities to which they belong. This information allows the companies to create specific messages for individuals.

If traditional industries such as tires, shoes, movies and entertainment, advertising, life and home insurance, and health insurance for those with long-term disabilities are moving in this direction, then as a manager you need to pause and ask: Why is my business any different? *We suggest that your business is, in fact, not different.* From cement to jet engines, education, and health care, from children's toys to delivery of parcels to your home or office by UPS, all industries are going through this transformation. If managers do not recognize this trend and get organized to compete in this new environment, they will be left behind. *This transformation is not a choice.*

What are the key elements of this transformation that we can identify from the examples given so far? There are five:

1. Value is shifting from products to solutions to experiences. In this new world, B2B and B2C will converge ($N = 1$).

2. No company has all the resources it needs to create unique personalized experiences. All companies will therefore have to access talent, components, products, and services from the best source ($R = G$).

3. Internal management systems can become an impediment. Flexible systems are a prerequisite and must be developed.

4. Resources in the ecosystem must be continually configured.

5. Specific models must be developed to enable organizations to focus on one consumer from the millions.

The competitive arena is shifting from a product-centric view of value creation (for example, tires) to a personalized experience-centric view of value creation (for example, pricing based on usage by application and driving habits that influence wear and tear). For example, we are moving away from a segment of consumers such as all class 8 (tractor-trailer rig) truck users to one driver (consumer) at a time. Now we can focus on Joe, who drives a class 8 on a long haul from Copenhagen to Madrid, and his specific driving habits. The basis of creating value is moving away from a single firm's housing all the resources needed (as in vertical integration, when a company may own its suppliers) to a firm's relying on a wide variety of suppliers who collectively provide the service. For example, the Finnish shoe firm, in focusing on $N = 1$, depends on Italian designers, Estonian factories, and Finnish scanner and software vendors. Resources are derived from a wide variety of sources. Continuous reconfiguration of resources becomes a critical element in serving in an $N = 1$ and $R = G$ world. In order to manage in a world of $N = 1$ and $R = G$, firms must deeply understand the internal impediments to change. Often, these impediments are posed by the legacy information, communication, and technology (ICT) systems, as we saw in the case of ING. Until the company confronted the limitations to competitive innovation posed by the internal business processes and real-time analytics, change in the business model was not possible.

DEVELOPING NEW PRINCIPLES FOR INNOVATION

As we have seen in the examples shown above, there are new principles of value creation as well as new capabilities that we need to build in order to compete. In this chapter, we will examine the implications of the two critical principles $N = 1$ and $R = G$.

Principle 1. N = 1

The individual is at the heart of experience. If the locus of value is shifting from products and services to experience, then, almost by definition, value creation must focus on the individual consumer. Contrast this to the manufacturing-oriented model we have inherited. Low cost (mass production) and differentiation (variety) were seen as clear strategic choices. In some quarters, this dichotomy still holds sway. However, the reality has moved on.

Our $N = 1$ world is not about the mass customization offered by large companies such as auto manufacturers that have allowed customers to choose their own color from a list of offerings or Dell that allows individuals to pick their computer options from a significant menu of components and essentially "build" their own systems. Mass customization has failed because, first, it is based on a firm-centric view of value creation in which product managers and designers preselect the possible options and say to the customer: We don't need to hear what you want; choose from the options we give you. Second, firms underestimated the complexity of the back end (business processes and logistics) that is required to fulfill that promise. Hence, many firms concluded that mass customization cannot be scaled economically.

However, digitization of business processes, a knowledgeable customer base, and ubiquitous access to information in recent years not only have made it possible to push beyond mass customization but have made it a competitive requirement. The way in which the principle $N = 1$ goes beyond mass customization is that it is about understanding the behavior, needs, and skills of individual consumers and cocreating with them a value proposition that is unique to them. Customers play an active role in cocreating value, and firms leverage a broader resource base to deliver value.

Consider, for example, that merely increasing the number of elective classes in a school is different from providing a learning experience that is personal and cocreated by the student and the instructor. Offering more shoe sizes and styles to choose from is different from taking exact digital measurements of individual customers' feet and allowing them to personalize their shoes.

In the $N = 1$ world, the traditional firm confronts several critical new demands.

Flexibility

By definition, if a company is focused on $N = 1$ and that value is cocreated with the consumer (for example, the diabetic patient), then the firm has to be flexible. For example, pricing is based on a risk assessment for each patient made periodically (say, monthly) based on his or her compliance and a resultant risk profile. The insurance company, in consultation with its ecosystem partners, may have to do capacity planning and ensure that eye, kidney, and cardiac care facilities are adequate in the geographical areas, based on a continually emerging understanding of the diabetic population it serves. Highly constrained resources will increase the cost of care. Underutilization of capacity will also lead to higher costs. So the insurance firm and hospitals may have to coordinate and continually adjust their capacities. Part of flexibility is the ability to reconfigure resources on the fly. The entire firm must embrace flexibility—be it for long-term capacity planning, monthly pricing, or daily counseling of patients. The focus is not just on traditional load balancing but on *continuously balancing the load and the nature of the task with appropriate resources* to maximize the experience of consumers.

Quality, Cost, and Experience

Flexibility does not mean poor quality or higher cost. The level of quality must be high. Six Sigma and low cost must be integral building blocks of the system. It must be a given. Consumers will not accept poor quality, nor will they accept a service that is not of "good" value. This means that price-performance envelopes will be constantly tested. The subscription to online movie rental model from Netflix or Apple cannot be out of line with traditional movie rental models such as Blockbuster. Furthermore, if our goal is to make the offering inclusive, then we have to make it affordable to the poor as well. For example, in the United States alone there are approximately 40 million people who are not served by banks and who are not insured because of their income levels or prior credit history. Affordability becomes a major criterion for success. The focus on the poor as active consumers will lead to breakthrough innovations in business models, as in a $25 cell phone or a $30 cataract surgery.

Collaborative Networks

No single firm can provide the range of skills to create the $N = 1$ world. In our example of the diabetic patient, in addition to the insurance firm, we need firms that develop diagnostic tools; firms that make the medications; specialized hospitals for kidney, eye, and cardiac diseases associated with diabetes; network operators; makers of special devices such as cell phones or watches with sensors; food processors who develop specialized food; and dietitians and fitness trainers. The insurance firm can be a nodal firm—at the center and influencing the entire ecosystem through a shared framework on how to serve the patients, as well as establishing the standards and customer interfaces. But all of them have to work together. The nodal firm, in this case the insurance provider, does not own the others; it collaborates and co-opts them to provide a complex solution. This is a shift from models based on ownership and control to models based on privileged access and influence. These nodal networks are becoming the norm. OnStar, the telematics network of General Motors, is a good example of a nodal enterprise.

Complexity

The need for flexibility and continuous resource reconfiguration and the management of a collaborative network of big and small players with valuable but fragmented contributions to overall customer experience can lead to a new level of complexity. This complexity can be managed only through a sophisticated system of technology architecture and its attendant business processes. This level of complexity also calls for all employees to recognize the need to cope with an interesting and continuously evolving set of opportunities and problems resulting from the focus on each individual customer. No two problems may be identical. In an $N = 1$ world, variations are constant, requiring significant analytical support that transcends the traditional dependence on managerial intuition.

Consider, for example, the revenue generation pattern of a new movie released on a DVD. It is known that 75 percent of DVD rental revenue happens within the first two weeks of a release, then 10 percent of revenue is earned during the next six months, and the rest over multiple years. If vendors do not align their resources to capitalize on the first two weeks, the release is a dead duck. How do we allocate resources every half day, across hundreds of branches and stores across a vast market such as the United States? What analytic understanding, in real time, is needed to pinpoint the opportunities to make a difference to revenue streams? How then do we get managers to use these actionable insights? This is not a back-of-the-envelope exercise. Procrastination in this case can translate into major shortfalls in revenue. Managers with access to a shared database and solid analytics will outperform human intuition most of the time!

Customer Interfaces

While managers have to cope with a complex system—be it the number of alliances and collaborations, the technological back end, or the analytical models used—the consumer's experience must be simple and intuitive. Given a wide variety of consumers and their skills and motivation levels, a simple interface is critical. Consider the OnStar interface. You simply press a button, and you are connected to a human being on the other side. Furthermore, for promoting dialogue with and among consumers, a simple interface is a prerequisite. Consumers are increasingly a source of competence. Accessing consumers as a source of competence also requires a focus on interfaces. The intuitive interface of Apple's iPod and iPhone are other examples that underscore the importance of interface in enabling consumers to cocreate their experiences.

Scalability

As organizations expand across the globe, the diversity of languages, customs, and norms must be matched with the sheer scale of operations. Wal-Mart, for example, has more than 100 million customers walk through its stores every week. However, every Wal-Mart store has different products on demand—umbrellas in rainy Seattle and shorts and tank tops in San Diego. The five different formats and sizes of stores need different configurations of resources. More than 100,000 stock-keeping units (SKUs) are involved. The supply chain is global. China alone supplies products worth $20 billion for Wal-Mart worldwide. These provide a dramatic example of scale, standards, global integration, and local responsiveness at the same time.

The implications of the $N = 1$ principle are profound. It is natural to ask if the $N = 1$ world is a very expensive proposition. How can businesses sell to customers? How will all this engagement translate to change? Can we make money if we move to this model? These are legitimate questions. Yes, $N = 1$ requires a new approach to access and use resources. This leads us to the second principle of the new approach to value creation.

Principle 2. R = G

The principle $R = G$ refers to the approach to understanding the nature of the resource base of large firms and learning how to access high-quality resources at low cost. The challenges facing business in adopting the $R = G$ perspective are the following.

Access to Resources

Historically, firms accumulated all the resources they needed in-house. Today firms have moved away from this model of vertical integration and have initiated programs to access specialized, global suppliers. For example, Flextronics provides world-class development and manufacturing capabilities to a large number of high-volume electronics companies. In addition, consumers are increasingly becoming a source of competence. They offer advice, suggestions, new concepts, and evaluations of existing products. Finally, any skilled person anywhere in the world can contribute.

Let us look at InnoCentive, which was started by Eli Lilly and is now a separate company. InnoCentive enables any firm or individual to pose a technical question that needs a solution to people throughout the world so that anyone in the world can solve that problem and can be compensated for doing so if his or her solution is accepted. InnoCentive is not alone in pursuing resources globally. We will present more examples later.

The idea of what resources are available to the firm, has moved

From what is available within the division

From what is available within the corporation

From what is available within the supply chain

From what is available within the consumer community

To what is available anywhere in the world

Outsourcing is just one way to access low-cost, high-quality talent. It is the globality of these resources that allows leaders to overcome the limitations in the building of low-cost, high-quality systems to meet the demands of consumers.

Speed

Cycle time and speed are critical elements of the $N = 1$ world. The opportunity cost of managerial procrastination continues to climb. Imagine company A working on product development on a 24/7 basis because of access to development centers in three time zones—United States, Europe, and Asia. Its competitor, company B, works on all of its development in one location—say, the United States. Irrespective of the cost differentials, company A can do it faster—if not in one-third the time, at least in half the time. It is a huge source of competitive advantage. It is not a surprise that several global firms are establishing research and development centers in India and China and inducting them into global projects. Simultaneously, Indian and Chinese firms are going global by actively buying firms in Europe and the United States.

Scalability

The need for the continuous scaling and downsizing of operations is a strategic imperative in the $N = 1$ world. New infrastructures may have to be built, demanding that a lot of talent be focused for a very short time. Global firms do not like to hire a large number of people and let them go after six months when the project is done. In contrast, the vendors, as they work for a large number of firms, can afford to focus a large number of talented people for short periods of time. Infosys can move 300 to 500 software engineers from one location to another or one project to another in a week. It also recruits 15,000 to 20,000 per year out of a candidate pool of a million plus. The selective outsourcing of work to others is a necessity for building scale in a short time period.

Innovation Arbitrage

While we focus on the large firms, large firms better focus on small firms as sources of innovation. New technologies are incubated and nurtured in small firms. Silicon Valley, Bangalore, Beijing, and other such centers are sources of innovation. Sensing what is available and leveraging the innovations that are coming out of laboratories of world-class institutions and small start-up firms are critical to staying ahead of competition. For example, there are more than 3,000 small firms in the IT industry alone in India, all of which have less than $25 million in revenues. They are a source of innovation arbitrage. Through selective licensing, collaboration, or acquisition, the quality and speed of innovation can be dramatically altered.

The nature of resources—financial, human, and technological has transcended the firm and its legal boundaries. Today, resources are global. The focus should be on access and influence, not ownership and control. It is all about leveraging a global resource base.

THE N = 1 AND R = G WORLD

As we look at the twin pressures—the focus on creating unique personalized experiences as the basis for value creation and the expanding sources of resources—we are confronting two trends that counter the traditional ways of managing. Firms used to focus on customer segments and large aggregates, not $N = 1$. Firms controlled most of the resources and were constrained by what they owned, not $R = G$. These opposing trends are shown in Figure 1.1.

Systematically, firms have spent the last century refining the models of segmentation of consumers at one end and "deverticalizing" the resource base (for example, manufacturing of components, design, and development) at the other end. Today, we are somewhere between where we need to be and where we started the journey. We have "global" supply chains and a host of suppliers. Not all resources and competencies are resident within the firm. Simultaneously, we have segmented the consumers in many ways, including in some industries moving toward mass customization. But our thinking about consumers does not reach the $N = 1$ standard. Nor are we fully able to leverage the global resource

FIGURE 1.1

N = 1 and R = G: The Journey.
(a) One firm focuses on aggregate customer needs. (b) Multiple suppliers address individual customer needs.

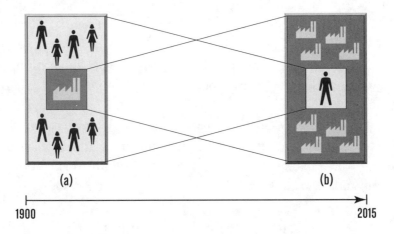

(a)   (b)

1900   2015

capabilities available to the firm. Outsourcing provides a model—a metaphor—that informs our efforts in manufacturing, design, software, and call centers, but it is only a start. In most cases, firms approach outsourcing as a primary means to control internal costs, not to find innovative approaches to reach $N = 1$.

The transformation of a firm from its current business model to $N = 1$ and $R = G$ will not be a smooth and well-balanced exercise. There will be lags. Some will move rapidly to $R = G$, as many have, to reduce costs. Some will move ahead on $N = 1$. The goal is to see the interrelationships between $N = 1$ and $R = G$. Managers approach cost reduction by leveraging the resources and the skills others have. Outsourcing manufacturing, design, services, and IT are the result. Most companies are moving rapidly toward the right along the resource dimension, sometimes motivated by cost reduction only. The movement to the right along the consumer dimension—to truly understand $N = 1$—has been slower. But "a segment of one" is a start. (It is still a firm-centric view of the consumer, not a "consumer cocreation" perspective.) It is obvious that the move toward $N = 1$ and $R = G$ will present new challenges in managing privacy and security of information. Firms need to develop new approaches to governing privacy policies and securing information with appropriate controls in their systems.

FORGETTING AND LEARNING

Just as we have to learn the rationale and the implications of managing in an $N = 1$ and $R = G$ world, we have to forget the approaches to managing using traditional ways of categorizing businesses such as manufacturing or services.

We traditionally recognize an automaker as a manufacturing-oriented business. GM and Ford are in manufacturing. And we recognize Oracle as a software-oriented business. But let us reconsider the car. Is OnStar, the telematics part of a GM car, hardware or software? Are the computers that manage entertainment, engine functions, climate control, and navigation to be considered software or hardware? Are new paints using passive nanoparticles hardware or software?

So the first distinction that we so often use—hardware and software—may be dated. The same thing may be said of a cell phone. Is it hardware or software? Yes, it's both. This shift is clearly visible with the new and emerging smart phones such as iPhones from Apple, where the entire user interface is software controlled and is likely to be upgraded to its next version through software downloads. In spite of this convergence, Nokia and Motorola in this industry have been selling these devices as products rather than as services. Apple now proposes to sell a subscription-based service to its customers for new features through software upgrades to the phone.

The second popular distinction traditionally made is that of a product business as compared to a service business. From that perspective, is serving hamburgers at McDonald's a service or a product (manufacturing) business? Without a well-developed and sophisticated manufacturing and logistics system, McDonald's cannot provide a consistent quality of service. Similarly, a credit card business has embedded in it a manufacturing process: Processing millions of transactions is a manufacturing operation subject to the same disciplines as making cars. It is not surprising that software and business process outsourcing firms in India have eagerly embraced the manufacturing system methodologies developed at Toyota. So, should we persist with the distinctions between product and service businesses?

Similarly, we could argue that distinctions between line and staff roles are becoming anachronistic. Consider the way Mr. Ramkumar, head of ICICI's human resources function, described his work:

> ICICI now faces a challenge in our aggressive growth and HR emerges as a strategic function in this increasingly competitive battle for talent. We run HR operations and recruitment as a production factory. We scan more than 350,000 applicants annually. We hold monthly recruitment planning meetings that resemble demand forecasting meetings by a manufacturer.
>
> In these monthly recruitment planning meetings, we assess the "product mix" needed as of now, and this mix is based on the demand by function—that is, x number of analysts and y number of back-office operators—and this is further segmented by geography similar to demand planning in manufacturing by SKU.
>
> We have specific "yield models" that take into account the current conversion rates in various levels such as financial analysts, tellers, and back-office support personnel. These yield rates are obtained based on prior data and further updated based on external shocks such as an MNC opening a large center in a particular city. In fact, we also proactively plan for attrition rates in various centers based on external events. The final number of résumés to be screened on a monthly basis is derived out of these yield models.

There is also a tradition in how firms categorize innovation, and that tradition has had a long-standing argument in some situations as to whether an innovation is in the product or in the process. Some people have gone one step further and wonder whether the innovation is in packaging, pricing, or something else. In reality, innovations that create significant value often incorporate all of the above. For example, is an iPod or an iPhone an innovation in product, packaging, pricing, distribution, or billing? As firms move toward the model of $N = 1$ and $R = G$ in this new age of innovation, as in the cases of Bridgestone, ING, ICICI Prudential insurance, and Google, these business models cannot be easily classified into the traditional categories of innovation.

Let us consider categorization in relation to our examples. Bridgestone is still a manufacturing company. It manages multiple plants around the world and manufactures millions of tires. But its transition to usage-based pricing forces it to incorporate software and sensors as integral parts of its offerings. The company is selling an experience, and embedded in that experience is a physical product. Finally, it has to make a significant number of work process innovations to make the price per kilometer of usage model work. As shown in Table 1.1, Bridgestone's move toward an $N = 1$ and $R = G$ world cuts across the traditional discrete categories in which we had pigeonholed a firm's activities. Hardware and software, manufacturing and service, product and service, and process and product innovations are categories of the past. As we can see in Table 1.1, in the Bridgestone Tires example, the tire is hardware and software (with sensors connected to a network to measure wear and tear). Yes, it is a physical product (a truck tire), but it is also a service to individual fleet owners, providing them with new information on fleet usage, cost of tires, and ways to improve efficiency. The innovation is both in the product and in the way it is configured with sensors and such, but it is also in the processes needed for continuous monitoring and feedback to the individual drivers and the fleet owners. Thus the discrete categories in which we pigeonhole business innovations become less relevant.

TABLE 1.1 **THE DEATH OF DISCRETE CATEGORIES**

	Traditional Discrete Categories					
	Core Activity		Type of Business		Innovation in	
Examples	**Hardware**	**Software**	**Product**	**Service**	**Product**	**Process**
Bridgestone Tires	Tire	Usage measure-ment	Yes (tire)	Yes (pay/use contract)	Yes (applica-tion specific)	Yes (workflow for measure-ment and pricing)
Pomarfin Shoes						
ING Insurance						
Netflix						
ICICI Diabetes Insurance						

You may want to consider where the innovations were made in the other four examples. This is instructive, since it forces each one of us to come to terms with our biases. We have, therefore, intentionally left Table 1.1 partially blank.

What really is the transition here? It is not that the discrete categories are disappearing but that a new set of requirements is emerging. For example, all businesses are becoming more *knowledge intensive*. A lot of the knowledge is not just in the physical product but in the embedded software that makes it intelligent, like the sensors embedded in a tire that can measure tire pressure and inform the driver if it is not appropriate. A significant amount of knowledge is built into the software that surrounds the product, such as the IT architecture and the analytics that are involved in sending information on tire usage and making specific interventions based on a pattern of usage. The need for creative harmonizing (hardware plus embedded software plus the ICT system plus analytics) represents the new knowledge intensity of businesses.

Simultaneously, the source of value is shifting from physical products (for example, tires) to solutions (for example, specific applications for managers of large fleets) to personalized experiences (for example, Joe, a tractor-trailer driver, for this application within this firm). This shift in value to $N = 1$ cannot be accomplished without increasing knowledge intensity. Similarly, not all of the elements of the knowledge intensity needed can be fully developed within a single firm. A multivendor strategy is required, which forces the firm to accept $R = G$. This is the key to innovation and value creation in the future. If we move toward $R = G$, we find that we can gravitate to $N = 1$. If we want to move to $N = 1$, we also will have to move toward $R = G$. This is the important takeaway. For example, McDonald's is experimenting with centralized call centers to take drive-thru orders at the stores. This may look like a purely efficiency-driven initiative to consolidate resources. It is. But it also enables McDonald's to enhance individual customers' experiences. For example, if a customer prefers to speak Spanish or any other language, the central pool of resources can provide an agent in that language for customers to interact with. That can also help in developing a deeper understanding of customer tastes and preferences. We suggest that firms start with an $N = 1$ view. This allows them to look at their migration to $R = G$ through a different lens. $R = G$ then does not become an opportunistic and a myopic cost arbitrage exercise but a thoughtful migration to $N = 1$. It suffices to say, for now, that $N = 1$ and $R = G$ go together.

N = 1 AND R = G: A SOCIAL MOVEMENT

It must be obvious to you by now that the new competitive landscape is not just a weak signal of change, but rather a social movement. Whether it is buying tires, renting movies, buying insurance, watching TV and consuming news, checking in at a kiosk in an airport, or self-checking out in a supermarket (even if it takes a little bit longer and more work), we are migrating rapidly to an

$N = 1$ world. We see this everywhere. If business leaders aggressively adopt these trends, we will witness historical new growth for businesses by 2015. We believe that a large enough sample of firms in critical industries will be successful over the next few years to provide the role models and confidence that will inspire many to follow this approach and adopt its strategic options.

We believe that the movement toward $N = 1$ and $R = G$ is not a choice. The focus of the young on Web sites like MySpace, YouTube, Orkut, Facebook, and others suggests that *a whole generation of consumers will grow up expecting to be treated as unique individuals, and they will have the skills and the propensity to engage in a marketplace defined by* $N = 1$. This movement is accelerating. Personalized and social networking sites are currently growing faster in numbers of customers than ever before. For example, MySpace reports over 200 million customers in four years, whereas Facebook reports over 47 million customers in two years. The fact that MySpace and Facebook in a very short time span have generated such a powerful following must tell us something about the speed of migration to $N = 1$. Further, Facebook, by opening its system to developers, has generated more than 5,000 applications in 18 months ($R = G$).

It does not matter whether Facebook as a business will thrive in the long run or will be run over by a consortium of Google and others who prefer an open-source approach. This is not about a single firm and its success. This is about the acceleration of a social movement toward a personalized cocreated experience. Value for this new generation of consumers is not embedded in traditional notions of quality. That is a given. These consumers want to be involved in shaping their own experiences. Similarly, the competitive imperatives of access to talent, speed (reduction of cycle time or, more appropriately, reaction time to changes in the competitive environment), and cost will drive most firms toward using multiple vendors across the globe, as have Facebook, Google, and others. $R = G$ is also inevitable.

This process of creating value with one consumer experience at a time will also permeate the way the firm is managed internally.

Within the corporation, engaging employees emotionally and intellectually in the mission of the firm will require that each employee is treated as unique ($N = 1$). Individual employees strive to seek different personal "meanings" in their work. They also bring unique skills and capabilities. Mobilizing global teams based on the unique skills of individuals to address unique tasks is no different from $R = G$. The social movement toward $N = 1$ will, therefore, affect not only how we deal with consumers but also how we deal with employees. Recognizing individuals as unique in all their roles (consumers, employees, investors, suppliers, and citizens) will become a prerequisite for success in value creation. Similarly, recognizing that resources are highly distributed—within the global firm, among suppliers, in consumer communities, and among people at large—is critical. Managers must build systems that selectively pull together teams that are uniquely capable of providing high-quality, low-cost solutions rapidly. This transformation is about the centrality of individuals, their choices, and their cocreated experiences. It is well underway. Digitization and emerging technologies (such as Web 2.0) are further aiding as catalysts in this movement.

We believe that the question for managers concerned about value creation is not "whether" but "when." The sooner firms learn to manage this transformation, the better it is.

This transformation will also touch all levels of management, from CEOs to call center operators. Ask yourself these questions:

> ➤ How can I connect these emerging strategic opportunities with day-to-day operations?

> ➤ How do I learn about specific consumers' desires, skills, and behaviors such that I can help create better experiences for them?

> ➤ What technical support structures do we need to create the capacity for flexibility and innovation at low cost?

> ➤ What changes do we need to make in the way we manage our human capital?

➢ Are we prepared for working across cultures and time zones in a seamless global network?

As we move toward an $N = 1$ and $R = G$ world, different capabilities become critical sources of advantage. Privileged access to capital, technology, and people is becoming less critical. The ability to develop flexible, transparent, and granular business processes that allow for continuous reconfiguration of resources ($R = G$) to serve the interests of $N = 1$ will indeed define the new age of innovation.

CHAPTER

2

A s firms transition to a world of $N = 1$ and $R = G$, the nature and sources of competitive advantage will change. So will the nature of managerial capabilities required to effectively compete in that market. Managers will have to ask themselves a set of questions that are the natural result of this transition: *How do we think about new sources of*

BUSINESS PROCESSES:
THE ENABLERS OF
INNOVATION

competitive advantage? What are the enablers of innovation in my firm?

Historically, access to capital and raw materials has been a source of competitive advantage. In some industries, it still is; access to low-cost ore and electricity is an advantage to firms in the aluminum and steel industries, and access to oil and gas is an advantage for an oil company. But access to raw materials is not a unique source of advantage in most industries. Although access to venture capital is not yet universal, capital is quickly finding its way to new opportunities. For example, technology venture capital firms in the United States and Europe are increasing their presence in China and India. Specialized manufacturers, such as Flextronics in high-volume electronics manufacturing, provide firms with world-class expertise in design and manufacturing. So do Infosys and Tata Consultancy Services (TCS) in IT services. If access to raw materials, capital, technology, and talent are rapidly becoming *table stakes*, what is the unique source of competitive advantage in an $N = 1$ and $R = G$ world?

In this chapter, we will identify business processes as the key enablers of an innovation culture. Second, we will focus on the twin dimensions of business processes—the technical and social architectures. We will demonstrate how some firms have leveraged this insight—the centrality of business processes—in building their unique innovation culture. Finally, we will illustrate how a firm can migrate to an $N = 1$ and $R = G$ world systematically by following the journey of one firm—the ICICI corporation.

THE EMERGING SOURCE OF COMPETITIVE ADVANTAGE

The global corporation can be visualized as a *logical thread of relationships between a multitude of moving parts*—ideas, information, knowledge, capital, and physical products. These relationships define an organization and its extended network of collaborators, including suppliers and consumers. The capacity of an organization to articulate the relationships selectively between these moving parts is at the core of an organization's ability to respond, in real time and cost effectively, to the demands of the $N = 1$ and $R = G$ world. The more explicit these relationships are, the greater the ability of managers to use them. We outline here the core elements of a framework that enables firms to enhance their innovative capacity and build their next source of competitive advantage.

WHY BUSINESS PROCESSES?

The new logic of innovation and value creation forces us to focus on the core principles. For example, ING, Bridgestone, Starbucks, and Google are all in different industries. But all of them, implicitly, subscribe to the core principles of $N = 1$ and $R = G$. We need to distinguish between the core principles of innovation and its man-ifestations in a specific industry or in a specific firm. We should avoid the temptation to imitate any one company's approach to op-erationalizing these core principles. We must not just focus on *knowing how* (how they did it) but on *knowing why* and *knowing what as well.* (Why does it work? What are the core principles? How do I implement these principles in my business?) Similarly, we need to discard traditional categories in our thinking, such as hardware and software (both as in GM's OnStar or cell phones), manufacturing and services (both as in McDonald's), and product and process in-novations (both as in iPod). These distinctions are not very useful.

Unfortunately, discussions of an innovation culture invite a plethora of similar distinctions. For example, are innovations strategic or operational? Let us assume that we have a new busi-ness model. We move away from mailing DVDs to a consumer's home as in Netflix. Consumers may want to get a preview of a movie before they order it, so we want to make it possible for them to do so and then order it afterward via the Internet and pick it up in any nearby store with a kiosk. This procedure will appeal to a wide variety of consumers. But in order to do this, we must install enough kiosks, develop business processes and tools of analysis to understand individual consumers, recognize their geographic lo-cations and suggest to them where the closest kiosk is, develop consumer credit analysis, and keep the kiosk full of blank DVDs. The video store would use blanks rather than copies of the movies themselves because with blanks it can write the movies that indi-vidual consumers have previously ordered onto DVDs when the consumers actually arrive at the kiosk ($N = 1$) to pick them up. This is a bank ATM type of application for movies. These and a million other details are critical for making this business model work. Is this a business model innovation? Or operational innovation? Or strategic innovation?

Similarly, any changes to the culture of the firm require a basic change to its business processes. Let us assume that we want to change performance measurement systems such that they better motivate employees. These system revisions must be translated into procedures for managers and human resource departments to follow. More importantly, these procedures must be transparent to the employees. If we want to change the capital allocation processes, the changes must be reflected in the procedures for submission of proposals. Product development projects that span multiple continents and time zones need procedures for hand-offs among the groups involved. Yes, we want people to be thinking of new ideas. So 20 percent of their time must be freed for blue sky projects. But we also need a procedure to know that 80 percent was spent on specific company-assigned projects.

Start-ups do not need well-developed processes. However, any firm of reasonable scale needs business processes to make its values, concepts, ideas, and business models operational. The human body needs the flow of blood to function—to think, to feel, to exercise, and to enjoy a gourmet meal. Therefore, we will not focus on the manifestations of innovations often categorized as strategic, operational, or business model innovations. As we did in focusing on the core logic of innovation—$N = 1$ and $R = G$—we will focus on the core enabler of innovations. Business processes are the bloodstream of an organization. The manifestations of innovations can vary. But underneath the veneer of differences are the enablers of all innovation cultures—well-developed and flexible business processes.

Business processes are critical to support an innovation culture. But if left unattended and not consciously adapted to the changing business environment, business processes can become *impediments* to innovation and change. Consider, for example, the IT services firms from India. They have had phenomenal success based on access to talented engineers at low cost. Their business models were built on doing work in India so that they can arbitrage the differences between on-site (U.S.-based) and off-site (India-based) wage rates. Over time, they have moved beyond the cost advantage to the advantage of cost plus quality plus technology. But their pricing policies still reflect a cost arbitrage model.

The economic model in most IT firms in India has not kept pace with the changing nature of the services they provide. As a result, revenue growth is tied to the number of employees—a legacy of the cost arbitrage business model. For a firm to go from $2 billion in revenue (60,000 employees) to $10 billion, it has to recruit approximately 240,000 more employees in a very short period of time. Needless to say, the time is ripe for a fundamental reexamination of this business model. We must add that we do not know a single senior manager in the IT industry in India who does not understand this problem at an intellectual level. However, all their business processes—be it estimation of work, assignment of people to a project, pricing, performance evaluation, and profit forecasting—are tied to the traditional model and are optimized to that model.

The change to a value-based pricing model (as opposed to a cost-plus model) needs changes to the underlying structure of business processes as well as changes in the way managers in this industry are socialized and in the way they keep score of their personal successes. The approach of a few industry leaders reinforces the business models in the industry—among both customers and vendors. The business processes that support that model get reinforced. These business processes, in turn, reinforce behaviors and the mental models, or the *dominant logic* of managers in that industry. This is the reason why an intellectual understanding of the need for change and a desire for change are not enough. The firm needs the *administrative capacity to execute that change*. In most firms, there is a gap between the capacity to think and the capacity to act. It is often like the millions who try to improve their health. While intellectually one can recognize the benefits of rigorous exercise, changing one's lifestyle and getting into a new discipline is another story. Organizations have similar problems in translating strategic intent into operations.

In most organizations, the evolution of business processes is undermanaged. This often creates major missing and broken logical links. Often, employees provide the missing links by making manual adjustments to the missing logical connections. In one large multinational firm, there were over 500 people entering incoming sales contracts. The contracts, spread over several years, were complex to negotiate and execute. On investigation, we found that more than 80 percent of staff focused on this task were supplying the missing links in the logical business process. This manual intervention was needed because as the business models and terms and conditions of sales changed, the necessary changes were not made to business processes. One of the impediments to these changes was their IT systems. The business process changes could not be accommodated within legacy IT systems in time and within budget limits.

It is not hard to see that business processes—the procedural articulation of various activities of the firm—are the core enabler of innovative capacity in the firm. They can also become the primary impediment to innovation. We recognize that business processes are not "sexy" in any company we have known. Few of the top managers want to be responsible for this area, much less pay attention to it. It is often an *organizational orphan*.

BUILDING A FRAMEWORK

We need to make an explicit connection between strategy, business models, and business processes. For example, the business concept of dealing with one diabetes patient at a time for insurance ($N = 1$) must be translated into a business model. The first requirement is remote diagnostics of a very large number of patients on a regular basis. This requires accessing patients in a secure and reliable fashion and downloading vital statistics. Issues of privacy and security are critical to patients. Furthermore, the insurance firm has to create a network of service providers, such as devices for sensing the vital statistics and transmitting them to dietitians, clinics, doctors and hospitals, pharmaceutical companies, diagnostic tools companies, and so on. The value created must be shared with all these providers in the ecosystem in some transparent and equitable fashion. While this insurance business may be part of a larger diversified financial services firm, it must, as a business, build its specific business model as distinct from the other businesses of the parent company. We will revisit this in detail in Chapter 6.

This broad understanding of the basic business model of how to compete must now be translated into business processes. For example, how do we handle individual billing on a monthly basis based on a changing risk profile for every patient? How do we alter business processes to pay the telecom carriers, an integral part of the network on this risk profile–based personalized billing? How do we deal with more selective use of other vendors—the doctors or the dietitians—who will help selected patients? What underlying processes and analytics are required to send specific messages to individual patients to improve their compliance? How do we integrate the unique business processes and the IT infrastructures that the participating vendors in the ecosystem may have? How do we train our managers so that they acquire new skills and exhibit new behaviors in this feedback-intensive relationship with customers and the network of partners? This chain of connections from idea to implementation—from the strategy to the business processes and their technical and social infrastructure requirements—is shown in Figure 2.1.

Business processes have had a long history in management literature and practice. The various approaches to business processes are captured in the chapter appendix. Our perspective on business processes is that they enable innovation. We define the term *business process* as follows:

> The *business process* is the link between the business strategy, business models, and day-to-day operations. It is the explicit and detailed understanding of the business model. Business processes define the logical relationships among activities within the firm (and its network collaborators, $R = G$) and its relationships with consumers ($N = 1$). Business processes impact and are impacted by both the *technical architecture*

FIGURE 2.1

The world of N = 1; R = G: A Framework for Capability Building

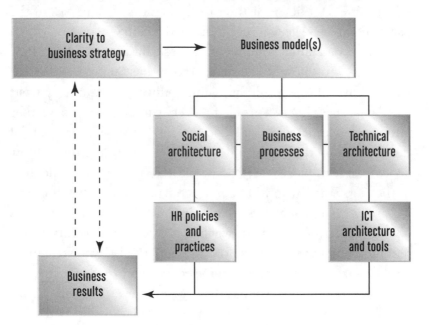

(such as information and communication technology systems—ICT) and the *social architecture* (such as organization structure, decision rights, and performance management systems of the firm).

It is important to recognize that business processes have two critical dimensions. One dimension comprises information technology architecture and its tools. Databases and enterprisewide systems—such as enterprise resource planning (ERP), proprietary and legacy applications, computers, and servers—get attention. This is an important aspect of business processes. But for business processes to be effective, we have to focus as much on the training, skills, and orientation of all employees. Business processes must become part of the social infrastructure. So in our discussion of business processes, we will cover the following topics:

1. We will show how the quality and the alignment of business processes to strategy and business models can become a source of competitive advantages. More importantly, we will focus on how flexible business processes can create the capacity to develop new business models and strategy.

2. We will discuss the analytical capabilities needed for an $N = 1$ and $R = G$ world in Chapter 3 and the requirements of the overall ICT architecture in depth in Chapter 4.

3. We will outline the organizational requirements of flexible business processes in Chapter 5.

The more detailed (granular) our understanding of the activities that constitute a business process and more explicit the logical linkages among those activities, the better. Granularity allows for fine-grained changes to the business process and enhances clarity to each activity and action. Similarly, the more modular the building blocks of the business processes, the better. Modularity of business processes enables easier change and connectivity to other processes.

BUSINESS PROCESSES
AND ICT ARCHITECTURE

As digitization permeates every aspect of business, most business processes are enabled by the ICT architecture. We will now focus on the ICT architecture that underlies business processes.

The ICT architecture is not a monolith. It can be divided into its components as depicted in Figure 2.2. It is useful to think of the ICT architecture in multiple layers:

➢ The lowest layer is Layer 4, which comprises the physical telecom connectivity and hosting architecture, wired and wireless cables and connections, and the server farms and routers that enable connectivity to the public telecom and data networks.

FIGURE 2.2

Building Blocks of ICT Architecture

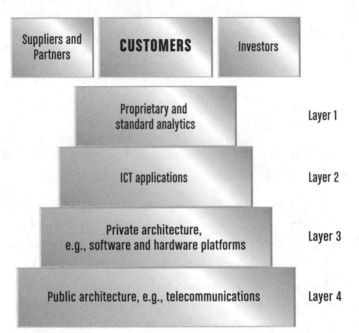

> On top of this public architecture is Layer 3, the firm's private IT architecture that includes the hardware boxes—that is, the computers and servers (database and application servers) and the systems software, such as the operating systems, databases, and any middleware platforms that the firm may use. The application software uses various pieces in the private and public architecture to enable the business processes within a firm.

The lower two layers of ICT architecture focus on standardization and efficiency. Often, some or all parts of these layers can be managed by third parties. These ICT layers also span beyond the firm to include suppliers and partners and increasingly even reside outside the firm. Firms can no longer differentiate themselves based on their choice of standard hardware boxes, operating systems, or databases.

While these layers are not a source of competitive differentiation, they can be a source of complexity. Firms recognize this. For example, Cisco and Dow Corning have standardized their desktop and laptop computers to specific models of IBM and Toshiba, respectively, throughout the organization. We will focus, in this chapter, on the top layers of the ICT architecture, primarily on the business processes and analytic applications that provide the basis for competitive advantage and competitive differentiation.

> Layer 2 focuses on business-specific applications and attendant business processes. Senior management is increasingly paying attention to some of these aspects of business process. The pressure for quarterly business results focuses senior management's attention on change levers, such as performance measurements, compensation, and organization structure. Now, with Sarbanes-Oxley regulations, many managers view business processes as a compliance headache. ICT applications get attention as a cost and a necessary evil. There is no one place where connection between the social architecture (managerial processes) and the ICT architecture come together. Business processes that influence both, as a result, evolve in a haphazard fashion. In very few firms is a senior executive accountable for business processes.

> Layer 1 represents the primary interfaces of a business with its customers, suppliers, partners, or investors. It is Layers 1 and 2 that can provide the source of competitive advantage. To describe ICT as important and a source of competitive advantage or otherwise without a detailed understanding of the layers and the relative contributions they make to competitive differentiation is inappropriate. Let us examine some examples where business processes have been used as a source of competitive advantage.

BUSINESS PROCESSES AS A
SOURCE OF COMPETITIVE ADVANTAGE

While few grasp the importance of business processes as a source of competitive advantage, several major firms recognize and leverage it to their advantage. Consider Wal-Mart, which uses its logistics capability to manage its global supply chains from China to the United States and all places in between. The company is able to stock its stores with varying formats and specific local demand and competitive characteristics. Wal-Mart revolutionized retailing by focusing on a new business model built on business processes and information technology to match. Wal-Mart protects its business processes and resultant ICT applications as a strategic asset. Its database is over 500 terabytes—the largest commercial database in the world.

Wal-Mart today creates value by managing the underlying information flows in a global supply chain. CIOs from Wal-Mart end up being CEOs of their own major business groups. For example, Kevin Turner, who was CIO at Wal-Mart, ran Sam's Club as president and CEO before moving to Microsoft as the chief marketing and sales officer. Linda Dillman, executive vice president of risk management and benefits administration at Wal-Mart, moved on to take over as the CIO of Wal-Mart. Such smooth transfers between business and ICT responsibilities at the senior levels are not common. At Wal-Mart, management recognizes that a deep understanding of how to translate the business model into its business processes and the role of ICT in enabling these processes (or using ICT and processes to build an effective and new business model) is critical for its success.

FedEx understands the critical importance of business processes. The fact that FedEx can cut its call center costs by allowing individual consumers to check on the status of their packages (or to allow large customers to reroute a package after it is in the system) suggests that the business processes not only are very well developed but also work with Six Sigma quality. Their ability to track the package at every event in the movement of a package—collecting the package from a customer, putting it on the truck, unloading it in the sorting station—has given FedEx an unprecedented opportunity to be focused on consumer experience. The fact that consumers can see for themselves how their package is handled increases confidence and trust in the company. FedEx has also partnered with several vendors in India and other countries to leverage resources to operate its global customer service centers. For example, the company ships international packages to over 150 countries, and the customs rules often change across countries. Their overseas partners have trained resources and processes in place that adapt to these changes promptly to meet the specific needs of each customer.

United Parcel Service (UPS) has also recognized the value of its systems. The company has spun off a new business, a logistics business, based on its internally developed capability. For example, UPS handles the reverse logistics and spare parts inventory and customer service for Toshiba's computer business. UPS has partnered with several local PC repair shops and contract technicians in various geographical locations to repair Toshiba PCs ($R = G$). But UPS is accountable for the final customer experience. UPS manages the entire process, from attending to a customer call to picking up the machine and getting it serviced at the local repair center. Execution of such complex logistics profitably is not possible without a visceral understanding of the connection between its business models, business processes, and ICT.

eBay goes one step further. By allowing its key customers, those who are veteran buyers and sellers, to participate in designing their systems, eBay has created a model user-friendly experience platform. The business processes are transparent because consumers helped to cocreate them. Every quarter, eBay makes an equivalent of 175 changes, most of which are derived from consumer suggestions. The quality of business processes and underlying infrastructure (both the social and the technical) is critical to eBay's success. The technical infrastructure is obvious. The fact that eBay's CEO and top managers meet with consumer groups through their eBay Voices program and read their e-mails daily is equally important. eBay also exhibits unique business processes for leveraging global resources ($R = G$). For example, eBay has over 60,000 independent software writers contributing to its platform. These developers have contributed over 9,000 applications that enable 25 percent of the product listings on the eBay platform.

All the examples—Wal-Mart, FedEx, UPS, and eBay—use their business processes as the core element of their competitiveness. Wal-Mart uses them to be the most efficient retailer. FedEx allows the consumer to be a part of the operations experience by sharing its databases and applications so that individual customers can track their packages. In eBay, the consumers cocreate the business processes as well. None of them uses a standard software package of business processes to run its operations. These companies' business processes reflect their unique business models and vice versa. All are built from inside. In these firms, business processes are clearly seen as a source of competitive advantage. The business processes are protected and nurtured. These four business models reflect the various stages of evolution toward $N = 1$ and $R = G$, as shown in Figure 2.3.

Each one of these examples illustrates the different competitive positions that firms have occupied. For example, Wal-Mart traditionally has paid less attention to personalization ($N = 1$) than to managing the back-end logistics. The company recognizes that it has to pay more attention to individual consumers and their experiences. Wal-Mart has to move beyond being a low-cost provider, and it recognizes this. eBay deals with a large number of customers as cocreators ($N = 1$). The company is increasingly using its customers as application developers ($R = G$) as well. FedEx is also focused on both dimensions. FedEx has constantly evolved in improving the customer experience at all touch points, starting with its Web interface and telephone service to the FedEx person at your door. Now the company is also leveraging global resources through high-quality customer contact centers around the world

FIGURE 2.3
Convergence of N = 1 and R = G

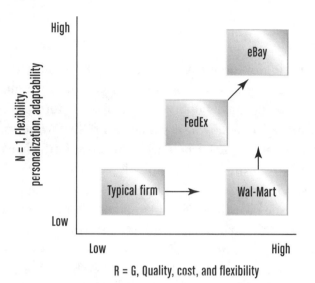

R = G, Quality, cost, and flexibility

($R = G$). Most typical firms, under pressures of cost reduction, are moving toward outsourcing their IT operations. While outsourcing of some aspects of the ICT stack (see Figure 2.2) may be justified, indiscriminate outsourcing may compromise these firms' ability to get to $R = G$, much less $N = 1$. While moving on both trajectories is important, senior management needs to assess their current capabilities across these dimensions and assign priority to their migration along these trajectories.

THE NEXT SOURCE OF COMPETITIVE ADVANTAGE

As Wal-Mart, FedEx, and eBay demonstrate, business processes are a source of competitive advantage in an $N = 1$ and $R = G$ world of competition. Can these advantages be built in a systematic way? We will use the case of the transformation of a bank—ICICI in India—as a way to build consciously the connections between corporate strategy, business models and business processes, and the underlying technical and social architecture to gain competitive advantage.

Migrating to N = 1 and R = G

We did not pick ICICI because it has done everything right. Indeed, it has had its share of missteps. Rather, we picked the company because it has transformed a public-sector-like institutional bank into a sophisticated, fast-moving retail powerhouse. Furthermore, the company has been one of the most innovative in the banking industry in India, working within a difficult regulatory framework. Many of its services, such as online banking and brokerage, were new to India at the time they were introduced. Some innovations are really new in the financial sector. The transformation of ICICI, with assets of over $79 billion in 2007 and a market capitalization of $35 billion (compared with a market cap of less than $2 billion in 2000) is an example of the capability-building framework depicted in Figure 2.1. Underlying this transformation was a clear strategy but, more important, a clear understanding of the need to embrace business processes and ICT as a basis of rapid transformation. We will interpret the ICICI transformation using our framework.

Clarity in Business Logic and the Choice of Corporate Portfolio

Capabilities to deliver a compelling experience for customers through the appropriate resource base begin with senior management's clarity about the choice of the corporate portfolio and the business logic. In the mid-1990s, the Indian banking industry consisted of two sets of players, in two distinct banking markets, serving at different price-performance (value and quality) levels. The first set consisted of the multinational banks such as Citibank, Grindlays, and Bank of America, catering to the affluent retail and corporate customers at a premium price. A group of public sector (state-controlled) banks was the second set of players attempting to meet the banking demands of the entire spectrum of corporate and retail customers with the legacy of banking as a public sector service. When the ICICI bank was launched in 1995, senior management at ICICI made the logic behind their business and corporate portfolio explicit.

ICICI identified two unique opportunities for banking business as a consequence of Indian economic liberalization in the early 1990s. First, it saw an uncontested opportunity in the rapid growth of middle-class consumers and Indian firms not served well by either of the two existing players at that time. Hence, ICICI started with two business units in its corporate portfolio—retail banking and corporate banking. The company's strategic goal was to give world-class service at affordable costs to middle-class customers. ICICI had to compete on cost with multinational corporations and match their quality. At the same time, the company had to compete on quality by matching costs with subsidized state-controlled banks. This meant that the company had to fundamentally rethink the *price-performance equation* (value) in banking in India. ICICI also recognized that scale and cost were critical to delivering this new value proposition.

For example, the average deposit of a middle-class consumer was about one-tenth that of a typical deposit in a multinational bank. Therefore, it was clear that ICICI had to build an ICT backbone that would deliver world-class quality or better at one-tenth of the cost (or better) of similar systems and processes at multinational banks. The company's ability to create unique consumer experiences would be determined by the quality and flexibility built into the information technology and analytics capabilities. Business processes, ICT, and social architecture were to become the backbone of the company's rapid expansion. This business logic was made explicit to all by the CEO's commitment and personal involvement in developing the business processes, technology, and human resources infrastructure of the bank.

The ICICI Business Model on How to Compete

In the mid-1990s when ICICI emerged as a player in both the retail and corporate banking fields, its business model was built around the following simple premises:

1. Focus on organic growth. Make few acquisitions.

2. Focus on providing value and at the same time minimizing cost.

3. Focus on the mass market, the emerging middle class and the emerging entrepreneurial Indian corporations.

4. Because ICT must become part of how ICICI would position itself in the marketplace as a high-tech innovator, create a new banking experience for consumers such as online banking, new branch hours, new devices for banking such as cell phones—offer a continuous progression of creative and new services. A list of financial service innovations in India implemented by the ICICI Bank is shown in Table 2.1.

ICICI-Induced Innovations in Financial Services in India

As depicted in Table 2.1, ICICI has been the first to bring a number of banking and financial services innovations to the Indian market. In 2005, ICICI reached more than 10 million customers with its network of over 600 branches and 3,000 ATMs. The CEO, K. V. Kamath, announced two major initiatives at the annual meeting to shareholders: *Going Global* and *Going Rural*. Since then, ICICI's increasing global presence in the United Kingdom, Russia, the Middle East, South Africa, Southeast Asia, and Canada has expanded its market of expatriates and international customers globally while at the same time helping to support rural self-help groups and community banks in India and other developing na-

TABLE 2.1 A LIST OF BANKING AND FINANCIAL SERVICES INNOVATIONS BY ICICI IN INDIA

1. First Indian bank to provide Internet banking.

2. First bank in the world to securitize microfinance portfolios.

3. First bank to make simultaneous equity offering in three markets—namely, United States, India, and Japan—in December 2005.

4. First bank to provide complete doorstep service for home loans (other players only partly provided this service).

5. First bank in India to introduce bill payment facility on ATMs in February 2002.

6. First bank to connect ATMs using wireless local loop (WiLL) technology in March 2002.

7. First bank in India to introduce solar-powered ATMs and also the first bank to connect ATMs through wireless networks.

8. First bank in India to auction nonperforming assets.

9. First bank in India to provide ATM interface in multiple regional languages spoken in India. Also the first bank to introduce voice only interface at ATMs to help visually challenged customers.

10. First bank to launch full-fledged statement printing on the ATM; also the first bank to have the capability to accept bulk cash at its ATMs.

tions. The two initiatives—global and rural—may appear as polar extremes; however, both initiatives, at their core, are based on common capabilities built over the last decade.

Migrating to the new logic of innovation was not a single giant step. ICICI adopted an evolutionary business model based on continuous innovation. These small steps reduced the company's risk in the transformation of the bank. Two umbrella principles guided the journey. First, ICICI embraced technology-mediated business processes and analytics to enable low cost, flexibility, and ease of deployment (as opposed to the traditional paper-based systems). Second, ICICI made sure that it had the capacity to experiment at low cost and scale rapidly. The bank ended up with low costs, speed, scale, and flexibility all at the same time. The series of specific products and services introduced in the company's migration to $N = 1$ and $R = G$ is captured in Figure 2.4. Let us briefly examine these innovation steps, during the period 1998 to 2007,

FIGURE 2.4

N = 1 and R = G Initiatives at ICICI

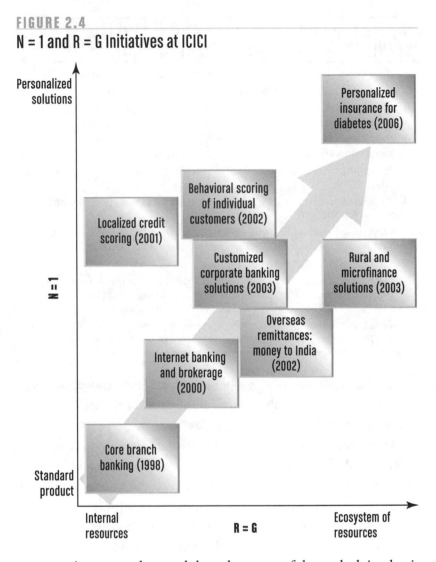

one at a time, to understand the robustness of the underlying business process innovations and the technical and social architecture.

Core Branch Banking (1998)

As ICICI emerged out of the highly regulated environment more than a decade ago, its core banking services began targeting a large segment of customers. The company's primary challenge in its new retail phase was quality and consistency in basic banking services (bedrocks of innovation in an $N = 1$ and $R = G$ world). These services, therefore, are depicted in the lower quadrant of the illustration in Figure 2.4 because they were standard offerings across customers and leveraged resources predominantly.

Internet Banking and Brokerage in India (2000)

ICICI was the first Indian bank to introduce online banking in India. The company started with less than a million customers in 2000, and it had nearly 9.5 million retail banking customers as of June 2006. ICICI tries to personalize its services for each customer right from the time of opening an account. The bank's representatives can visit customers at their homes or offices at times convenient to them to open new accounts, and the representatives even fill up all the required forms, leaving only the signature to the customer ($N = 1$). The bank soon followed its online banking initiative with an online brokerage platform—for the first time in India. This platform integrated its business processes in cash management, banking, and brokerage to present *one single window* for its customers. The ICICI trading platform with 5,000 customers in 2000 had grown to over a million customers in 2006.

This initiative democratized trading in securities and unleashed a huge middle-class market from homebound educated housewives to small entrepreneurs and brokers with direct access to the market for the first time. Unlike in the United States, ICICI sells this online brokerage as a premium service, and customers are willing to pay for it. This trading platform currently executes more than 320,000 transactions per day on average with peak loads exceeding a million transactions. This online trading platform was developed by the bank's internal team in 12 months. The entire day-to-day operation behind this platform is now managed by just five full-time employees. These online channels to ICICI's customers are an integral part of its overall business model with emphasis on leveraging the Internet to bring a new level of access and value to its consumers. The online trading platform of ICICI is the third largest in the world. This platform has provided visibility of its accounts online for every customer and has also enabled portfolio assessment tools for customers to track the performance of their accounts. This capability has required partnership with electronic exchanges, and hence this initiative is placed in the middle of the grid in Figure 2.4.

Localized Credit Scoring (2001)— Customized Credit Rating System in the Indian Context

As noted earlier, when ICICI entered the retail banking and credit card business, the dominant players in the credit card business were the multinational banks catering to the affluent while the rest of the market had almost no access to credit cards. Since India lacked any central credit tracking system, it was a safe bet for multinational banks to mandate a high minimum deposit with the banks providing a credit card facility. The multinational brands were strong and very aspirational. They lured the rich. It was therefore a necessity for ICICI to experiment with a new credit rating system to capture the growing middle-class market and at the same time mitigate risk. Since no prior data existed, ICICI had to develop a credit assessment system to help it develop risk profiles of a new consumer category for credit cards in India.

In less than six months, a new application platform was built with a rules engine that included both standard credit rules and rules that were customized to the Indian context. This credit assessment engine incorporated declared income and lifestyle parameters with constant updates of rules based on default and spending data. While the distribution of credit status among consumers may remain stable in a developed economy, the reality is far different in an economy that is growing at 8 to 10 percent annually with a rapidly emerging middle class. The credit profile of these emerging consumers is far more dynamic. Hence, credit scoring is updated more than once a year through regular updates as new information becomes available on income and spending patterns. The capability to customize the credit assessment system to the Indian context and build personalized credit histories for individual consumers based on their financial and lifestyle parameters enabled

ICICI to expand this line of business from less than a million customers in 2001 to 5.6 million customers as of June 2006. This capability demanded a deeper understanding of the profiles of individual customers. The profiles were built using primarily internal resources, and this step is thus depicted in Figure 2.4.

Behavioral Scoring of Individual Customers (2002)

Credit scoring based on the behavior of individual customers helps ICICI to understand customers and enables it to cocreate strategies for value creation across its customer lifecycle. ICICI, in this effort to understand its evolving consumer base, works with multiple partners with specialization in analytics to derive contextual insights and enhance consumer experiences. For example, this initiative maps a 360-degree view of its customers in terms of their engagement with the bank and searches for opportunities to better inform customers and cocreate value.

Overseas Remittances: Money to India (2002)

Money2India is a remittance service offered by ICICI to capture the market of funds transferred to India by Indian nationals residing across the globe. Remittances from Indian expatriates back to India, through formal channels, were not a significant business till 2002. However, given the growing number of affluent Indian expatriates in the United States, Europe, and the Middle East and the restrictions on money transfers through unorganized sectors after 9/11, managers at ICICI saw a huge opportunity.

Public sector banks from India such as the State Bank of India had a remittance business. They followed the traditional banking business processes and operated on a paper-based system for remittances from expatriates. It was a very slow process with no transparency, and obviously the consumer experience was not good. For example, on average it took around 10 days for the money sent by an expatriate in the United States to reach its final recipient in India. If the recipient was in a small town or village, the transfer could take even longer. ICICI created a digital bridge to integrate

the U.S. and Indian markets through transactions between an
ICICI account with JPMorgan in the United States and an ICICI
bank account in India. ICICI leveraged the electronic transfer
through JPMorgan and its electronic network of various branches
across India to increase transparency to the expatriates and cut the
cycle time from 10 days to less than 48 hours. ICICI currently en-
joys over 30 percent market share of the $25 billion plus remit-
tance market to India. ICICI has, more recently, introduced Indian
rupee–denominated remittance cards usable in any ATM or over
100,000 merchant establishments in India.

Customized Corporate Banking Solutions (2003)

As noted earlier, the ICICI Bank has placed its ICT capabilities at
the center of its value creation process, and it has an R&D lab with
a small team of 40 people drawn from business and technology
groups to experiment with new ideas. This combination of business and technology expertise enables the company to understand
customer concerns and deliver unique solutions. These teams are
provided incentives to identify unique solutions that enhance value
to consumers. We illustrate with a few examples of how they have
adapted products and processes to create unique value for customers.

ICICI was the first bank in India to introduce a check-scanning
machine with its ATMs. All customer acknowledgment receipts
for regular transactions include a small scanned image of the
check, making it easier for consumers to track their transactions.
Most banks in the United States still provide receipts with unique
identification numbers, but consumers seldom use them due to the
additional work needed to reconcile these receipts with their state-
ments. The ICICI Bank integrated its magnetic ink character
recognition (MICR) and image-scanning applications to provide this service. Similarly, for corporate banking, the bank has
developed unique customized software applications to connect directly with enterprise systems of some of its large clients. ICICI
has also developed unique solutions for its corporate customers.

For example, large two-wheeler manufacturers in India, such as Bajaj Auto and TVS Motors, who sell over a million vehicles annually, face the challenge of reducing the float in clearing checks from their dealers countrywide. ICICI has delivered a cash management feature connecting dealers of these firms with their corporate offices so that information from a dealer's check is itself treated as collection and directly linked to the financial systems of these manufacturers. This has reduced the collection time from weeks to a few hours.

This approach is closer to $N = 1$ and $R = G$, since the bank's corporate customers in the past have had their own unique financial systems in different software platforms. ICICI has had to work with multiple global partners to customize this service and enhance its unique value to its customers. In another example, ICICI has partnered with the Austrian multinational firm Efkon, which specializes in electronic payment systems, to provide collection and cash management at over 2,500 retail outlets of Hindustan Petroleum Corporation Limited (HPCL), the second-largest oil marketing firm in India. In the first three years of its operation, the retail customer base for this payment solution has grown from a few thousand to over a million.

Rural and Microfinance Solutions (2003)

The government of India mandated that every bank open rural branches. For every two urban branches that were licensed, the bank had to open at least one rural branch. Most established banks saw this as a burden and as a cost of doing business. In contrast, ICICI recognized, fairly early, how to effectively leverage this requirement into a new business opportunity. The bank realized that in order to reach the rural poor, it needed a new distribution system.

ICICI acquired the Bank of Madura, a regional bank in South India that had pioneered the concept of rural lending through self-help groups (SHGs)—groups of 20 village women who are organized to provide support to each other. As the women become a tight-knit unit, the bank then lends to the SHG, which in turn provides loans to its members based on locally developed criteria. The SHGs prioritize, monitor, and collect dues.

ICICI recognized that rural community organizations and village self-help groups have a deeper understanding of customers in this market. ICICI has developed processes to efficiently screen, borrow, and manage loans as little as $100 at sites located every 6 to 10 miles in rural India. These borrowings include loans for crops, buying a buffalo or tractor, irrigation, education, health care, and mortgages in rural India.

ICICI has also innovated services such as biometric cards and digital kiosks to improve personalization and access to services. ICICI's rural lending doubled in 2006 to reach $3.6 billion with over 3.2 million clients. These loans are personalized based on the earning potential of the borrower. For example, the terms of payment for a "buffalo loan" may be adjusted based on the milk yield from the buffalo. Biometric devices were introduced to protect the identity of each member in these self-help groups.

ICICI has partnered with thousands of community-based organizations and cooperatives to tap the microfinance market and provide unique solutions to finance different types of rural consumers at their convenience. In designing these services, ICICI has pushed along the $N = 1$ and $R = G$ axes (see Figure 2.4) through personalization and resource leverage in collaborations.

Personalized Insurance for Diabetes (2006)

As discussed in Chapter 1, this initiative from ICICI Prudential is another powerful example of the many serving the needs of the one. ICICI has built an ecosystem of partners that includes pharmaceutical companies, local gyms, doctors, and nutritionists to provide access to its consumers. The company adjusts premiums based on individual levels of conformance. ICICI is building analytical models to understand the unique behavior of each patient and at the same time gain deeper understanding of the disease to further improve the services that it offers to customers.

These examples provide a remarkable range of business models at ICICI—many reaching "scale" in a short period of time. These initiatives combine access to resources from JPMorgan, analytics firms, self-help groups, and community banks (beginning of $R = G$) with portfolios of customizable products and services for the individual ($N = 1$). ICICI also allows rural self-help groups to decide their own priorities. Often, most of these initiatives have moved from conception to reality in one year. ICICI is still primarily an Indian bank with a growing appetite for global growth, and it is mastering the business of serving customers at every level of the economic pyramid.

ICICI's Core Capabilities

ICICI's capabilities are built on three core capabilities:

1. Business process flexibility to reflect evolving business models

2. Synchronization of strategy, business process, and ICT architecture

3. Senior management leadership in shaping social infrastructure and culture

Capability 1. Business Process Flexibility to Reflect Evolving Business Models

Senior managers at ICICI consider their capability to enable flexible business processes that support organic growth coupled with a flexible social structure to execute their strategies as a major asset. This flexibility allows constant experimentation on new products and services. Resilience in their business processes is reflected in their capacity to adapt credit assessment systems in retail banking, to connect directly with thousands of dealers around the country, and to scale up with microfinancing to self-help groups in rural banking with adaptive pricing. More important, all these initiatives begin as low-cost and low-risk experiments that take only a three- to four-month period to prove viable. Scaling of such successful experiments is a continuous process at ICICI. This flexibility in business processes does not mean that there is a lack of process definition at any given time. All of the processes and their output metrics are well defined and monitored.

ICICI has balanced the tension between well-defined business processes and the capacity to alter business processes to seize new opportunities. In 2004, ICICI identified opportunities to compete with Internet-only banks such as ING Direct in some developed markets. Since this did not require opening branch offices and success was largely defined by the flow of information and improvements in business processes, it was a viable opportunity. For example, ICICI manages the entire operations of direct banking to its customers in Canada from India.

The bank adheres to all the regulatory norms as set by Canadian authorities, and it offers 1 to 2.5 percentage points more in interest than other Canadian banks. The efficiency of its business process and ICT backbone fused with its base in India allows it to create a surplus (compared to its Canadian competitors) and share it with its customers. It is not surprising that the bank has been adding 2,000 customers per week in Canada (as of June 2006) and has over 500,000 international customers (as of that time). A study by a major consulting firm revealed that the ratio of operational costs in salary terms between ICICI and other Internet banks in Canada was 1:7 while IT costs per customer was 1:15. One senior manager at ICICI argued, "While large MNC banks are trying to push their back-office operations to India to leverage resources here, our entire operation is in India, and hence, we are well positioned to offer competitive services in the international market." They call this *reverse business process outsourcing* (or reverse BPO).

Capability 2. Synchronization of Strategy, Business Process, and ICT Architecture

ICICI's chief executive officer, K. V. Kamath, identifies the bank's ICT capability as one of the two pillars of the company's organic growth and ability to rapidly deliver new products and services to its customers.

ICICI differs significantly from other banks in how it manages the synchronization between IT and business. First, it does not have a CIO. The bank's head of IT has several years of experience in domestic and international banking, where he learned the strategic assets of ICT. Second, the entire senior management team, starting with the CEO, K. V. Kamath, has a deep understanding of the business implications of ICT. Synchronization between business needs and ICT investments is governed by a small group called the Technology Management Group that consists of both bankers and IT professionals.

The portfolio of ICT applications at ICICI contains only a few "packaged applications," with the rest being customized applications to enable the dynamic business process capability that the strategy mandates. In reference to the building blocks shown in Figure 2.2, ICICI has deployed standard pieces of hardware and software in the lower two blocks of the infrastructure while it has customized the ICT applications that support business processes. The application layer enables the business processes that help ICICI execute its business model and strategy. For example, the Technology Management Group at ICICI decided to abandon packaged software from a leading enterprise software vendor because the functionality in that product was restricting its capacity to change its business processes rapidly at low cost. The company opted to codevelop a customized system by partnering with one of the largest IT vendors in India. This codeveloped banking application is now offered in the international market.

Yet another distinction in the case of ICICI is the two-way flow of ideas and information between business units and IT. It is not just the traditional model of requirements emanating from business units that lead to demand for investments in IT. As noted earlier, the tech R&D lab and senior management constantly scan new technologies and developments in ICT for their business relevance. They engage commercial and academic partners to seed low-cost experiments.

For example, ICICI has partnered with the Indian Institute of Technology, Chennai, to develop a new electromechanical ATM machine customized to the rural Indian environment at a much lower price point. The climate in many parts of India makes the currency notes soggy with moisture and soiled with rough usage. Hence, the traditional ATM technology used in the West or in cities may not be suitable, since the makers of those ATMs expect cleaner currency notes. The new ATM from ICICI is being designed to deliver currency notes to consumers in collated bundles of cash similar to the way in which soda vending machines work.

Customized ATMs for rural markets, biometric devices for rural markets, and corporate cash management applications are some of the examples resulting from this exercise. ICICI has always been on the forefront of adopting new technologies. While business groups pull ICT projects on a need basis, the ICT team and the tech lab push new technologies through low-cost experimentation. In a typical large firm in the United States, various industry reports suggest that discretionary spending on IT is in the range of 15 to 25 percent of the total IT budget, while the rest—75 to 85 percent—is spent on the incremental maintenance of legacy applications to keep current business operations running with minor changes. However, in the case of ICICI, only 20 percent of the total IT budget is spent on maintenance, while nearly 80 percent is spent on new business applications. One of the reasons for this distinct difference is that unlike traditional international banks, ICICI has no legacy systems. The business implication of this difference is significant because it unleashes resources for experimentation with new business processes and technology solutions.

Capability 3. Senior Management Leadership in Shaping Social Architecture and Culture

We stated earlier that ICICI had no legacy in terms of software systems in its ICT architecture. But it did have a legacy in terms of social norms. The company had to transform an environment that was similar to that of a state-controlled bank. A legacy in how a company organizes its decision-making process—consisting of the authority structure, roles, decision criteria, and capabilities of senior management—can determine how that organization copes with complexity.

The social infrastructure and culture fostered by the bank's senior management since 1996 have been decisive factors behind its capacity to constantly experiment and seize new opportunities. The senior management recruited a young and dynamic management team. Team members were empowered to "kill" old legacy systems. These young managers turned themselves into change agents. In their new culture, managers were willing to share their best people for new initiatives that may not have been directly under the managers' control. Winning as a corporation became a critical goal. One senior manager used the metaphor of "donating blood" to describe the sharing of the best people in her group for new corporate initiatives. It was not suicide, nor was it stealing. Few were likely to "hoard" key skills. The willingness to share skills reflected the bank's confidence in its strategy and its willingness to experiment and grow rapidly.

The social architecture within ICICI depicts a sense of urgency and a need for real-time insights from transparent processes and data in all decisions. While hierarchy is used as a substitute for transparency in traditional firms, ICICI tries to use IT to cut as many unnecessary layers as possible from its decision chains. While the bank may not have a formal CIO, the head of IT has a visceral understanding of the bank's business processes and needs and a similarly deep understanding of business processes and ICT capability as critical elements of senior management. For example, ICICI has aggressively adopted open-source software and has deployed open-office software across the organization, including the senior management staff (for internal communication), and the company is comfortable with it. In summary, the company has created a culture of boldness to constantly seize new opportunities and at the same time mitigate risk through transparency in processes and information.

Business Results at ICICI

Over the last decade, senior managers at ICICI focused on strategy, business models, and business process—the technical and social infrastructure to rapidly grow and become global. Their business results are impressive by any standards. They moved from a few thousand in 2001 to almost 10 million banking customers by 2006. The total number of customers they now touch through all their products exceeds 20 million. Total assets managed by them has multiplied 250 times in the last decade, starting with an asset base of around U.S. $250 million in 1996 to nearly U.S. $80 billion in 2007. This phenomenal growth has not been achieved without profits. Their net profit also presents a significant rise, from U.S. $4 million in 1996 to U.S. $620 million in 2006. An interesting trend underlying this phenomenal growth is the reduction in their nonperforming assets from 4.7 percent in 2002 to 0.71 percent in 2006.

A WORD OF CAUTION

ICICI allows us to walk through the entire framework of capability building (see Figure 2.1) and identification of business processes and the supporting social and technical architecture as sources of advantage. ICICI's performance has been stellar. But such growth and increase in scope also carries their own seeds of risk. The robustness of the ICT enterprise architecture must allow not only for rapid change but also for compliance. A large firm is subject to the requirements of Sarbanes-Oxley. Furthermore, a bank should also be compliant with the requirements of Basel II. It is not only about external compliance. Compliance with internal delivery norms and policies are critical as well. Even if the processes are robust, training a very large number of new people (ICICI recruited 20,000 new employees in 2006) will strain any system. The risks are around the following parameters:

1. As the number of customers and vendors increases, how can ICICI retain its $N = 1$ and $R = G$ orientation? What analytic capabilities are needed to make this work? We will discuss this in Chapter 3.

2. Can the architecture of the ICT system automatically identify all the cross-impacts of any single change to a single subprocess such as minimum balance requirements? As the systems become complex because of the variety of products and services, as well as the choices that individuals can exercise, the architecture of the system must automatically sense and adjust itself. Can the system self-monitor? Will the ICICI face the same challenges that legacy systems face? How can the firm overcome this? We will discuss this issue in Chapter 4.

3. Can social infrastructure keep pace with the rate of change—new business models, scale, and scope with a large number of new employees? As the battle for talent in India intensifies, what is the quality control process for retaining the best talent and protecting the company's culture? We will discuss this in Chapter 7.

ICICI has been used as an illustration because its strategy is still evolving and its competitive advantage both in India and increasingly in its global operations is based on its deep understanding of the business models and its links with business processes.

CONCLUSION

So what do the experiences of Wal-Mart, FedEx, eBay, and ICICI tell us? The success of these firms is based on building a unique business model that is reasonably robust. The robustness of these business models depends on the underlying business processes, the ICT infrastructure, the analytics and applications, and the social infrastructure that supports them. This conclusion challenges the assertion that "IT does not matter." The popular argument is that ICT capabilities will become akin to utilities such as power in a manufacturing plant, which is necessary to conduct business but may not help in any way to compete better. Our examples suggest that that argument can only go so far as the bottom two layers of the ICT stack as shown in Figure 2.2—that is, the hardware, communication links, systems software, and database utilities. The business processes and the analytics provide unique and clear competitive advantages to the firm. Managers must recognize the distinct differences and implications of a firm's ICT foundation.

APPENDIX:
BUSINESS PROCESS DEFINITIONS

The term *business process* (BP) has been defined in different ways by industry experts and academics. The reason for the diversity in definitions stems from the differences in orientations of the authors. For example, the term has often been defined from an industrial engineering or operations perspective. Alternatively, it is seen from a technology vendor and/or computer science perspective with clearly defined inputs and outputs. The temporal aspect of the BP has been captured by some who define it as a specific ordering of work across space and time with a beginning and end. Some believe that not all BPs have a defined end and a beginning. Further, some definitions are grounded in business process reengineering work that emphasizes processes in workflows with a focus on operational efficiency, including efficiency at the customer and stakeholder interfaces. Those focused on the behavioral aspects in organizations emphasize the importance of collaboration and coordination in business process definitions. We list below sample definitions for BP. Our list is only indicative of the diversity and is not intended to be exhaustive:

> A business process is most broadly defined as an activity that carries out a series of steps, which produces a specific result or a related series of results.

> A business process is a collection of related, structured activities, a chain of events, that produces a specific service or product for a particular customer or customers.

> A business process is a recipe for achieving a commercial result. Each business process has inputs, method, and outputs. The inputs are a prerequisite that must be in place before the method can be put into practice. When the method is applied to the inputs, then certain outputs will be created.

> A business process is the complete and dynamically coordinated set of collaborative and transactional activities that delivers value to customers.

> A process is a structured, measured set of activities designed to produce a specified output for a particular customer or market. A process is thus a specific ordering of work activities across time and space, with a beginning, an end, and clearly identified inputs and outputs.

> Business process implies (1) organization of work to achieve a result; (2) multiple steps and coordination of people; (3) an element of design or implementation that renders a business process as distinctive as a competitive asset as research and development or product development, a "firm-specific asset" (in the words of institutional economists), "core competence," or "dynamic capability"; and (4) management as the enabler and sustainer of process advantage.

CHAPTER

6

n the last chapter, we identified business processes as the enabler of an innovative culture through their impact on both social and technical architecture. As a critical intermediate step between strategy and operations, the quality of business processes (granularity, flexibility, and clarity) determines the capability of firms to compete ef-

ANALYTICS:
INSIGHTS FOR INNOVATION

fectively. By definition, in a rapidly changing competitive environment, business processes cannot be static. The dynamics of an industry dictate the rate of change in business models and strategy. Business processes must keep pace with this rate of change in the strategy of the firm. More important, business process capability may suggest new ways of competing.

Competitiveness favors those who spot new trends and act on them expeditiously. Therefore, managers must develop insights about new opportunities by amplifying weak signals. These weak signals emerge from insights derived through a deep understanding and interpretation of a wide variety of information. For example, recognizing that SMS (text) messaging using a cell phone will be an important method for settling small payments is critical for the long-term success of Visa and MasterCard.

Spotting new trends requires comprehension of consumer expectations and behaviors and technological changes, as well as the nature of the supply chain and opportunities for its improvement. How does one spot trends early? Can a firm develop tools that aid in building insights? The new competitive landscape requires *continuous analysis* of data for insight. Analysis that is only episodic and ad hoc (as when a senior manager commissions a specific study, say, to assess the impact of oil prices on shopping patterns) or periodic (such as actual sales compared to forecasts) will not suffice. Traditional analytical approaches are often asynchronous with business changes. Hence, delays in recognizing, interpreting, and acting on the trends are emerging as critical impediments to competitiveness.

Every firm accumulates a voluminous amount of transaction data (for example, sales transactions) and equally large volumes of unstructured data (for example, video clips and advertisements). Managers need a mechanism to understand the accumulated information and extract valuable insights. Real-time analytics seize the opportunities and mitigate the risks in seeking to have global resources serving single customers.

We use the terms *analytics* and *analytical models* to describe a class of mathematical applications that permits businesses to crunch everything from picking stocks in trading rooms rapidly (in less than a millionth of a second) to identifying specific advertising messages based on your search at any time in Google. Some recent trends are helping firms build this capacity. Algorithms and quantitative methods used in analytics are evolving to help managers derive insights, often combining structured transaction data (numbers) and unstructured data as in documents, images, and video. Digitization of business processes, the Internet, and evolving ICT architecture enable real-time predictive modeling. These capabilities, as we will demonstrate in this chapter, are at the heart of effective management in an $N = 1$ and $R = G$ world.

The link between data, analytics, and insights is shown in Figure 3.1. As you can see, the quality of insight depends on both the quality of data and the quality of analytics. Models that are not built specifically to inform on strategic priorities are of little value to line managers. More important, insights that are not available when decisions have to be made are of little value. In this chapter,

FIGURE 3.1

FIGURE 3.1
Business Insights

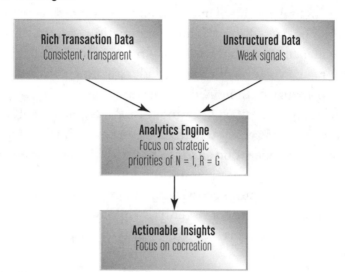

we will assume the availability of high-quality data that capture the millions of transactions in a company—be they sales, warranty claims, orders placed, or payments to suppliers. (We recognize that the quality of data is a major concern in many firms. Data collection often is not standardized across the firm. Increasingly, data are also collected in a highly decentralized fashion, for example, by delivery agents with handheld devices. Rather than engage in a detailed technical discussion on how to "clean up databases," in this chapter we will assume that the data quality is acceptable to perform analytics.) We will explore a range of analytics, with examples, that can help you recognize the usefulness of these tools in migrating to an $N = 1$ and $R = G$ world of innovation.

ANALYTICAL TOOLS PROVIDE BUSINESS INSIGHTS

Traditionally, managers depended on experience and intuition to develop insights—"gut feel," if you will. Most often a gut feel is based on past experiences. Gut feel and intuition are important, but in a fast-changing competitive environment, experience of the past is less and less valuable. *Foresight, not hindsight, is of value.*

Foresight is a result of understanding, through structured and unstructured data, the unfolding of competitive dynamics. There is value in identifying new patterns of relationships, predicting the behavior and evolution of systems, and mitigating risk. In an $N = 1$ world, the behavior of individual consumers as well as broad patterns of change must be understood. In $R = G$, the capabilities of each vendor in the ecosystem in terms of costs, time, and quality levels must be understood and matched with the specific demands of a single consumer at a point in time. Furthermore, given the complexity of the entire ecosystem, the impact of change in any single variable, such as order entry, will have a ripple effect on other related subsystems such as inventory, spare parts, and manufacturing lead times.

A "small change" in order entry could trigger multiple changes in the totality of business processes. Managing the systemwide impacts of changes cannot be left to the gut feeling of managers. However, individual managers can, based on their experiences, interpret the signals differently (especially in a rapidly evolving system). Hence, foresight based on the real-time analyses of both structured and unstructured data is indispensable. Intuition and gut feeling are still useful, but not as a substitute for analytics.

Keeping business processes current and compliant with all changes and at the same time gleaning insights about the evolving behavior of consumers and the supply network require a commitment to analytics. Consider, for example, the Indian IRS. It is known that not everyone in India pays his or her taxes adequately. The IRS can safely start with the assumption that there is significant tax evasion in the country. In order to deal with widespread tax evasion, India's tax agency is building a database of declared income and consumption patterns, such as travel, purchases of big-ticket items such as cars, plasma TVs, deposits and withdrawals from banks, stock market activity, and the like, to spot patterns of tax evasion. The focus is on identifying individual taxpayers

($N = 1$) for further investigation. This project calls for deriving insights based on data from multiple sources.

A similar initiative is in place at the IRS in the United States as well. In the United States, the cost of tax avoidance is estimated at $350 billion. Tax evasion, around the world, is a moving target. In order to predict these behavior patterns, complex analytic models have to be developed. Data from a wide variety of sources must be pulled together to see the emerging patterns. Microsoft recently announced its purchase of a small start-up health search engine called Medstory, Inc., that applies advanced analytics to structured and unstructured medical and health information in journals, government documents, and the Internet to present an enhanced customer experience in access to health information. The desired result is a personalized information search based on one customer's family history, prior medication, age, and gender.

Analytics must be driven by strategy. For example, in order to price health insurance for each diabetic consumer (patient), we need analytics, which in real time monitors behaviors (compliance on predetermined routines) but can also forecast likely behaviors. Analytics can also show where to allocate resources and how to optimize the "resource network." Should a call from an irate and important customer in New Zealand be routed to India or Australia? This is a real-time decision, one of thousands, to which the firm must respond creatively. Insights also result from consumer concerns and comments. Understanding and researching blogs and chat rooms is another important source of insights. The capability to use analytical modeling tools is critical in every aspect of value creation, from understanding customer preferences and behaviors to supply chain management, global resource reconfiguration, skill management, and risk mitigation. We will illustrate the power of analytical tools with applications focused on leveraging global resources to serve individual customers in global markets first ($R = G$), followed by illustration of such tools in moving toward $N = 1$.

GLOBAL RESOURCE ACCESS (R = G)

The capability to leverage global resources will demand new levels of visibility and agility in managing logistics of physical goods and resources (globally) to meet unique demands of customers.

Visible Global Supply Chains

Let us start with a well-known example. Access to global resources requires the capability to tap into a complex web of resources, expeditiously, and at the best global price. Li & Fung, a premium global trading group covering high-volume, time-sensitive goods including fashion accessories, furnishings, handicrafts, and home products, is a good illustration of process innovation through analytics. Li & Fung started as a pure trading company, sourcing its products from China for exports. However, within a decade Li & Fung had put in place a global network for managing supply chains for a large number of retailers in Europe and the United States. Unlike the traditional trading business model, Li & Fung does not own any production facility or large warehouses. As stated by Victor Fung, the CEO:

> Everybody thinks that a trading company is just taking an order from the right hand and giving it to the left hand. The idea is that, maybe foreigners don't know which factory to go to, so you perform an introductory role, maybe a quality control role, and there it stops. . . . Whenever we go in, we don't just give them [the suppliers] an order and hope that they know what to do. We hand-hold them through the whole process. That's why we say we almost are a virtual factory. . . . It is the way we orchestrate the production, come up with samples, and feed them information. All that is going way, way beyond that original matching function.

Li & Fung manages a large number of quality-conscious, cost-effective producers who can effectively deliver orders on time for customers such as JCPenney. More recently, the company identified the need to expand in locations near Europe and the United States to cut lead time for delivering physical goods. The overall business model of Li & Fung is based on the "end-to-end business process knowledge"—that is, from the point-of-sales data emanating from a specific branch of JCPenney in the United States (for example, how many white shirts, cotton, size 16 inches/32 to 33 inches, pattern XYZ) to its ability to replenish the inventory in that location through articulating its supplier network in maybe three countries.

The complexity of the company's supplier network demands a capacity to manage information regarding regulatory restrictions across countries, managing the skill base of its suppliers and hiring in specific locations, and finally, integrating all this information to provide a seamless one-stop shop for its customers. The insights derived through the company's accumulated data on various markets and individual supplier capabilities enable the company to deliver unique value. This system cannot function without a detailed, constantly updated understanding of all the suppliers—capacities, capabilities, costs, skills, and distances. This also demands a detailed understanding of the customers' needs—urgency, quality, locations for delivery, and profitability. $R = G$ must start with this level of visibility to all variables that can impact the appropriate resource configuration—"plant A in Thailand to serve JCPenney in Dallas for this order"—decisions.

In an $R = G$ world, establishing the visibility to the entire chain is a good first step. Schneider Electric is the world's largest manufacturer of electrical distribution systems and components. The company has a healthy growth rate; sales are U.S. $8.8 billion, and it has 70,000 employees in 130 countries. Schneider's purchasing organization procures for four leading markets (each worth U.S. $1 billion): raw materials and means of production, fabricated metallic and plastic components, electronic and electrical devices, and nonproduction services. The global purchasing operation works with these four markets and a total of 33 commodity groups and multiple country organizations. The complexity of a supply chain such as this makes business analytics a necessity to effectively compete. Many large companies operate such supply chains without full visibility, and the consequences are obvious as they expose their supply chain to unknown global sources. For example, Serge Vanborre, a senior manager at Schneider Electric's purchasing headquarters, says, "We want to know who is buying what from whom. We want to know the global purchases, be able to do an analysis in order to repartition our purchases and verify if the supplier policies are followed."

As introduced earlier, a well-known example of visibility in a global supply chain is exhibited by leading logistics firms such as UPS and FedEx. For example, Atlanta-based UPS moves over 15 million packages around the world in a day, and it provides complete visibility to the end consumer on each and every packet. FedEx recently integrated the software systems of its ground, air, and freight businesses to provide full visibility to all of its customers and employees for the 6 million plus packages it handles every day.

Similarly, in one of the largest radio frequency identification device (RFID) projects implemented so far, Unisys has created full visibility for the global supply chain of the U.S. Department of Defense (DOD). Prior to this new system, the department operated three different supply chains for the army, navy, and air force with minimal integration. Furthermore, there was almost no visibility. In contrast, the new system connects global suppliers with 30 centers of DOD to any location in the world from Taiwan to Tacoma, providing complete visibility through RFID tags. As a result, when the military runs out of spare parts for a tank in Iraq, it has the capacity to locate the floating warehouse in the nearest ship instead of having to source the parts from the nearest depot, which in the past has often been far away.

Similarly, Homeland Security demands that it know where the cargo shipments that reach U.S. ports have been. So far, this has been an elusive goal. For example, a Sara Lee innerwear shipment manufactured in Pakistan and loaded in a container at Karachi can travel through a feeder ship to Mumbai, India, and then to Sri Lanka, through the Suez Canal, to Nova Scotia, and finally to New York. The items in the ship are invisible during their circuitous course of travel in the sea for almost a month!

Dynamic Real-Time Reconfiguration of Resources

Visibility in the global supply chain is almost a prerequisite for managing the complex web of product and information flows. The capacity to reconfigure resources globally can start with a simple trend analysis of the key metrics across different markets and product categories. But this beginning should be expanded to a capacity for rapid response to changes in either external market demand or internal process capabilities available at a given point in time.

For example, U.K.-based Aviva plc, the largest insurance company in Europe, is architecting its global customer service processes to constantly search for innovation and efficiency gains to deliver value to its customers. It is common for customer support call centers to use technologies to route calls to appropriate agents (agents with specific skills and temperament based on customer needs) within an office. Aviva's insurance underwriting and claims business processes are designed to dynamically leverage the appropriate competencies from its global service centers, ranging from Australia to the Philippines, India, Europe, and Canada. Aviva's focus is on enhancing the consumer's experience ($N = 1$) by dynamically routing customer service requests to different parts of the world to provide the best service for that customer without compromising the cost of that service. This requires a capacity for real-time matching of customer profiles with agent skill profiles on a global basis.

In its global customer support processes, Aviva worked with its partners, including a business process outsourcing (BPO) firm called 24/7 Customer in India, to capture metrics in every subtask of the entire customer engagement process to better understand its customers. The process adopted by 24/7 Customer is visible with performance metrics such as customer satisfaction and time to resolve the problem. Outcome measures such as cross-sale and transaction completion are tracked in real time for each call. In order to accomplish this dynamic routing, Aviva must have visibility to the type of customer, loads, and the quality of agents and their skills in various locations. In an article published in the *Economic Times* in India in 2006, Richard Harvey, Aviva Group CEO, says, "Because we take a lot of care to measure customer satisfaction on a completely arm's-length basis, we can demonstrate that our customer satisfaction from India is as strong as or even stronger than the United Kingdom."

An additional benefit of this transparency in its global processes is that it enables Aviva to constantly monitor the best-in-class process execution across its global centers and disseminate that knowledge to other centers. John Ainley, HR director at Aviva, admits that the company is building a culture within the organization to promote competition in process performance across its global centers, to prepare its employees to emerge out of the "not-invented-here" syndrome and to accept process innovations from other centers. This leads to continuous improvement across all centers. Aviva has certainly taken a lead in reconfiguring global resources to create customer value in the insurance industry. But it is not alone.

A visit to the Chennai (India) office of the Dallas-based Perot Systems reveals a new level of visibility in its processes and a capability to predict and reconfigure resources for its global clients. The business process service unit of Perot Systems provides back-office support to a number of hospitals and health insurance clients. Its Chennai center has developed a customized technology platform that integrates operations, HR, and finance business processes in a single portal. The Chennai team has disaggregated every process assigned to them and carefully identified both the skill requirements and performance metrics around each task. For example, each claim can be broken into subtasks. Each subtask requires a specific skill. One can identify the performance metrics appropriate for each subtask. Such a detailed understanding of the business process (granularity) is a key ingredient in their success.

Granularity is as important as visibility. Granularity allows managers to examine in depth the process steps, as well as the appropriate skills needed to perform them. The training modules required for each task at Perot Systems processes are digitized so that individual agents can take a set of e-learning courses at a time convenient to them. As the back-office business processes for large health insurance clients are executed in its Chennai office, the integrated platform automatically tracks the performance of every process step by every agent in every work shift. The best and worst performance levels across the organization are derived in real time through live data. Performance goals for each agent are redefined periodically with an analytical engine to enable continuous improvements in their processes and hence value for their global client. The same analytical engine also computes profitability for every client at the end of each shift.

Anurag Jain, vice president for business process services at Perot Systems in Dallas, states that this integrated platform in the company's India office allows it to assess the performance of its employees in a direct and transparent way by which individual employees are presented with their performance in a task as compared to the mean, best, and worst 10 percent of performers in that task within the organization. It is not surprising that this BPO unit of Perot Systems has bagged several awards. And Mr. Jain has now been promoted to the position of India head at Perot Systems, which means he is leading the overall consulting, applications, insurance, and BPO units in India. Perot Systems has also extended into a new business service that helps engineering services firms apply lean manufacturing concepts to their operations.

While this may be viewed as an invasion of privacy, the reality is that firms are beginning to operate at a new level of visibility to individual performance, a performance that is measured and com-

pared with others in the organization. In a high-performance organization, there may be no place to hide for the employees,
agents, or their managers. Vardhman Jain, heading the offshore
BPO Chennai center of Perot Systems, claims that its primary motivation was to create a transparent culture in which there is constant
peer pressure to perform as well as incentive to improve processes.
A majority of its process improvement effort emanates from its
own agents, akin to a Toyota production system. He adds that the
company immediately spots development areas of employees who
are unable to perform at expected levels and assigns training modules that specifically improve performance in targeted areas.

This same transparency in the company's processes and analytics also enables it to accurately measure the cost incurred for
each global client, and hence, the related client profitability. *Per-
formances of individuals or the profitability associated with a customer
are not exercises performed periodically; rather they are performed continually.* The company's platform provides instant profitability of
each client as it executes its processes. The analytical model can
also predict future run rates of revenue based on demand patterns.
This creates a capacity for Perot Systems to know profitability levels of potential engagements. This level of granularity and the
capacity to execute the engagements allows Perot to submit proposals of great accuracy.

Large IT systems vendors in India, such as Infosys and TCS,
have developed capabilities to constantly monitor the demand and
resources needed for new IT services in their global markets.
These firms recruit about 25,000 people annually, and their business models demand that they train these new recruits rapidly.
These firms manage around 3,000 projects on site and offshore
globally. They need to build capabilities to track latent demand for
expertise in specific IT tools such as J2EE (Java to Enterprise Edition) or technology such as RFIDs and use these insights to manage their talent supply chain. Their annual training budget exceeds
half a billion dollars. They need to understand resource needs and

performance at the project level and profitability and experience at the customer level. Their challenge is to anticipate global demand for services, recruit and train for the right skills rapidly, and deploy resources to the right projects for the right clients globally to maximize long-term profitability. This is an analytical problem akin to a quantitative assignment problem familiar to operations researchers.

Nirvana, an emerging BPO company in Bangalore that serves global financial services clients in customer support and other back-office processes, is yet another example of a company's unique applications of analytics and process discipline to constantly improve its understanding of customers and deliver value through global resource leverage. In addition to business process visibility and metrics- and measurements-based decisions in daily management, Nirvana has further integrated analytics-driven insights into its decision processes to build a capacity for dynamic resource reconfiguration. For example, while typical BPO organizations record at most 10 to 15 percent of the customer calls for customer support from India, Nirvana records 100 percent of the customer calls. This enables Nirvana to build a real-time customer profile based on both transaction data and keywords searched from customer conversations recorded digitally and mined for insights.

In addition, Nirvana's IT infrastructure also tracks the voice amplitude of each customer during the service call to sense the customer's frame of mind or temper. For example, the voice of a male customer calling from Dallas is tracked and compared to the typical voice profile from similar callers. The variation in a customer's voice amplitude is tracked in real time to be used as one of the inputs to build real-time customer insights and alter the company's services appropriately, if needed. For example, Nirvana's analytics engine based on data from multiple sources (transaction data, voice recordings, and keywords used by customers) has helped a large U.S. financial institution predict propensity to switch to a competitor at an individual customer level. This information has enabled the company to proactively alter its services to some of the high-risk customers and reduce its customer churn rate by 15 percent.

Similarly, consider the collaboration between the multi-billion-dollar online retailer Overstock.com in the United States and 24/7 Customer in India. Virtual stores and sales chat agents are common in online retail sites because they try to enhance customer experience through either automated or human support "online chats" with customers. Unlike physical stores, online retailers, such as Amazon.com, eBay, or Overstock.com, have millions of visitors every day, and the majority of these visitors have no intention to buy and can easily switch to other shopping sites at the click of a mouse. Hence these retailers look for analytics to identify the right customers to engage in chat.

In this partnership with online retailers, 24/7 Customer experimented with analytics to crack the science of determining the right filters to apply in inviting customers to chat and at the same time matching the appropriate resources (that is, agents) for a given customer to enhance overall customer experience. First, the process of selecting customers and assigning agents is made *visible* to the U.S.-based retailer, and performance outcomes are transparent. Second, for individual customers who are invited to chat, the past data about those customers and their current requests or queries are combined to identify the appropriate agent to be assigned to that chat, illustrating real-time reconfiguration of resources.

The performance of agents, in terms of closing sales and overall customer experience and loyalty, is constantly assessed as feedback inputs to this analytics engine. The goal here is not to optimize product-agent selling output but to develop a real-time analytics engine that uses data from multiple sources to assess agents based on a set of customer, product, and experience attributes to determine the best available agent to talk to a given hot-lead customer. This process has also improved the performance of some agents by over 60 percent because it matches the right agents (based on their strengths and knowledge in specific product and customer categories) with the right customers. Now, if the company extends this by allowing customers to define profiles of the agents it would like to chat with, we will be moving closer to anticipation of demand and resource needs and cocreation of value.

It must be obvious that in order to perform analytics for insights, we need to focus on the visibility, granularity, accuracy, and timeliness of data. Visibility to the processes is a necessary first step. The premium paid by large businesses for logistics services offered by UPS or FedEx is not for mere visibility. These businesses are also paying for accuracy, timeliness, and the ability to reroute the businesses' packages based on their current needs—that is, the capacity to reconfigure resources. Dave Barnes, senior vice president and CIO at UPS, states that his company has undertaken several time and motion studies to continuously optimize every step in the package delivery processes. These studies have revealed methods for loading the trucks in better ways through new heuristics and analytical methods such as training their drivers to fasten their seatbelt with their left hand while turning the ignition key with their other hand. Package routing information is constantly tracked and planned for each delivery truck, allowing for any changes in the routes if required either by the customer or by other interferences such as traffic or weather.

The examples of Li & Fung, UPS, the Department of Defense, 24/7 Customer, Perot Systems, and Nirvana illustrate increasing sophistication in the means available to create visibility and transparency to business processes. These examples also highlight the learning capability to reconfigure resources in real time, continuously improving the skill base of employees such that consumer needs and employee skills can be matched, and finally, building a personalization component in activities that appear simple and commonplace, such as delivery of parcels. These advances call for the integration of analytics with explicit business processes defined

FIGURE 3.2
Building Blocks of R = G Capabilities

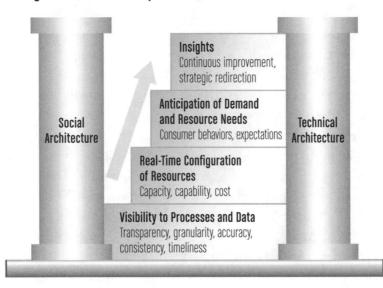

with fine granularity. Such integration demands extreme levels of training and intense measurement of both people and business processes. These systems are measurement intensive, and they prosper with the capacity for real-time feedback and corrective actions. $R = G$ needs to be appropriately configured to serve $N = 1$. The building blocks of analytic capabilities for $R = G$ are depicted in Figure 3.2.

It should now be obvious that visibility to processes and data within global supply chains ($R = G$) is crucial for building the multiple layers of capabilities that are critical for dynamic reconfiguration of resources. This visibility also helps managers anticipate consumer behaviors such that they can add or subtract appropriate resources to the whole supply network. In this process, we will also be able to get new insights—be it for operational improvement as in the case of UPS or for strategic redirection and course correction as in the case of the DOD supply chains that require integration of three distinct supply chains into one.

COCREATION OF VALUE: N = 1

The capacity to serve individual customers—that is, personalization and cocreation of value—will demand capabilities to work with customers to anticipate and predict their preferences on a continuous basis.

Let us return to UPS. Years ago, customers would deliver their package to the nearest UPS collection center and wait a few days for an acknowledgment of delivery. Next, UPS and other logistics companies opened a number of physical centers where the packages could be dropped off and created online process visibility for customers to track the packages in transit. Following this, UPS and other leading companies offered home or office pickup of packages at predetermined times in a day. More recently, UPS is working on its business process capabilities to pick up packages from individual customers' premises at the times specified by its customers.

This is a significant transformation from a business process focus on the firm to a business process focus on each unique customer experience. A careful attention to business processes, integration of analytics, and capacity to dynamically reconfigure resources is behind this transformation. UPS starts by focusing on the business processes at the individual truck and route level to load and route each truck in an efficient manner such that it improves the convenience for both its employees and its customers. For example, the routes at the truck level are planned to meet delivery times despite weather and traffic conditions. UPS's new routing analytics engine analyzes package delivery, weather, and traffic data to route each truck, minimizing left turns so that trucks are not held up at traffic junctions. This process improvement has reportedly saved the UPS fleet 1.9 million miles of travel per year. Dramatically reducing costs, simplifying work for employees, and maximizing personalization of the customer experience are all compatible goals in this instance.

UPS has developed a new ICT system to enable visibility of a packet even before the packet is picked up. Customers can engage with UPS at the UPS site www.ups.com and print out their smart delivery slips; so the demand for the pickup service is visible to UPS even before the package is picked up. The UPS system tracks this information and schedules a pickup. The requisite business processes in the company's new pickup system will be enabled by satellite GPS features to track each truck and package (within minutes) to know exactly when a driver will arrive at a destination. This capacity to reconfigure its resources will allow the company to enable customers to schedule an appointment for either pickup or delivery at the customers' convenience because the nearest truck can be routed for pickup. This is a definite shift to a more customer-centric view of delivering services in a business that involves physical goods and supply chains.

The shift toward a more customer-centric view of delivering services is also evident in the business of information goods, where deliveries are more direct. Online news portals, social networking sites, and search engines such as Google, Facebook, and Yahoo! allow customers to design their own choices of news topics and sources. In this new model, consumers rate specific Web sites or news items of interest to them, and a back-end analytical engine applies a range of qualitative and quantitative techniques, such as collaborative filtering and pattern analysis, to anticipate the likes and dislikes of those consumers to further refine the quality of their personalized information. For example, a Web add-on tool called StumbleUpon allows consumers to create a community of users with common interests and rate the Web sites and news items for their appropriateness so that only Web sites and items rated high in the community are displayed in the active lists. The online social networking news site Digg is another example of a Web site for which top news items are chosen based on the number of votes (Diggs) from members in the community as opposed to the traditional media companies' relying on a small editorial team to make these choices.

FIGURE 3.3
Building Blocks of N = 1 Capabilities

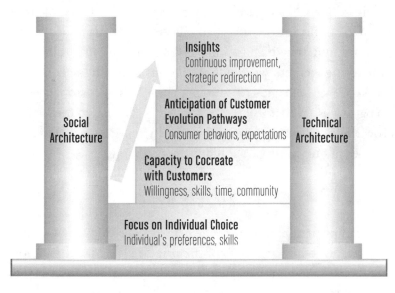

These examples illustrate the democratization of the process of identifying sites that may be of interest to individual customers based on insights derived from collective opinion in their peer group. Such analytical capabilities are now widely used by leading online retailers and auction sites (such as Amazon.com and eBay) to build personalized products and services for their customers based on deep insights derived from their past choices and behavior. We believe that the transformation to a business model of personalizing experiences for individual customers has only begun. Firms may not have a choice but to move in this direction to compete. We believe that this transformation will call for rigorous business process capabilities, integrated analytics, and focus on training and measurement. The building blocks of $N = 1$ capabilities are shown in Figure 3.3.

Needless to say, we need a system that focuses on individual customers and their individual preferences and skills. Consumers base their choices on their skill levels as much as their desires. For example, an Internet-savvy consumer is more likely to use all the capabilities that UPS offers online than a consumer who is not. Depending on individual consumers' willingness to engage as well as their skill levels, they can participate at various levels of cocreation. Cocreation also assumes that individual consumers are part of a community in which members share a common interest. The intimate engagement with individual consumers in the cocreation process allows managers to anticipate patterns of customer evolution pathways. "What will they want next?" "What do they value?" "How do they want to engage with us in cocreation?" These are the types of questions we should be focusing on.

N = 1 MEETS R = G

The transformation to a customer-centric cocreation view of value pushes firms to new frontiers of the price-performance envelope. (The focus should not be just on price or on performance. It is the relative performance delivered for a particular price. Value to individual consumers is the relationship between the price they pay as compared to the performance they receive.) This transformation in combination with global resource leverage through visible business processes and integrated analytics provides an opportunity for new customer insights and unique value creation opportunities.

Let us consider the case of JPMorgan, a leading global bank that uses 24/7 Customer, a leading customer support BPO firm in Bangalore, India, for customer support and outbound sales of its new products in financial services. JPMorgan had initiated a normal outbound telemarketing contract with 24/7 Customer primarily to arbitrage the cost advantage of doing the work in India. The team at 24/7 Customer spotted ideas to improve the effectiveness and efficiency of the bank's processes. Their premise was that new customer insights may be derived by combining very large databases (terabytes of data) on customer support transactions with other customer-related data through analytics to improve business processes.

On approval from the bank, a dedicated team at 24/7 Customer consisting of business analysts, statisticians, and functional specialists conducted an in-depth analysis of the customer database and cross-selling process to arrive at a predictive analytical model to improve service quality and selling effectiveness by matching the right products and services offered to the right customers with the right agents. This model combines customer attributes, such as gender, income, other products used, and service transaction data, with agent characteristics, such as age, experience, and functional knowledge, so that a customer is contacted by the "right" agent at the "most convenient" time for the customer with the "best" product to suit the needs of that customer. Here, the primary focus of this analytical engine is to deliver a personalized experience for the customer instead of a mass blast of outbound calling for all customers. The initial results from using this model were fine-tuned by both the 24/7 Customer team and managers at JPMorgan through a judgment process. This predictive analytical model improved selling effectiveness significantly, and the team at 24/7 Customer beat monthly sales estimates of JPMorgan consistently for several months. This example illustrates how firms have combined analytics, business process focus, and global resource leverage to enhance value and experience for individual customers.

The engagement between Wyndham Worldwide, the hospitality company (a division of U.S. Cendant Group), and Marketics (now a part of WNS Global Services), a novel marketing analytics company in Bangalore, is yet another example of how firms are transforming their business processes to gain consumer insights. Wyndham owns a number of premium vacation properties and hotel brands, and it had a customer base exceeding 3 million as of June 2006. The scale of the sample made it complex for Wyndham to understand its customers even in groups or segments. Marketics provided back-office analytics for Wyndham by integrating multiple sources of data such as prior transactions, online engagements, demographics, and focused surveys. Based on the data available and the pattern of missing links from these sources, the team at Marketics built analytical models to deliver insights that can be acted upon.

The analytical models from Marketics predict a probability score for a given customer's interest in a specific property during a certain part of the year. Aided by this analytical engine, Wyndham modified its outreach to its large customer base and thus improved significantly its campaign effectiveness. This capability from Marketics is not limited to selling new properties or new offers. Marketics is also able to integrate structured data from transactions and surveys with unstructured data in focus group interviews to deliver new customer insights. Similarly, Marketics has built a financial simulator for Wyndham to engage with its property builders to time the building and renting of these properties with price bands based on data on local demographics, financial information on the builders, risk profiles, and cash flow details of the project.

Sri Raghavan, senior vice president of revenue management and analytics at Wyndham, states that beyond cost advantages, the biggest benefits from engaging with a firm like Marketics are skills availability, business process flexibility, and fast turnaround. Marketics allows Raghavan to ramp up and down the number of his research consultants working on analytics at an attractive price. He says, "If I have a concept or idea, I have the capacity to experiment with 25 consultants overnight at Marketics. If I look for this talent in a single city in the United States, it may take me several months to get the team together even if I am willing to pay the higher wages." This capacity for continuous low-cost experiments is at the core of the innovations required. For this continuous innovation to become a culture of a company, the focus should be on the intersection of managing the tension between $N = 1$ and $R = G$.

It is easy to get the impression that a company has to be big to capture the benefits of $N = 1$ and $R = G$. On the contrary, as discussed in Chapter 1, TutorVista is a start-up. At TutorVista, tutoring is done between one teacher and one student through the Internet, working on improving the student's skills interactively.

The learning platform deployed over the Internet has been customized with specific add-on devices to allow tutors and students to make freehand drawings and graph charts in subjects such as mathematics. TutorVista manages schedule algorithms to match thousands of independent tutors to the specific needs of individual students. This calls for new analytical capabilities to derive insights based on specific profiles of individual students' needs and the tutors' capabilities. Building such capabilities can be easier for start-up firms because they don't have to overcome organizational legacies.

Netflix is a successful online video rental business. Using the Internet, Netflix created a business model that was an alternative to the traditional movie rental operations then in existence at brick-and-mortar stores. For a monthly subscription from Netflix, requested movies are delivered by mail, and customers can watch as many movies as they want. And there are no late fees.

Furthermore, Netflix, over time, has accumulated data on customers' choices and knows their preferences. To make accurate movie recommendations, Netflix needed and developed a sophisticated analytical engine to understand individual consumers and their unique sets of preferences. Netflix believes that this capability is such a crucial part of its business model that it has issued an open challenge to mathematicians and software developers around the world. Anyone who can measurably improve the performance of Netflix's current analytical engine by over 10 percent will get a $1 million prize. The company is trying to tap into the global market for sophisticated modeling expertise. This is a move to $R = G$. Thus far Netflix has received thousands of suggestions. About 10 of them came close to beating the target. It is reported that a couple of them made it to an improvement of 7.5 percent over Netflix's current performance.

Embedded in these examples of firms such as JCPenney, JPMorgan, UPS, Aviva, Perot Systems, FedEx, Netflix, and Wyndham Worldwide is an underlying trend for large companies to search and engage with small firms and in some cases individuals.

These relationships are focused on access to specialized talents and skills required for moving to $N = 1$ and $R = G$. We capture a representative sample of such emerging relationships in Table 3.1. It must be clear that the ability to collaborate between large and small firms as well as to tap into the unique skills of individuals is a critical requirement. Further, the analytics required to migrate to $N = 1$ and $R = G$ can be mutually reinforcing. The greater the ability to dynamically configure resources ($R = G$), the greater the ability to support $N = 1$. The migration to $R = G$ is also fueling the development of highly specialized suppliers of specific skills such as Marketics. Ubiquitous connectivity makes real-time communications a reality.

TABLE 3.1 EXAMPLES OF LARGE FIRMS' RELATIONSHIPS WITH SMALL FIRMS AND INDIVIDUALS

Nodal Firm	Global Partners	Specialized Skills and Capabilities
JCPenney and other large retailers	Li & Fung	Applies business process execution capabilities to leverage global suppliers for $R = G$
U.S. Department of Homeland Security	Sara Lee and Unisys: Manufacturing units in Pakistan and other locations in Asia	Provides visibility to the shipment of products across multiple carriers and ports. Visibility to global supply chain $R = G$
Aviva	24/7 Customer: Customer support centers in India, the Philippines, and Australia	Provides access to the right global talent for meeting specific customer engagement requests for $N = 1$ and $R = G$
Perot Systems (United States)	Perot Systems (India) in Chennai	Leverages global talent to build a deeper understanding of business process performance at new levels of granularity and visibility

Nodal Firm	Global Partners	Specialized Skills and Capabilities
Netflix	Individual analytical experts across the globe	Leverage specific statistical and qualitative modeling skills to build a deeper understanding of individual consumer preferences for $N = 1$
Overstock.com	24/7 Customer in California	Leverages global talent and tools for specialized expertise in real-time analytics models to drive foresights on individual consumer buying intent ($N = 1$)
Wyndham Worldwide	Marketics (now a part of WNS Global Services), Bangalore	Quick access to high-quality research consultants to work on specific analytics projects from line managers
UPS	Global UPS analytics teams and individual truck drivers	Scheduling, bin packing, and routing algorithms to map customized routes for each driver and customer delivery route to optimize overall fuel consumption

CONCLUSION

In this chapter, we have considered the importance of analytics for providing actionable insights. But insights must be built on a platform of clear strategic direction. We have advocated an $N = 1$ and $R = G$ framework for thinking about analytics. The justification for this was provided in Chapter 1. This clarity in strategy must be combined with clarity in business processes. Granularity, transparency, and flexibility must inform business processes because processes mediate between the desire to act and the ability to act.

FIGURE 3.4
Building the Analytical Capability

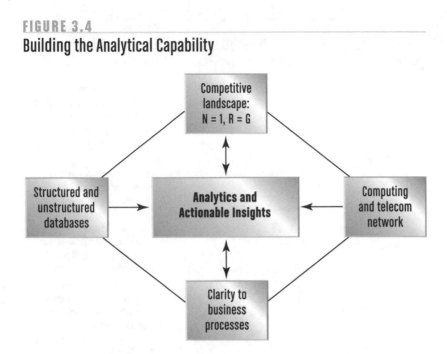

We discussed this in Chapter 2. Analytical capability is the bridge between the competitive landscape and the clarity of business processes to enable action. Analytics also helps improve both strategic direction and business processes, as we have discussed in this chapter.

Another prerequisite for good analytics that we did not discuss in depth but that must be obvious to you is the need for richness and quality of data—both traditional transactional data (structured) and unstructured data (text and video). The capacity to combine different types of data enhances the richness of the analytics, as you saw in the Marketics example. It is also obvious that using powerful mathematical models requires computing capabilities. What is often less obvious is that for a global firm, getting real-time data from multiple sources—point-of-sale systems, RFID tags, consumers, suppliers, and other stakeholders—requires an investment in telecommunications and network capabilities as well. (See Figure 3.4.) Data quality is a critical necessity for building analytical capabilities. This is an area where most firms face problems. In most firms, the situation is akin to drinking from a fire hose. They lack a strategy to link data architecture with the logic of their business models and business processes. Once the data are stored in the archives, they are rarely accessed. The move to $N = 1$ and $R = G$ adds a further layer of complication, as data sources will become highly distributed, reflecting touch points for customer cocreation and supplier connections. Managers need a method and clarity in approach to ensure data quality. The process of cocreation and real-time analytics can help in improving data quality, since data collection becomes an integral part of the value creation process. We have intentionally not dealt in detail with either the architecture of databases or the configuration of networks because these subjects can become quite technical. It is sufficient to know that these capabilities are relatively easy to build.

In the next chapter, we will delve into the need for a clear technical architecture and the criteria for developing one that is supportive of a rapidly evolving $N = 1$ and $R = G$ world. The discussion is not about technology. It is about the nature of the architecture that managers must demand of their ICT organizations. No longer can the demands on the ICT be left to the technical community in the organization. As so much of the competitive advantage is derived from understanding the business processes and the analytics, senior leaders must recognize the capabilities that they are building in their ICT architectures. For example, K. V. Kamath, CEO of ICICI, and Gary Loveman, CEO of Harrah Entertainment (a well-known example of customer analytics in the entertainment industry), are known for their depth of awareness and priority for ICT architecture and analytics as enablers of business innovations. Just as CEOs cannot totally delegate the finance and human resources functions, they should not, as we will argue in the next chapter, delegate the technical architecture of the company.

CHAPTER

4

As we discussed in Chapter 2, business processes that link strategy and operations are key enablers of innovation and sources of competitive advantage in the emerging global economy. But continuous fine-tuning of strategy and the business model requires that managers focus attention on analytics that allow them to gain new insights

IT MATTERS:
TECHNICAL ARCHITECTURE FOR INNOVATION

as the consumer's needs, interests, and skills, as well as the capabilities and reliability of suppliers, change. Having the capacity to act on consumer insights and reconfigure resources dynamically means that the entire network—consumers, the firm, and its collaborating suppliers—*must be seen not as a static system but as a system in continuous flux*. For example, Amazon.com, Apple, and eBay make several changes to their consumer interface pages in a quarter to initiate new features for dialogue and interaction with customers. The ability of individual consumers to shape their experiences via access to a flexible and responsive global system is at the heart of value creation.

In this chapter, we will discuss the requirements of an information and communication technology (ICT) architecture and the governance mechanisms that can connect business processes and analytics to data and applications. These systems must accommodate the apparently "contradictory" demands of consistent quality and low cost, capacity for change and extreme efficiency ($R = G$), and capacity to cope with complexity and ease of use ($N = 1$).

The new ICT architecture extends beyond the enterprise. The new architecture should embed the enterprise in the Internet, connecting to external devices, sensors, and products (as in the RFID example in Chapter 3 or the tire example in Chapter 1), customers (as in the ICICI insurance example), and supplier systems (as in the Wal-Mart example). This enables an $N = 1$ customer experience executed in an $R = G$ environment.

In this chapter, we will first define the four broad categories of business specifications of such an architecture illustrated in Figure 4.1. We will then match these specifications to the technical requirements in the top layers of the ICT stack we briefly described in Chapter 2 (see Figure 2.2) and discuss the extended enterprise that will be embedded in the Internet. This extended ecosystem of firms and individuals demands flexibility in internal business processes and must connect to sensors, devices, and content sources through new platforms that can include blogs, wikis, contextual data, and video.

We have to start with two assumptions. First, no firm today has the systems in place for being fully compatible with the innovation demands leveraging global resources to serve individual customers uniquely. Firms are in varying degrees of progress toward that goal—either because they have understood the emerging requirements of value creation described in this book or because they have focused on managing one part of the equation, $R = G$ through global supply chains, as in Wal-Mart or Li & Fung, or $N = 1$ through consumer cocreated business processes, as in eBay or Apple. Second, unless senior managers start with a clear point of view on the specifications of such a system, this migration from where they are to where they need to be will be costly and time-consuming. We will explore this point of view in this chapter and subsequent chapters in the book. This transformation of the firm requires not just strategic clarity but also clarity to the underlying linkage between strategy and operations that converts assets into value.

FIGURE 4.1

Business Specifications for the New ICT Architecture

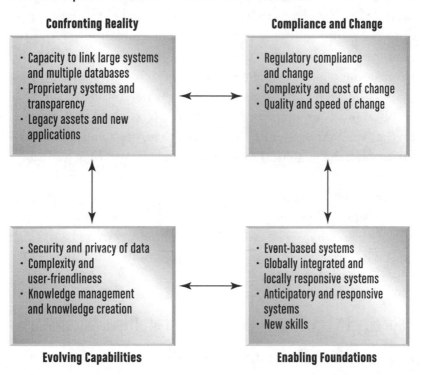

Confronting Reality

- Capacity to link large systems and multiple databases
- Proprietary systems and transparency
- Legacy assets and new applications

Compliance and Change

- Regulatory compliance and change
- Complexity and cost of change
- Quality and speed of change

- Security and privacy of data
- Complexity and user-friendliness
- Knowledge management and knowledge creation

- Event-based systems
- Globally integrated and locally responsive systems
- Anticipatory and responsive systems
- New skills

Evolving Capabilities   **Enabling Foundations**

Let us start with the business specifications. We have organized them in four buckets, as shown in Figure 4.1. These will inform the development of the overall ICT architecture for the firm. We will first discuss the four categories and how they link to the capacity to innovate. We will then map these business specifications to explicit ICT requirements and develop an approach to building the ICT capabilities to compete.

CONFRONTING REALITY

As companies develop specifications for their new ICT architecture, they need to deal with several realities. All large firms start with significant legacy assets in their ICT architecture. These legacy assets are in the form of software packages and custom or proprietary applications, systems, databases, and processes. The ICT architecture familiar to most firms is the result of (a) the freedom that was given to individual business units in different geographies, (b) the legacy of mergers and acquisitions, and (c) a continuous stream of "patch-ups" to systems. So the first step in confronting reality is to perform an audit of the existing ICT systems and develop an understanding of the magnitude of the task involved in migrating to an $N = 1$ and $R = G$ world. As firms focus on the experiences of one customer at a time, the volume and variety of data, the analytical capabilities, and the need for flexibility will grow. As firms try to build their own insights about individual customers and partners in the ecosystem, proprietary systems and analytics capability will become a source of competitive advantage, as we saw in Chapters 2 and 3. We will briefly outline below the typical ICT architecture tasks stemming from these historical realities in an established firm.

Capacity to Link Large Systems and Multiple Databases

As end consumers, we have all had our share of frustration with the inability of businesses to integrate databases. Such breaks in continuity are reflected, for example, in a call center–based customer support system in which the person responding to your query asks you to repeat your problems three times or routes your call to a new service specialist who has no clue about your prior transactions and/or encounters with the firm. Often, this problem is a result of incompatible databases and applications. These problems will escalate. As the global economy demands ever greater attention to individual customers, the size of the databases will increase enormously. Google, for example, accesses 40 billion distinct pages to create unique personalized experience for its customers.

In an $N = 1$ world, managers must have the ability to access multiple databases, both within the firm and outside—public databases as well as databases of collaborators. Many of them are often incompatible. Acting in real time to solve the problems of a consumer requires that we have the tools and methods to access databases to gain insights and provide a service in a specific consumer context. For example, OnStar must be able to access multiple databases to send help in case of an accident—the local police, the ambulance, family, insurance, and the like. Access is not just a problem imposed by the size of databases but, more importantly, by the multitude of databases that must be coordinated for a real-time response.

Proprietary Systems and Transparency

We discussed in prior chapters that most firms that have built agility and efficiency in their business processes have done it through in-house proprietary systems. As illustrated in Chapter 3, analytical solutions often must be and are proprietary for the firm. Managers migrating to an $N = 1$ and $R = G$ world recognize that business processes and analytical tools provide the basis for competitive advantage. However, they also realize that they rely on a large number of suppliers and their consumer communities to help improve their service offerings. This implies that their systems must be simultaneously proprietary and transparent such that others can participate effectively.

Meeting this requirement creates a tension: How much of the system must be transparent? And to whom? If Wal-Mart represents 16 percent of Procter & Gamble's (P&G) sales in the United States, what visibility to point-of-sale (POS) data from Wal-Mart should P&G receive in order to create a seamless supply chain? The tension between "openness" and "proprietary intellectual property" is not easy to deal with. Neither is there one formula that fits all. Even within an ecosystem, there may be multiple levels of "openness." This is an evolving issue in most firms. The nature of the tasks, the criticality of the relationships in serving consumers, and the level of trust based on learning about each other can determine the level of openness. We need to recognize that in an $N = 1$ and $R = G$ world, collaboration to create value is commingled with competition to extract value. This tension is a reflection of the inherent nature of the emerging value creation process. We will discuss this tension further in Chapter 6, as this tension manifests itself in other forms such as in balancing efficiency and flexibility in business processes. The new ICT architecture should be capable of providing the required transparency as well as being capable of controlling access where needed.

Legacy Assets and New Applications

All large firms have significant legacy assets—databases, operating systems, and applications. For example, at one time GM was reported to have had more than 1,700 financial accounting packages working worldwide. Under the leadership of its CIO, Ralph Szygenda, GM over the last decade has spent thousands of person-years of effort to streamline some of the legacy assets—from cleaning the databases to streamlining applications. The job is still not complete. Legacy assets are a reality. The question is, how do we build on legacy assets and use them in new applications? One approach is to suggest that the firm build a new data warehouse for a specific application such as Oracle's Siebel Customer Relationship Management (CRM) Technology. This could cost hundreds of millions of dollars and several years of effort with uncertain payoffs. Very few managers and CIOs are willing to walk that route again. Protecting and leveraging legacy assets without compromising the quality, cost, and speed of new application development will be a source of advantage. Hence, the approach to the new ICT architecture should embed a capability to selectively integrate legacy assets in terms of data and applications in the new platform for business processes and analytics.

COMPLIANCE AND CHANGE

As discussed in Chapter 3, building capacity for real-time reconfiguration of resources to cocreate value with customers is the stepping stone to $N = 1$ and $R = G$. The capacity for change in business processes needs to be built as part of the new design of ICT architecture. The demand for change in business processes will stem from a wide variety of sources—the regulatory environment, changes in the competitive landscape, technological disruptions, and the need for a unique approach to personalized value creation. This implies that managers must focus on the system's capability to adapt rapidly at low cost and without sacrificing quality. We will briefly elucidate these specifications for the new ICT architecture below.

Regulatory Compliance and Change

The Sarbanes-Oxley Act (SOX) of 2002 is focused on ensuring that the underlying business systems are explicit and tested to ensure consistency and performance reliability. All large firms have approached SOX requirements with the same sense of urgency and dedication that the Y2K problems evoked. For firms that have had prior visibility in their business processes and ownership of these processes, SOX did not require a significant effort. However, most large organizations lacked this visibility, and for them, complying with SOX was a multiyear project costing several millions of dollars. Most firms now are compliant, meaning that they have checked all processes once and have fixed the broken links and bugs.

As a result of SOX, companies have established elaborate procedures for making changes to business processes. However, such a single-minded focus on compliance can lead to paralysis. Business conditions change. In a multibusiness (diversified) global firm, someone somewhere is making changes to how he or she conducts business—trying to differentiate, to catch up with competitors, or to be responsive to consumer requests. Changes are unavoidable. This leads to a tension within the firm. We need to find mechanisms that will make it easier to change the business processes; and as we make a change to a subprocess, we need to recognize all the impacts it will have on other related processes automatically and change them. This will ensure that there are no missing links in the logic chain and that the systems are always compliant. As of now, ICT architecture in most firms falls short of meeting the requirements of dynamic compliance—compliance in a constantly changing world of business models and processes. We will pursue this issue further in subsequent chapters.

The Complexity and Cost of Change

As systems get more complex, there is bound to be acceleration of the need for change and the costs associated with change. The more moving parts in the system, the more difficult it is to implement changes in a cost-effective manner. For example, consider firm A with its customer-order-to-cash business process integrated right from customer sales to the company's internal processes (including operations, finance, and human resources), and finally reaching the processes of its suppliers and partners who collaborate to complete a customer's order.

The impact of a change to a business process in firm A can be significantly higher than in firm B, where there is not much integration and systems operate in silos. While the speed of response to change in the market conditions or customer needs can be far superior in firm A, any business process change in firm A can impact areas ranging from within a function in the firm to across the processes reaching its suppliers, who could be possibly in a different continent.

In most firms, ICT systems provide little clue to the specific interconnections and dependencies across their business processes, even within that firm, and much less across their suppliers. As a consequence, there is seldom any transparency to the cost of a potential change, especially changes in business processes that touch multiple functions or span the total supply chain. This difficulty can handicap managers in their efforts to build a resilient and agile operation. This results in a visible tension between business unit managers and the CIOs in most firms.

The Quality and Speed of Change

Managers are critically concerned with the cost and speed of change, knowing that quality must never be compromised. One example would be the ICT demands of SOX reporting and compliance. A system supporting millions of users and collaborators requires zero tolerance for errors in matters of regulatory and financial compliance—these expectations won't change. Methodologies used for developing new applications and changes to existing applications must have Six Sigma quality built in. For example, IT firms from India, which use distributed workforces and remote delivery systems, spend a significant amount of time and effort to build quality by adopting total quality management (TQM) methods and processes as integral parts of their work. Quality, speed, and cost as critical parameters of change require strict adherence to clearly defined and articulated methodologies.

EVOLVING CAPABILITIES

As discussed earlier, reaching $N = 1$ and $R = G$ requires capabilities for the cocreation of value with each customer and also the dynamic reconfiguration of resources. The new levels of transparency demanded here pose unique challenges for managing security and privacy in the ICT architecture. Systems should be flexible, anticipatory, and responsive. Anticipation of new trends such as patterns of customer preferences in an $N = 1$ world demands management of both explicit and tacit knowledge. We will explore the demands from these business specifications below.

Security and Privacy of Data

While the new business models, such as insurance for diabetics by ICICI Prudential or personal accounts in Facebook or MySpace in an online environment, as discussed earlier, provide a unique personalized experience for each customer in an $N = 1$ environment, they also create enormous challenges in managing security and privacy of data. Data ubiquity is a necessity. But controlled access to that data is important. While individual customers may like the quality of personalization in their pages by Google, they certainly may not be comfortable with this profile being shared without their knowledge. The backlash against Facebook for sharing information with advertisers without permission of customers is a good example. Hence, protection of customer privacy will be a critical requirement of the new ICT architecture. The exposure of physical and information assets to global vendors and partners presents new security challenges, requiring new approaches to protecting data and individual privacy. For example, the traditional approach to security akin to castles, moats, and mountains may be necessary but not sufficient. Firewall protection is important, but in addition there is a need to proactively spot patterns in data access or system usage. The capacity to anticipate potential breaches in security or privacy is a must in this new ICT architecture.

Complexity and User-Friendliness

Needless to say, as firms move toward $N = 1$ and $R = G$, their ICT architecture will be complex irrespective of what dimensions we use to measure complexity—size of systems, interfaces needed to harmonize multiple collaborations around the world, the need for compliance and change, the need to facilitate insights at the individual customer level, or the need to accommodate complex analytical models. However, this complexity should not make the system unusable to all but the very savvy and skilled. The system must be accessible to all—from those with low levels of skills to those who have the time and the appetite for complexity. As we have discussed, user-friendly systems, such as OnStar and Google's "iGoogle," are examples of simple interfaces that allow consumers to access a complex system. The next phase of this transformation is to make the interfaces iconic so that even people with little literacy can participate. The goal for the new ICT architecture should be to create a platform for user interfaces with globally recognized icons such as those used to indicate handicap ramps, elevators, and no-smoking areas.

Knowledge Management and Knowledge Creation

In building capabilities for innovation in an $N = 1$ and $R = G$ world of competition, managers need to leverage their knowledge. We know how to reuse explicit knowledge stored in digital form—the essence of most knowledge management systems. However, firms need to focus as much, if not more, attention on leveraging the implicit knowledge continually generated in their ongoing interactions with consumers, global suppliers, and partners. More important, creating *new knowledge* is critical. So the system must know whom to tap to solve critical problems that are encountered. This means that the system must not only focus on archived knowledge but also be able to access experts in the entire ecosystem.

Creating new knowledge requires that managers be able to generate a hypothesis. Consider, for example, a sales manager who wants to understand the pattern of sales decline around the world. She may consider a query such as this: Show me all the locations where sales were less than 80 percent of our forecast. This query has three dimensions: *Where* (all branches around the world), *when* (last week), and *what* (sales less than 80 percent of forecast). This question, simple as it sounds, may still be a difficult one to handle for some firms coming out of recent mergers and acquisitions. A coordinated search of multiple databases will be required to cope with this. Add to this the next question: Show me all the competitors' activities in these locations. Or show me where our inventories are tied up. This way, we build a *knowledge thread* across the organization, which leads to new insights. These questions are an integral part of developing a hypothesis on what may be going wrong and what possible courses of action are open to the firm.

The new ICT architecture should enable a platform for managers to get visibility to data and information across functions to build an integrated perspective. Blogs, wikis, real simple syndication (RSS), and podcasts allow for new kinds of transparency and capacity to leverage tacit knowledge contextually. For example, Massachusetts-based Eastern Mountain Sports, one of the leading outdoor specialty retailers in the United States, with over 80 stores, recently implemented these Web 2.0 technologies to build contextual real-time alerts for business managers on exceptions in process performance and specific drill-down capabilities to support insights. The CIO has also enabled internal blogs and wikis so that the company's product designers, customers, and marketing experts across various sites can collaborate and share tacit knowledge. But, in reality, few large firms have platforms to extend visibility even to business process metrics in a user-defined format across functions. Getting real-time responses to these questions is becoming a prerequisite for ICT effectiveness. At this time, in most firms, this process is mostly a result of face-to-face meetings, and these often occur without supporting data.

ENABLING FOUNDATIONS

The current approach to ICT architecture in large companies falls short of meeting the new business specifications of $N = 1$ and $R = G$ discussed above. We will discuss below the nature of transitions that most firms have to make so that their ICT systems are effective and strategic.

Event-Driven Systems

Almost all of the existing business systems were built as a way of archiving and managing the large volume of transactions that capture the activities of a firm—from sales to purchasing to employee benefits to manufacturing. This *transaction orientation* is also a result of history—how the ICT architectures evolved since computerization of business started four decades ago primarily with automation of transactions and data capture at the transaction level. However, in an $N = 1$ world, the mandate to create unique personalized experiences requires that systems capture the essence of interactions, not just transactions.

Business prospers if it is aligned with events in the lives of individual customers. For example, consider the context of taking a family holiday. An airline today has the capacity to identify if a trip is for business or a holiday. If, for example, a business traveler books four tickets with the same last name to a popular vacation destination, it is an easy guess. Should the airline, recognizing that this is not a business trip, offer to book not just hotels and rental cars but also children's entertainment and reliable babysitting? This implies that the system knows from the tickets booked that it may be a trip to Walt Disney World or to Yellowstone National Park. This should allow the airline to tag it as a unique event and suggest options that could create a personalized experience for that family. The sources of competitive differentiation are the sophisticated rule-based analytics that can identify both the event and the services that could enhance consumer experience. Analytics, as we have argued in the last chapter, provides the insights. Integrating analytics with ICT software applications enriches the transaction data.

Globally Integrated and Locally Responsive Systems

All global firms face a dilemma: How much central control should we mandate and what freedom should we give to local operations? In a global business, we have to deal with heterogeneity of business practices around the world, such as credit terms, employee benefits, and sales cycles. At the same time, there are benefits to having one standard set of rules for all to follow. Global standards make the systems simple to understand and manage.

The pendulum swings constantly between global standardization and localization. Firms set up task forces to standardize such core processes as order-to-cash. After a few years, due to the rigidity of systems and losing some sales to competitors—either local or global—the pain starts to build. The constraints get relaxed.

These swings are not healthy. We need to focus on "global standards" of quality, transparency, interoperability, compliance (with SOX or Basel II), speed, and cost. But we must also provide space for the local operations to be flexible. If all flexibility is "outlawed," then we will lose the very basis of experimentation and learning in the system. *What must be global, and therefore nonnegotiable, and what can be local is a critical consideration in building flexible business process and agile systems.*

Firms now begin to recognize that their approach to ICT can be a huge impediment to building this capability. As firms attempt to comply with SOX and Basel II, managers are confronted with different versions of enterprise resource planning (ERP) packages across their global units by different implementation partners without a common view to their global processes. In some cases, even ERP packages are from different vendors. A common exercise undertaken in many large firms is to match their business processes and practices across their global units and arrive at a common template for some of the standard processes and allow for unique local flexibility in other required processes.

The leading enterprise systems vendors, SAP and TCS, are undertaking joint projects to "reimplement" SAP at a global level for large firms. The goal is to get global business process templates right and also to track local flexibility in their business processes. Often, these initiatives are viewed as "one-off efforts." Inevitably, the visibility to global process standards drifts with time. The new ICT architecture must allow for continuous changes in global processes and at the same time central visibility for control.

Anticipatory and Responsive Systems

Most often, CIOs are asked to be sensitive to their customers—the business unit managers—which is as it should be. The goal of the system builders should not be to just be reactive and responsive. Speed, cost, and quality are the right attributes of a responsive system that allows the business units to compete effectively today. But we have to start with a point of view about the likely changes in the value creation process and therefore the new demands that will be imposed on the system. A system builder must build robustness into the ICT so that it may continually incorporate a wide range of changes over time. Since an application becomes a legacy as soon as it is deployed, builders must keep the legacy from becoming a problem and make it an asset instead. This capability will stem from the capacity to integrate legacy applications at the business process level with new initiatives. The system must provide end-to-end visibility in data and processes. Some evolving standards in ICT, such as Web services and the use of extensible markup language (XML), allow for such integration, and the new ICT architecture should include a common fabric to integrate new processes and legacy systems at both the logic and data levels.

New Skills

New systems require new skills on the part of managers to fully deploy the systems for competitive advantage. Further, not all managers—even those at the same level and performing the same function—behave in the same fashion. So the system must allow managers to be themselves (some are more risk averse than others; some like a lot of detail and others don't). This imposes at least three distinct demands on the system:

1. Does the system allow for customization for individual managers? Can they decide how they want to manage as distinct from someone else's deciding what all regional sales managers must look at?

2. When new applications are introduced, how easy and intuitive are the interfaces? How long should it take for individual managers to be comfortable with the output as well as develop the ability to navigate through the intricacies of new applications?

3. How easy it is for the individual managers to build their own miniapplications or information dashboards on the system without violating quality, compliance, and cost parameters? Should application development be demystified and the capacity for flexible design of analytics interface shift from the IT organization to business line managers?

SPECIFICATIONS FOR ICT ARCHITECTURE

The specifications for the ICT architecture that we have so far identified appear to be very onerous and impossible to achieve. But we believe that the opposite is true and that these specifications are perfectly achievable. We will approach the development of the ICT architecture by first summarizing the specifications in Table 4.1 below and then extracting the critical elements of the architecture. We will then identify an approach to building such a comprehensive architecture.

TABLE 4.1 SPECIFICATIONS OF THE NEW ARCHITECTURE

Requirements of $N = 1$ and $R = G$	ICT Architecture Requirements
Confronting Reality • Capacity to link large systems and multiple databases • Proprietary systems and transparency • Legacy assets and new applications	• Integrate and mine large databases both internal and external to the firm. • Present the flow of information and data across processes in a transparent manner. • Wrap legacy applications into business process components that can be integrated into the enterprise business process framework. • Use a common integrated fabric in the ICT architecture that allows the firm to continuously integrate new business processes and emerging technology standards with the existing legacy systems and processes.

Requirements of $N = 1$ and $R = G$	ICT Architecture Requirements
Compliance and Change • Regulatory compliance and change • Complexity and cost of change • Quality and speed of change	• Dynamic compliance. • Assess and test the impact of each change at the process and data levels. • Track the interdependencies in logic and data across various business processes through a metadata framework. • Predict the effort required for each business process change with fair accuracy. • Develop the capability to deploy new business process applications rapidly. • Develop the capability to predict quality levels in defects across business process applications.
Evolving Capabilities • Security and privacy of data • Complexity and user-friendliness • Knowledge management and knowledge creation	• Develop the capability for controlled access to transparent business processes, and develop an audit trail for the access controls. • Use standard interfaces that are simple and easy to understand. • Develop the capacity for managing content with a central portal that is linked to live transaction data and information flows in the business processes. • Develop the capability for common standards for known business documents. • Develop the capacity for managers to rapidly define new templates and interfaces to view data for a given context.
Enabling Foundations • From transaction-driven to event-driven systems • Globally integrated and locally responsive systems • Anticipatory and responsive systems • New skills	• Develop the capacity to deploy analytics on top of the transaction business processes. • Develop the capability to integrate structured transaction-based data (for example, sales data) and unstructured data (for example, advertising videos) from multiple sources.

TABLE 4.1 **SPECIFICATIONS** *(cont.)*

Requirements of $N = 1$ and $R = G$	ICT Architecture Requirements
Enabling Foundations *(continued)*	• Make global business processes transparent.
	• Develop the capacity to rapidly integrate new technologies and legacy assets to the ICT platform.
	• Develop the capability to track the changes and deviations in business processes across business units and global locations through a central control to support business process governance.
	• Develop the capacity for business managers to detect new patterns in data with ease and experiment with new process changes with miniapplications.

The above specifications combine the *business demands* of an $N = 1$ and $R = G$ world with the *technical demands* it imposes on the ICT architecture. It is important to identify the centrality of the business demands when developing the ICT architecture. The interdependencies of the business and the technical demands can be identified in a spline chart, as shown in Figure 4.2. In this figure, the *dark solid lines represent the basic business issues* that must dominate decision making in ICT architecture. These business questions about such characteristics as quality, speed, or cost of change and flexibility are obvious by now.

The second set of issues (denoted by dashed lines) concerns questions that have both a *business and a technical dimension*. For example, the ease of the line manager's involvement in rapidly developing new applications or the nature of the databases, such as size, type, and number, is one such choice. So is the ease of line manager involvement and flexibility of interfaces. These reflect both the business and the technical requirements of ICT architecture.

For example, flexibility of interfaces is a business concern. How people with *different cognitive patterns and risk profiles* can adjust in-

FIGURE 4.2

Enterprise Space: Where Is Your Center of Gravity?

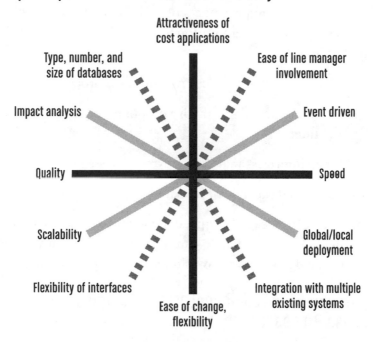

terfaces to suit their needs is a critical question in a global firm with multiple cultures. It is also a technical question for the experts.

The third category is the purely technical questions that the CIO and the ICT technical folks have to resolve. These are represented by the lighter solid lines. For example, event-driven architecture is a CIO concern. So is ease of cross-impact analysis of any changes made to any of the subsystems. The spline chart, therefore, represents the pure business, business-technical, and technical capability dimensions of an ICT architecture.

As you read this chapter, you can identify where you are as a company along these dimensions (the center of gravity of your systems) and where you ought to be if you want to be a true $N = 1$ and $R = G$ player. That may give you a framework for determining the journey you ought to take. All the implicit assumptions about the speed and direction of change needed for competitive effectiveness can be brought out by this simple exercise.

While this is not the place to get into a detailed discussion of the requirements of such a system, we will provide what we consider to be the minimum requirements of an ICT platform capable of delivering capacities for innovation in an $N = 1$ and $R = G$ world of competition:

1. A component-based design of business processes

2. Ubiquitous access through a corporate intranet and the Internet

3. Open interfaces to data and external systems

4. Integrated capability for analytics

The following can be easily skipped if you do not want to be bothered with the technical details. But we recommend that you read and understand it, since we have simplified the technical details.

Requirement 1. A Component-Based Design of Business Processes

The migration in the ICT architecture of firms from an archipelago of tightly integrated legacy systems to a loosely coupled component-based architecture that is modular to support the flexibility needs of $N = 1$ and $R = G$ is depicted in three phases in Figure 4.3.

As shown in Phase 1, in the traditional ICT architecture of large firms, applications that enabled business processes often tightly integrated data, business logic, and user interfaces. These applications also reflected the business or functional silos within the firm. They also tended to be large. For example, applications that bundled business processes in sales, production, and finance were quite common. The interdependencies and linkages across these processes were often implicit. Often, some of these interdependencies were manual and plagued with data redundancies and inconsistencies. For example, the definition of a "customer" in terms of attributes and data could be different across applications such as the sales order system and the inventory application.

FIGURE 4.3

The Evolution of Business Process Architecture

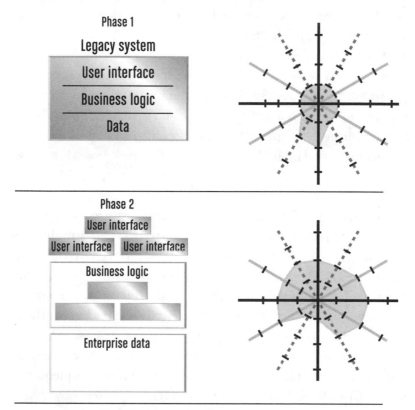

Phase 1

Legacy system

User interface

Business logic

Data

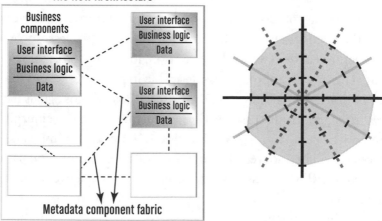

Phase 2

User interface

User interface   User interface

Business logic

Enterprise data

Phase 3

The New Architecture

Business components

User interface
Business logic
Data

User interface
Business logic
Data

User interface
Business logic
Data

Metadata component fabric

Furthermore, while the business processes were clearly defined, either on paper or in an online business process modeling tool, before they were developed, these process definitions tended to be static. They were the requirements captured at a point in time—that is, at the initial design phase of the systems. Since these business processes were interwoven with multiple interdependencies (other linked processes), the boundaries of a business process and its user interfaces and data were often invisible. Thus, the capacity to meet the multiple dimensions of the $N = 1$ and $R = G$ environment outlined in the spline chart (see Figure 4.2) was low across all dimensions. Let us call this our point of departure (Phase 1 in Figure 4.3).

As firms moved to the large enterprise software packages depicted as Phase 2 in Figure 4.3, the separations among the user interface, business process logic, and data were achieved and the dependencies across processes and data were made explicit. A single view of the enterprise data also helped in eliminating inconsistency and redundancy in data. These enterprise packages offered choices for firms to configure their business processes. While the boundaries of the business processes were well defined through configuration of these packages at the time of initial implementation of large-scale ERP, in most cases, the processes were frozen in time, allowing little room for flexibility.

It is often argued that the vendors of these packages were bringing to their customers the best-in-class industry processes. However, the vendors also decided how the business processes would be structured and therefore, by definition, forced the basis for competitiveness. This approach was desirable in processes where standardization and efficiency were the primary goals. Those goals have since changed. As discussed earlier in Chapter 2, in the emerging competitive landscape of $N = 1$ and $R = G$, flexibility in business processes will be a source of competitive differentiation. The packages from ERP vendors fell short here. Hence, while overall architecture improved, the capabilities in dimensions such as ease of line manager involvement in developing new applications, flexibility in interfaces, and process logic were not at par with the demands of the new competitive landscape. The need for a new and a different approach to ICT architecture is obvious.

We have to move to Phase 3, a component-based architecture of business processes. Because *component-based architecture* is a loosely defined term and can be interpreted in multiple ways across the technical community and among vendors, it is important to define our perspective clearly.

In this new architecture, *business components* are the core building blocks of the business processes. We list below some of the key attributes and roles of business components in this architecture:

1. A business component includes a logical set of relationships and rules of a subset of repeatable subprocesses, data specific to these rules (logic), and a choice of user interfaces to expose this logic and data. An example of a component would be a "customer." This customer component would include the data and logic on customers required in various business processes, such as name, address, and credit limits for different contexts, and a set of user interfaces linked to customer information. This component can then be reused multiple times, as it is an integral part of several major processes, such as sales order processes, invoicing processes, and shipping and delivery. While these separate processes may access different logic and data related to customers, the same component can be used with the appropriate interfaces in different processes.

2. Business components can be strung together in a logical sequence to create a logical chain—a business process. For example, a sales order business process will be built by a logical sequence of steps using multiple components such as *customer* and *order*.

   ➢ Because components have been *tested and are self-contained*, stringing them together to build a total business process becomes easy and cost effective, and it guarantees Six Sigma quality.

   ➢ Business components have *open linkages*, meaning that they connect with other components or external systems through standard and open interfaces such as XML and can be invoked by Web services.

A business component–based approach to ICT architecture disaggregates business processes into their logical building blocks and standardizes each of the building blocks with respect to its internal logic and its access to data and hooks to other related components. This allows anyone with little training in software development to articulate a business process and build it with modular components strung in a sequence. This approach reduces the skill level necessary and the cost of change, and it improves the quality of the finished business process. Since the components are pretested, the chances of errors are minimal. Six Sigma is built in. This approach leads to high quality, speed, and low cost of changes in business processes. Because of the impact analysis that is built in, it keeps the system dynamically compliant.

Visibility to the Business Process Logic through a Simple Interface

The component-based ICT platform is capable of presenting business process logic in a transparent manner—what you see is what you get—through a simple interface for business managers to easily track the flow of information in process execution.

In the traditional method of systems development, specifications for a system were solicited from the managers at the initial requirement definition stage. It is often difficult for managers to explicitly state their requirements without experiencing the look and feel of the system. Hence the specifications were always only partially right. Once the requirements were frozen, line managers often got to see the system only after several months, at the time of acceptance testing of the full system. This long gap failed to keep pace with competitive realities. Therefore, managers struggled with disconnects between what was really needed by business managers in their processes and what was actually delivered. Partial acceptance of systems was the norm, motivated by the desire to protect the investments in developing the system.

If custom development creates this disconnect, buying a pack-aged enterprise system as in Phase 2 of Figure 4.3 creates different but equally difficult problems. In opting for a packaged solution, managers need to accept the level of visibility provided by the re-spective vendor and lose the capacity to change the processes. While there are some rapid development methodologies that al-low managers to view prototypes of the system, managers often do not get to experience the actual system. In addition, rigid user in-terfaces in some packages do little to invite managers to use the system. It is not surprising that these large systems are often used only for automating the processes, and firms often need to incur additional investments to integrate other information warehouses, portals, or flexible reporting tools for managers to really use the data and derive insights for their decision making. The new busi-ness component–based architecture that leverages Web services and contemporary Web 2.0 technologies allows firms to overcome these challenges through significant capabilities embedded in this architecture, as shown below:

1. Capability to define the business process in a free format with specific user interfaces as designed by the end users to suit their preference

2. Active inputs from final users of the business system to provide inputs on the information flows in the business process (that is, business process knowledge is explicit)

3. Interface with the system as it is being developed, prefer-ably on an online platform

4. Capability to map the business process, user interfaces, and data access onto business components with inter-dependencies and the data model needed to support the process needs

Such direct automated mapping, aided by software designers who identify the right granularity of components and data, will enable significant reduction in the time taken to deliver. End users of the system will also be able to get exactly the same interface and information flow they articulated at the time of the joint system design with the IT team members. This rapid delivery of WYSIWYG (what you see is what you get) systems goes beyond traditional prototyping and takes the shape of a perpetual beta. It is the live system that they see. As the business process model definition is integrated with the business component design (with interfaces and data linkages) and rendering of the final system, managers get visibility to the real process that is running as opposed to a version of the business process frozen a few months or even years earlier in a document or tool. This visibility to the live processes will also help meet the requirement of dynamic compliance.

A Common Fabric to Automate and Track the Interdependencies in Business Components and Process Logic through Data and Interfaces

A component-based modular approach to ICT architecture and mere visibility to the live business processes may not be enough to meet the business specifications of the emerging competition. The new ICT architecture, as depicted in Phase 3, must deliver more. It must include capabilities to conduct what-if analysis of a proposed change to a business process.

This can be achieved only through visibility to the interdependencies—interface, logic, and data—across business components. For example, if a manager in a large firm is considering a change in how customer information is used in a business process (for example, a sales order), she should be able to explicitly view the impact of this change on other business processes, such as invoices, shipments, and customer service.

This can also extend to dependencies across processes adopted by a different business unit within the same diversified, global firm. To enable such a capability, the new platform must capture the linkage among all business components, data, and user interfaces in a common metadata fabric that can be queried in real time to assess the impact of any change. This common fabric is a data model

about how the system is designed and how the business components come together to deliver the interface and information flow
needed. Once such a model is built, it helps in assessing the impact
analysis of any changes to the business process. This will also make
the process of production, testing, and delivery of the business
process changes both efficient and effective, thus creating the capacity for flexibility in business processes.

These collective sets of capabilities make the component-
based architecture score high in almost all the dimensions of the
spline chart demanded by the $N = 1$ and $R = G$ environment. We
will next discuss three additional requirements of the ICT architecture for an $N = 1$ and $R = G$ environment.

Requirement 2. Ubiquitous Access through a Corporate Intranet and the Internet

In order to leverage global resources and cocreate experiences, it
is critical to get visibility to business processes and their interdependencies. The ICT platform, therefore, must provide ubiquitous access with selective controls. Such ubiquitous access can help
meet several requirements listed in Table 4.1. First, such a platform can facilitate global standards for business processes templates, and it can also make the flexibility added in local units of a
large firm globally visible. Ubiquitous access enables transparency,
faster delivery, and efficient changes in business processing. As
managers define requirements in terms of interfaces and information flow for a new application, their IT team in India, for example,
could convert these requirements into business components and
data models with the required logic overnight, thus rendering the
system live rapidly. The work done by the IT team in India or any
other location is experienced live by managers online in the United
States or Europe. Platforms that integrate new technologies, such
as Web services, in their architecture can deliver these capabilities.
This access should not be limited to business processes and structured transaction data. The platform should enable integration with
emerging Web 2.0 technologies such as wikis and blogs, leading to

a capability to leverage tacit knowledge and to shift from mere transactions to interactions, as discussed earlier in the case of Eastern Mountain Sports.

Requirement 3. Open Interfaces to Data and External Systems

The new ICT platform should support open interfaces such as XML and Web services for data and process access. It should also allow for open standards in the emerging service-oriented architecture to connect with external systems and devices. For example, the ICT architecture behind the personalized pay-as-you-go insurance scheme offered by Norwich Union in the United Kingdom requires that customer processes in the enterprise architecture are connected to the GPS device installed in individual vehicles. These standards need to be open to enable flexibility and governance. It is the same as the personalized shoe company in Finland, which needs to connect with digital scanners across retail outlets to get digital footprints of customers.

As discussed before, legacies in existing systems are unavoidable. The new platform should have a capability to wrap the whole or parts of existing software packages and legacy systems and the corresponding data as a business component into the platform. While in some cases it may not be technically possible to make internal dependencies embedded in packages or legacy systems explicit, the architecture should be able to account for these business processes as modules in the overall end-to-end visibility. This will help in building an integrated view of the business processes and hence the business model.

A central repository of all the interfaces used for external components will help in impact analysis of the proposed changes. This will also facilitate the overall governance of multiple standards adopted for data and interfaces, a growing problem as firms adopt new technologies that come as part of the overall service-oriented architecture. Further, this requirement is almost critical to accommodate mergers and acquisitions smoothly. Mergers and acquisitions are a common culprit for the state of disconnected business processes through disparate systems in large firms. This requirement is also a must for scalability of the system, both in data and in new applications. The open interfaces also help firms to migrate to new database platforms without incurring major changes to the component logic and interface.

Requirement 4. Integrated Capability for Analytics

The new platform should present a dashboard for managers to conduct rapid experiments with analytics to detect new trends and changes in business process performance metrics. This interface should provide an ability for the firm or its external partners (through ubiquitous access) to drill their large databases for insights through appropriate analytics. The platform should also provide capacity for overlaying unstructured data (and tacit knowledge) with transaction data to derive insights.

Controlled access and other security measures should be a given. For example, in the case of Eastern Mountain Sports, tacit knowledge about product performance from the internal wikis and customer blogs is combined with other structured transaction data to derive insights. This firm also provides real-time business process performance data as RSS feeds to its analytics engine and enables timely alerts for its managers. For example, a trend in sales targets slipping or inventory buildup will appear as a contextual alert to the respective managers.

In the case of personalized insurance offered by Norwich Union in the United Kingdom, the ICT platform enables micro-billing, as in billing for a song downloaded to your iPod, and analytics at the individual customer level based on data on driving habits (through GPS sensors) and past history of customers. In the current model of ICT architecture in most companies, analytics is often disconnected from the live business processes. Instead, it is conducted by a dedicated team of analysts and statisticians outside the line of business. This often increases the latency of response to insights derived from analytics. This is not sufficient for the flexibility and agility required in a $N = 1$ and $R = G$ world of competition.

The new platform should provide the capability for analytics linked to the live processes and data so that feedback actions can be immediate, as seen in examples in Chapter 3. As the importance of analytics evolves as a source of competence, the need for integrating analytic modules with core business components will be more pronounced. Firms may need to also assess the impact of business process changes on the specific analytic modules deployed for decisions. Such a capability will also mitigate the emerging risks from the scale and complexity that are part of the $N = 1$ and $R = G$ environment.

The requirements listed above are prerequisites to meet the business specifications listed in Table 4.1 and the spline chart in Figure 4.2. We do not suggest that the examples of firms quoted in prior chapters have such a fully developed architecture. Some of these firms do have some parts of these requirements and hence are able to partially meet the demands of either $N = 1$ or $R = G$. Our goal here is to make the requirements of a new ICT architecture explicit. We believe that recent advances in software technology make such an integrated platform possible. We discovered such architecture in a couple of unexpected sources. We are aware of at least two global firms—Chennai-based Ramco Systems in India and Unisys in the United States—that have developed a capability for delivering an ICT platform very close to what we describe here.

The Ramco Virtual Works platform is primarily a business process–driven architecture that integrates software delivery with business processes visibility through assembly of business components. Ramco Systems started as a traditional ERP vendor and at one time had more than 800 installations of its products globally. The company learned from its experience as a traditional ERP vendor that its customers constantly required changes in product offerings and underwent the costly exercise of customizing the product. Five years ago, senior management at Ramco spotted this trend and set to work on creating a platform that will allow for flexibility with ease of use, efficiency, and quality at the same time. The Ramco Virtual Works platform supports most of the requirements listed here.

The 3D Visible Enterprise from Unisys is another such platform that enables visibility to enterprise business processes, and, similar to Ramco Virtual Works, it is business process driven. It provides a common blueprint of business processes to everyone in the enterprise, starting from business leaders and including technical architects and end users, so that all of them can speak the same language. This platform also provides a capability for impact analysis through a common fabric, as discussed earlier. We will discuss below two live business cases in which these platforms have been successfully implemented.

DYNAMIC ICT PLATFORM AT ITC

ITC is a successful, $3.5 billion Indian conglomerate involved in such diverse businesses as tobacco, hotels, paper, and foods. ITC, as part of its food business, procures soya bean and wheat from a large number of subsistence farmers. ITC, as a method of accessing these farmers more efficiently, developed a unique digital business platform to procure and distribute agricultural products in the Indian rural market. This solution transformed the rural economy in India by creating new livelihoods, enhancing consumption and income, and empowering the rural population with information and access to high-quality products and services.

As part of this platform, ITC provided a PC to every large village (or to a cluster of smaller villages). It enabled these farmers to check market prices of their produce and sell it at a favorable price, bypassing the traditional "mundi auction" system. The farmers were able to increase their profits, and at the same time ITC was allowed to procure at a lower cost by eliminating the logistics inefficiencies. A detailed description of the ITC case is reported as a University of Michigan case study. This electronic marketplace was called an e-Choupal (literally the electronic meeting place). The ITC e-Choupal is an information center (with a PC connected to the Internet) in every village. It provides farmers a unique experience through information access and interactive applications to cocreate value.

ITC soon realized that its network of over 6,400 e-Choupals covering thousands of villages could also be a strategic distribution asset to reach millions of customers in rural India. ITC decided to set up village supermarket stores (Choupal Sagar) at the procurement hubs and convert its contact points at the village into retail outlets to sell various products ranging from fast-moving consumer goods (FMCG) to coffee, apparel, consumer durables, and components for farm equipment and farm inputs such as fertilizers and seeds. A majority of these products were manufactured by non-ITC companies, and ITC was primarily looking to leverage its access and physical presence in the rural centers.

ITC created a digital platform that supports multiple businesses (incorporating various vendors using ITC's network to access the villages) and supports both the procurement and selling of a variety of products to farmers. It was very clear that given the variety of users and products to be supported, the system had to be intuitive, easy to use, and flexible to support a variety of applications. For example, procurement of aqua products (such as shrimps) in bulk, estimating yields, and separating them based on size and quality is a different business process from selling farm equipment or partnering with financial institutions to sell insurance and savings products. It was clear that the platform had to support a multitude of business models and, therefore, business processes. ITC had plans to expand to 20,000 villages, and hence the new platform had to be scalable and provide traceability of products across the entire logistics chain. ITC designed a portal using a component-based framework with the help of its infotech subsidiary and Ramco Systems to deploy a scalable and flexible ICT architecture, as discussed in this chapter.

Another challenge that ITC faced with this new platform was a need for an interface that would be intuitive for farmers to use. Needless to say, it needed user interfaces in multiple languages, as different languages are spoken in India. In addition, the concept of futures and options in the Indian commodities market was evolving. This led to continuous changes in regulations and tax laws. The architecture had to reflect the need for the system to accommodate changes easily. ITC searched for standard ERP products for developing this platform. It was clear that a standard package was nowhere close to the needs of business process diversity and the cost-effective way of accommodating the ongoing changes to the processes. After a considerable due diligence and assessment of various vendor products, ITC selected Ramco's Virtual Works platform for this implementation. The system was large—about 100,000 function points. The platform went live in December 2005 with almost no defects reported postdeployment, which is unusual in such a large-scale implementation.

The system has the following capabilities:

1. It can accommodate business process changes cost effectively. In the first six months, the company has been able to implement several significant changes with variants of business processes for new product segments.

2. It can work with other ERP systems. Integration of the Virtual Works platform with the SAP system at ITC is in progress.

3. It has accommodated the needs of several vendors who use the ITC e-Choupal network to access farmers ($R = G$).

4. It has five language versions and customized interfaces to make it useful for managers and farmers alike ($N = 1$).

5. The entire system was developed in 10 months. Traditional ERP systems of this complexity and size usually take twice the amount of time.

The entire system was implemented ahead of schedule, and the company has successfully rolled out the new system in over 800 centers in its rural distribution network. Since the Virtual Works platform also allows for integration with other systems, ITC is in the process of integrating its new rural distribution platform with its SAP financials, providing real-time visibility to the financial implications end to end in its retail chain.

CONSUMER CENTRICITY AND FLEXIBLE BUSINESS PROCESSES AT ING BANK

ING Group is a large global financial services conglomerate with several million customers and net profits of $10 billion in 2005. ING identified the need to build flexibility in its business processes in the insurance-related products in 2004. The problems in its insurance business were many. First, the group faced intense competition. Second, it operated through more than 5,000 insurance brokers who were the distribution agents for its products. These intermediaries needed faster access to information. The system at that time provided only offline and manual integration, and it therefore took around 10 days to complete a transaction. In addition, the insurance business in ING's global markets was facing a number of regulatory changes.

To be ahead of its competition, ING needed to roll out new products across various sectors in insurance, such as life, general, and personal insurance. Like many other large firms, it found its IT architecture was an impediment to rapid change in its business processes and therefore new product rollouts. The legacy of growth through acquisitions common in the financial services industry had left ING with disparate and sometimes redundant systems in its core insurance businesses. The linkages between business processes were invisible. As a result, they could not get a single view of a customer across products. Furthermore, changes to their business processes were very expensive and were not possible in some cases.

Age Miedema, chief operating officer at ING, stated, "It was clear that one of the things we had to do was to innovate in our application landscape." ING looked to maximize the use of common processes across its general and life insurance products and also to create a platform to make its business processes visible. It needed a capacity to enable fast and low-cost changes to its business processes. As discussed in Chapter 2, business processes are the core enablers of innovation. Hence, inability to make changes to the business processes will be a major roadblock in the path to $N = 1$ and $R = G$ transformation of any business. Firms that do not take a proactive initiative to build this capacity for flexibility in business processes will be left behind.

ING assessed various alternatives and decided to partner with Unisys to create a new platform that can enable the capabilities discussed above. Based on its component-based platform called 3D Visible Enterprise, Unisys and ING jointly deployed a system of core components such as claims management and contract engines for insurance policy delivery and administration in ING's life insurance business. As discussed earlier, the nature of component architecture is such that ING could reuse these components from life insurance to general insurance and other products and markets. Similar to the Ramco Virtual Works platform, the Unisys platform also allowed ING to integrate its new systems with its legacy systems and SAP environment. The platform-based system developed for ING was first deployed to internal users in ING and later extended to its network of over 5,000 brokers through the Web (over the Internet). Now brokers can quote, submit policies, process contracts, and make changes to existing contracts in real time through this Web-enabled system. More than 80 percent of the administrative activities in ING's general insurance business are now online, thus significantly improving its quality of service to its brokers and ultimately to its customers. The latency to handle a broker's request for a product has been drastically reduced, from 10 days in the prior system to a few seconds with the new system.

The visibility and flexibility in business processes enabled by the new platform also allow insurance agents to package policies to meet the unique requirements of individual customers depending on their age and lifestyle preferences. The company's new ICT platform based on component architecture allows it to interconnect with other systems and adapt to regulatory changes. ING now runs both its Netherlands and Belgium operations in one instance of the processes on the same platform. This provides a new visibility in processes across geographies as identified in our business specifications for $N = 1$ and $R = G$. The latency and cost of changes to the business processes are reflected in ING's ability to change the premium rules engine every few weeks as compared to the routine of at most once a year change in the industry. This enables ING to rapidly adapt its policy and premium structures to meet the specific needs of its agents and their customers. While the ING model is not fully $N = 1$, this new ICT platform is a step in that direction.

CONCLUSION

In the first four chapters of this book, our intention was to identify the emerging nature of competition and the value creation process. We suggest that the new world of innovation and value creation is knowledge intensive and oriented toward personalization of experience. This world is best described as $N = 1$ and $R = G$, the opposite of the Model T view of the world. In this emerging value creation space, business processes that link strategy and business models to its operational manifestations become a source of competitive advantage.

Business processes allow for rapid, real-time, and personalized responses to individual consumers ($N = 1$) and at the same time link and coordinate the complex supply chains that weave multiple collaborating firms and the consumer communities into a seamless source of innovation and experience (product and service) delivery ($R = G$). Furthermore, analytics provides the insights that are required to continually fine-tune the strategy and the business models.

In this chapter, we looked at the ICT architecture, the backbone of processes, and the capacity for analytics. We developed the specifications for a future-oriented ICT architecture and the basic requirements as determined by business needs as well as the business-technical and the technical needs. Finally, we illustrated how two platforms—Ramco Virtual Works and Unisys's 3D Visible Enterprise—provide us the reality test of such an architecture. These platforms are still in their infancy, but they have already proven their usefulness in competing in an $N = 1$ and $R = G$ space.

In the next four chapters, we will explore the process of migration of systems—social and technical—to conform to the demands of an $N = 1$ and $R = G$ approach to value creation.

CHAPTER

5

P ropelled by technological changes and changing consumer expectations (especially those of the young), the value creation process is rapidly moving toward an $N = 1$ and $R = G$ world. Many firms find themselves not ready to accept the challenge posed by this new reality. Managers face organizational legacies—both social and

ORGANIZATIONAL LEGACIES: IMPEDIMENTS TO VALUE CREATION

technological. Here we are referring to managerial mindsets, skills, incentives, behaviors, and decision structures in a firm as well as its social architecture. This architecture is a result of a long period of socialization within both the firm and the industry.

Managerial responses to new opportunities such as those presented by $N = 1$ and $R = G$ are conditioned by the existing social architecture. It is a truism in organizational life that "what you see depends on where you have been." That is, the past influences the perceptions of the future. Similarly, the technological architecture—the applications, databases, and systems—is often a patchwork representing the pattern of evolution of the firm. For example, mergers and acquisitions bring with them disparate systems. The history of applications, developed over time, also adds to the problem. It is common to find archaic Cobol programs in many large firms. The Sarbanes-Oxley Act, and before that Y2K, exposed many of these system infirmities of the firm. While most of the significant accounting deficiencies are documented and remedied in firms because of the need to comply with Sarbanes-Oxley, the legacy applications and incompatible systems continue to persist. The social architecture of how managers think, interpret market signals, and act, as well as the capabilities in the technical architecture of the firm to cope with the new competitive demands, can become impediments on the way to capturing the $N = 1$ and $R = G$ world of opportunity.

Organizational legacies can erode the capacity of an organization to innovate and create value. In this chapter, we will deal with an approach to identify the state of the social and technical architecture and the interactions between these two systems in a firm. We will suggest a methodology for migrating out of organizational legacies toward a system that is more supportive of value creation in an $N = 1$ and $R = G$ world.

SOCIAL ARCHITECTURE AND THE DOMINANT LOGIC

Social architecture is the sum of the systems, processes, beliefs, and values that determine an individual's behaviors, perspectives, and skills in an organization. It includes managerial behavior determinants such as organization structure, performance metrics, reward systems, career management, training, beliefs, and values. These processes collectively influence managerial mindsets and behavior. Reinforced over time and embedded in the organization in standard operating procedures and rules, they lead to a predictable way of thinking about opportunities, competitiveness, consumers, and performance. We call this the dominant logic of the firm.

The dominant logic becomes the lens through which managers in that firm see the world. For example, in the past, auto firms ignored appealing to children because they assumed that adults make the decision on which car to buy. However, children, as any parent who has recently bought a car knows, have a disproportionate influence on the family decision. They decide "what is cool."

FIGURE 5.1
The Evolution of Dominant Logic

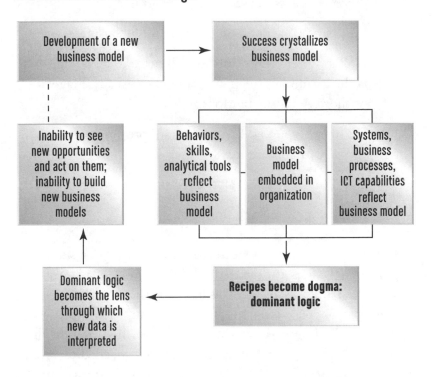

Children don't pay, but they influence. The evolution of the dominant logic in a firm is shown in Figure 5.1.

The development of a new business model in a start-up or an established firm creates a new business opportunity, as occurred in Google, eBay, Bridgestone, ING, and ICICI. The new business model breaks the mold and creates a new opportunity. As the business model becomes successful, managers start embedding processes that are optimized for that business model. We briefly mentioned in Chapter 2 how large and successful Indian software firms are confronted with a need to change their business model. For example, the business model that got these Indian software firms started on their very successful growth trajectory nearly a decade ago can be captured as follows:

➤ We win on price.

➤ Our advantage is based on cost arbitrage.

➤ We assume one operating margin for all businesses.

➤ Doing work in India (offshore) is better than doing work at the customer's site (onshore). The cost advantage in offshore work is better for the firm.

➤ We must respond to all requests for proposals: no specialization.

➤ Customers must bear all the risks: We do what they want.

➤ Every project must be profitable.

This model obviously helped them to become great successes.

Imagine the implications of this business model and its underlying logic. The cost arbitrage was based on the contribution (revenue to cost) per person. So to grow, these firms had to recruit and train more people every year. More important, the larger the firm, the larger the increments of people that were needed to sustain double-digit growth rates. It is not a surprise that most of the larger software export firms in India presently recruit and train about 20,000-plus people every year. Of course, there are natural limits to this process.

We will examine the implications of each element of the dominant logic. For example, pricing based on cost is likely to undervalue significant intellectual property because it is based on time and materials and not necessarily on the value delivered to the customers.

Over time, the skills of managers and the capabilities of the organization become focused on preserving their dominant logic. For example, all large IT firms have developed unique skills in screening over 1 million applicants to recruit 15,000 to 20,000 employees per year. They have perfected the system to train engineers with varying backgrounds—from civil engineering to electronics— to become software developers. Each of them has made massive commitments to training and skill development. All of them are concerned about effective project management—coordinating on-shore-offshore teams across the globe. Their IT systems and social architecture reflect the implications of the business model. Indian software firms were able to grow rapidly and also challenge Accenture and IBM in delivering effective software solutions. However, IBM and Accenture have also moved a significant portion of their operations to India to leverage advantages of access to talent at low cost. The question for Indian software majors is whether they will be able to rapidly build front-end consulting capabilities to supplement their back-end delivery capabilities. They may also need to further innovate in their back-end delivery capabilities as wages in India escalate with entry of multinationals and India's rupee continues to appreciate.

Developing these new capabilities is not just about investments; it is about a new way of thinking about these new opportunities, skills, performance metrics, and pricing practices. For example, IBM, Infosys, and TCS in India are experimenting with new ideas through partnerships with universities to leverage raw talent in India to counter the continuing escalation of wages for software professionals. The challenge is to convert, in a very short time, fresh graduates from universities to industry-ready assets that are deployable in global projects. Finding the motivation to effect change is very difficult when the existing business models seem to be working well, as evidenced by consistent double-digit growth and 30 percent–plus profit margins. The question is, is their dominant logic holding them back? Will their zone of comfort force them to wait too long before they make the transition?

Every organization has its own version of dominant logic. For example, the major pharmaceutical firms are so focused on protecting their intellectual property (IP) that they are exposing themselves to criticism of ignoring human suffering in Africa. While their social legitimacy is increasingly being challenged, their right to protect their patented positions in AIDS drugs is being revoked by countries like Thailand and Brazil. Microsoft, in another example, assumed for too long that the PC would be the device of choice rather than the cell phone. Thus the questions for managers are the following:

1. What is the dominant logic in my firm? How did it evolve?

2. What are the key elements of that dominant logic? How relevant is it in an $N = 1$ and $R = G$ world? What parts of it help the move toward that future? What are the impediments?

3. How do we develop a social architecture tuned to the $N = 1$ and $R = G$ world?

The dominant logic of the firm is easy to identify. It is never explicit, but it is never too hard to unearth. All managers can identify it. Ask yourself the following simple questions:

1. What types of managers are valued in the company? Why?

2. What projects get easier access to investment dollars? What is hard to "sell up"?

3. What is considered superior performance? What must you do well to get that rating?

4. Which companies, other than their own, do managers admire most? Why?

5. What is the background of top managers? Did all of them grow up in the same company?

6. How does the company deal with managers from outside? What is the process of assimilation of outsiders? What impact do they have? How long do they last?

7. How do top managers cope with dissent? What is the role of hierarchy in settling differences of opinion?

8. How does the company handle and evaluate risk? How is failure handled?

You must get a feel for the drift of the answers to these questions. The issue is one of surfacing deeply embedded beliefs about good management practice as seen through the lens of the dominant logic of the company. We will, later in this chapter, describe how to specify the requirements of $N = 1$ and $R = G$ such that managers can see the mismatch between what capabilities and orientations they need and those that they already have. Taking this step can help start the migration process—that is, developing the capabilities that are needed to compete in the new environment.

ICT ARCHITECTURE AND LEGACY SYSTEMS

The ICT architecture of a company is equally fraught with implicit legacy problems. For example, no established financial services firm is without legacy systems. Financial services firms, due to significant transaction volumes, were the first to embrace computerization of their processes. As a result, they have a significant number of old applications and systems. Archaic software programs, multiple incompatible systems, and multiple incompatible databases are all too common. Legacy systems, just as in social architecture, represent an investment. CIOs and top leaders are unwilling and often unable to accept the cost and the risk of moving away from the legacy.

Legacy systems are a result of some or all of the following:

1. Mergers and acquisitions often result in the proliferation of legacy systems. Each merger brings with it its own systems, values, and ICT architecture. While all mergers will have to transition to a common financial reporting format, other systems may or may not be integrated. Even while the systems appear to be integrated, they may just be held together by Band-Aid solutions.

2. Freedom for subsidiaries and business units to develop their own systems can lead to, over time, a proliferation of incompatible systems.

3. As approaches to applications development have evolved over
   time, a wide variety of applications can be operational in a firm,
   each one supported and maintained but incompatible with other
   systems.

Periodic approaches to cleaning up using an enterprise resource planning software product such as SAP or Oracle do not
fully solve the problems, as many versions of ERP can be found in
most diversified firms and those that have grown through acquisitions.

The challenges arising from such unplanned growth in the
legacy architecture of the firm are not just technical in nature.
The results of unplanned growth manifest themselves as impediments to business process clarity and capacity to change business
processes to reflect new business models. In most firms, business processes are not the responsibility of any one executive.
Organizational and administrative hierarchy is often aligned with
business, geography, and/or function. But end-to-end business
processes such as order-to-cash often cut across these boundaries.
As a result, business processes tend to be "organizational orphans."
Changes to business processes, therefore, are not well managed,
leading further to multiple and, often, incompatible systems.

The causes are many, but the net result is the same. Managers
who manage the technical architecture—such as the chief information officer in many firms—are very sensitive to the risks of
making big and sudden changes in systems because the systems
have become "mission critical" to businesses. In addition to the
risks, they see a huge investment and long time frames for these
changes to be implemented. As a result, seldom do we see a willingness to take a fresh look at the entire system. This reluctance
also stems from how the performance of the CIO and his or her
unit is assessed in the firm. Furthermore, we believe that there is a
growing disconnect between the needs of the business and the capabilities of the ICT system. We will explore this in greater detail
in the next chapter. An insidious result of this "paralysis" is that
most of the ICT budgets in large firms are oriented toward main-

tenance of existing systems. It is estimated that more than 70 percent of the ICT budget goes to maintenance, leaving a small percentage for developing innovative solutions to address emerging opportunities. Firms need to close this disconnect between business and ICT teams *before* they start their journey toward $N = 1$ and $R = G$. If they try to migrate without closing this disconnect, this gap will further widen and become a significant impediment.

We can outline a long list of reasons, but the reality is that incompatibility of applications and processes can affect a firm's ability to migrate to the new model of innovation and growth.

BUSINESS PROCESSES: THE MEDIATING GLUE

Business processes mediate between and are influenced by the social and technical architectures, as shown in Figure 5.2.

All aspects of the social architecture are reflected in the business processes, including performance management, compensation, career management, and the seamless sharing of information. So business processes influence managerial perceptions and act as lenses through which people view competitive opportunities and threats. Similarly, as discussed in Chapter 4, business process capabilities are determined by the flexibility and resilience built into the technical architecture of the firm. Business processes also determine the technical capabilities needed by the firm. As such, business processes are at once the enabler of rapid change as well as the impediment to progress.

MANAGING THE MIGRATION OF SOCIAL AND TECHNICAL ARCHITECTURE

We like to consider organizational change as an orderly process of migration and evolution, not as a revolution. A systematic approach to change allows managers to take small steps, which reduces the risk of change and increases the capacity to learn. As we established earlier in the book, winning in the new competitive space will require a systemic change from the inside out. In order

FIGURE 5.2
Social and Technical Architectures

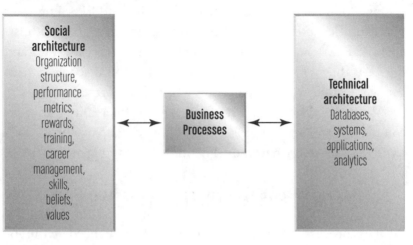

to manage migration, managers must start with a set of criteria. We outline some of them below.

Creating Transparent and Flexible Business Processes

The task of transformation to an $N = 1$ and $R = G$ world must be clear by now. It starts with the transformation of the underlying business processes into a transparent, flexible, and predictable system that can provide the capacity to change (support innovation) and maintain cost competitiveness (efficiency and consistent quality). These are critical requirements in assessing the process and the direction of change. We have already outlined in depth the specifications of the ICT architecture for an $N = 1$ and $R = G$ world in Chapter 4. We can, similarly, identify the specifications of the social architecture that allows for real-time capacity to act—be it reconfiguring resources on the fly, establishing a culture for transparency, or making other changes based on the requirements of competitiveness.

Expanding Engagement with Consumers

The transformation to $N = 1$ by definition demands a capacity to engage customers in a wide variety of activities, such as product development, pricing, and logistics. This cocreation nature of engagement can enable firms to learn about customers as a part of the value creation process. Internal decision-making processes and the supporting technical architecture need to reflect this need.

Coping with Complexity

As discussed earlier, complexity is a given in the transformation to $N = 1$ and $R = G$. In addition to the enormous diversity and scale, real-time reconfiguration of resources and globalization add to complexity. The social and technical architectures need to build capabilities to manage risks arising from this complexity. Imagine a firm operating in 150 countries with 10 large product groups. The company will be addressing a staggering array of business models, competitors, cultures, and channels. Leaders must encompass multiple microcultures and capabilities in advancing consumer-centered change. The social and technical architectures need to reflect this reality and support it.

Building Consensus Rapidly

While multiple microcultures may be needed to manage in the new world of competition, these cultures cannot be incompatible with each other. They must subscribe to an overarching and a common unified logic. Solutions will often transcend microcultures. For example, the social architecture needs to build capabilities to spot deviations and rapidly build consensus to achieve coherent actions in geographically fragmented organizations. As resources are reconfigured and relationships among organizational actors and suppliers change, consensus in action must be developed at low costs. The emerging information technologies such as wikis and social networking tools allow firms to build a capacity for rapid consensus building globally across the organization.

Recognizing Organizational and Information Silos

Firms need to recognize that organizational and information silos naturally evolve in large organizations. Managers must accept that silos trap organizational resources, including information. Managers love to hoard information. This reality must be acknowledged and addressed. Organizations create redundancies, and sharing information across organizational boundaries is a hard process for managers. The social architecture needs to directly address this issue.

Creating Knowledge Rapidly and Sharing New Knowledge across All Levels

As organizations acquire new strategic knowledge, these organizational silos can be bridged across boundaries to cocreate new approaches at the nexus of $N = 1$ and $R = G$. The social architecture in the firm needs to build capacity for rapid knowledge creation through appropriate culture and incentives. The technical architecture needs to build capabilities to enable this.

These specifications are not as onerous as they may seem here in this list. Our vision is of managers moving from "here to there" in careful steps, not in one massive reform. We acknowledge that attempts at business process transformation are far from new. As we noted in Chapter 2, most large firms have attempted this exercise in some form at least once in the last decade. Indeed, few of these initiatives succeed, and many are terminated prematurely. At best, large firms have improved efficiency in some of their processes.

As reported in a recent article in the *Wall Street Journal*, leading U.S. firms have voiced their concerns on diminishing returns from a process focus—be it TQM or Six Sigma. We believe such disappointments in managing processes are not surprising. What is missing in adopting most of these initiatives is a perspective that includes innovation and value creation, not just cost reduction. Some of these process-focused initiatives are blindly adopted across the organization and miss the critical need for balancing demands of innovation and efficiency.

Unless managers start with a point of view about how they want to compete and drive change day by day, meeting by meeting, report by report, to create that reality, they are likely to be disappointed. Further, it is often forgotten that making business processes strategic to results requires managerial and cultural, as well as technological, change. Before we introduce our methods for reforming the logic of innovation and the firm, we must first discuss why and how business process initiatives fail in large firms.

FALSE STARTS IN THE BUSINESS PROCESS TRANSFORMATION

The reasons why business process transformation initiatives do not bear fruit in many organizations are largely managerial and social. There are technical failures as well. We briefly outline some of the reasons below:

1. Lack of senior management evangelism

2. Weak accountability

3. Misalignment of goals

4. Lack of discipline and underestimation of the connection to ICT

Lack of Senior Management Evangelism

Inability to sustain senior management evangelism and commitment is one of the primary reasons why process transformation efforts do not meet the desired goals. Business process reforms typically receive significant attention and resources from senior management at the initiation of the project. Most of these initiatives represent a massive one-shot attempt to redefine a major chunk of processes and systems. However, most process changes are multiyear projects. Few CEOs have the stamina to stay the course. Other new initiatives and priorities often take over their attention during this time. Many CEOs recognize the pattern, but they lack a framework for motivating managers to stay with the effort. Business process issues do not lend themselves to the top-line metrics that dominate the dialogue of senior managers. In manufacturing rationalization, management counts the number of factories closed or inventory in the warehouses. In raw materials logistics, management measures costs and time to market. In business process work, we are not always measuring a physical reality, but rather the effects upon physical reality. Hence, the ownership of business process transformation is often lost midway.

Weak Accountability

While the scale of these initiatives can be vast, managers often fail to address ownership of the initiatives and decision rights. For example, when the discussion of process transformation started in a large high-tech company we know, various functional areas all promised support. However, when it was time to assign responsibility for ownership of the new initiatives, there were no takers. Why? Because every unit was aware that incentives were not clear or aligned with the view of performance in the company. Additionally, taking ownership was viewed as too risky because the project required managing across silos within the firm and cutting across roles and responsibilities. Managers realized they would have to step on too many toes to get the changes completed.

Misalignment of Goals

Business process transformation is not solely about pushing a standard and a new template to lower costs or improve transaction speed, which is the dominant logic in many firms. While efficiency is a powerful valence of the strategic change we proffer, customer-facing processes must be designed for continuous innovation and responsiveness to customer value. All stakeholders should grasp the fluidity and transparency of customer value offered by the $N = 1$ and $R = G$ model. We will provide a portfolio approach to aligning goals in business process capability in Chapter 6.

Lack of Discipline and Underestimation of the Connection to ICT

Business process transformation initiatives also fail because stakeholders lack discipline in execution. While this may sound recursive, the reality is that process inconsistencies stem from a lack of standards for how business entities are defined. In addition, design of new processes is often handed over to external vendors and consulting firms to bring benefits from best-in-class processes. As a result, the teams that spent months designing the new framework move on while a different team of consultants and internal members implement the reforms as best as they can as an entire system.

Managers are familiar with the thick binders delivered to them by vendors with all the details of business models and process designs. These binders provide the requirements and specifications for the next vendor or an internal team to implement. The handover is seldom smooth and can compromise final implementation. This resulting lack of clarity further intensifies as new incremental changes are made to these processes to meet changing business demands. More recently, the use of business process management system (BPMS) tools has contributed significantly in aiding the definition of business processes. A disconnect between process definition during design using a BPMS tool and the enactment of the processes in IT applications still exists in many cases. As noted in Chapter 4, the new ICT architecture needs to support not only the definition and enactment but also the capacity to change and assess the impact of change in one business process on other interconnected processes.

This is a subset of the representative reasons behind the failure of many business process transformation initiatives. We have begun to show that the path to lasting success demands that managers understand that the migration to $N = 1$ and $R = G$ requires several iterations be taken in small steps. The organization and its leadership must simultaneously make changes in social and technical architectures.

Global competition has thrust challenges in business process upon many large firms. Many leaders and managers recognize the need to learn from past failures and undertake a fundamentally new approach. As noted earlier in Chapter 2, GM, under the leadership of its CIO Ralph Szygenda, cleaned up the staggering number of applications in GM's legacy architecture, reducing 7,000 applications to less than 2,500. Furthermore, GM is now working companywide to define different organizational structures, roles, and responsibilities to assure stronger control and management of critical global business processes—the new dominant logic of the firm.

GM is moving rapidly to streamline its certified list of global ICT vendors, reducing the complexity generated by engaging multiple small vendors. Senior management is shifting managers from functional and geographic spans of control to global, process-oriented roles. For example, senior leaders are redirecting managers from their roles as regional operational heads responsible for local supply chains to roles as single management units that are located in the corporate office and are responsible for global supply chain processes. This change is expected to drive standardization and achieve clarity and transparency in global business processes. Once the business processes are transparent and clear, managers can begin governance of such processes to manage the tension between flexibility and efficiency in an $N = 1$ and $R = G$ world of business. We will discuss this more in the next chapter.

Cargill is a $60 billion–plus conglomerate—and another example of how and why a large firm is shifting its focus to business processes. This large conglomerate has inherited from its acquisitions a legacy of processes and systems. Prior process efforts resulted in a patchwork of processes. That patchwork approach to their social and ICT architecture, managers believe, is now limiting their ability to compete globally. Cargill has recently appointed a vice president for "noticeably better processes" with the responsibility of process improvement and process design throughout Cargill. Cargill has taken the approach of starting with standardization of internal processes first, an inside-out approach. This approach allows them to focus on the inefficiencies in their internal processes first.

There may not be one right path to migrating the business processes for $N = 1$ and $R = G$. Depending on the current state of social and ICT architecture and the nature of the business and markets covered, firms need to find the right approach for them and the balance between efficiency and innovation in their business processes. Business process transformation efforts in large firms are often motivated by a threat from globalization and low-cost global competitors. Our argument is that firms must view globalization and digitization of business as an opportunity to compete in an $N = 1$ and $R = G$ environment.

AN APPROACH TO ORGANIZATIONAL EVOLUTION

We suggest the following approach to organizational evolution (migration) to seek $N = 1$ and $R = G$ opportunities—small calculated steps, learning from those and consolidating by scaling. The whole process of change must focus on "derisking big changes." The methodology for systematic change is shown in Figure 5.3. We will discuss this methodology and illustrate it with an example: the journey in business transformation through processes by a large cement manufacturer in India.

The transformation process must start with a shared and a consistent point of view. In this book, we have identified a point of view that is based on an $N = 1$ and $R = G$ world of value creation. We have given a large number of examples from a wide variety of industries where transition to this new value creation perspective is afoot. Once there is agreement on the point of arrival, as it were, we can develop specifications for the new world of value creation and competition as we did for ICT architecture in Chapter 4 and for social architecture in this chapter.

FIGURE 5.3
How Do We Approach This Transformation?

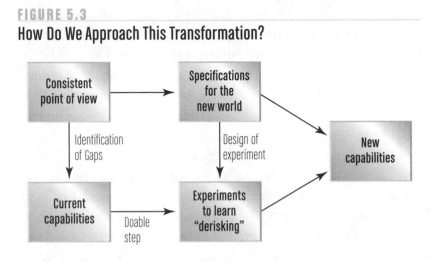

These two starting points allow us to calibrate current capabilities (as in the spline chart in Figure 4.2 in Chapter 4) as benchmarked against the new approach to competition and the specification for that world. This will let us know where the gaps are. We can then begin to develop small, contained organizational experiments to learn about how to build new capabilities. These need not be giant steps nor encompass the entire organization as a first step. These must be doable steps. The whole point is about derisking significant changes in the capabilities of the firm through small steps taken with a great deal of urgency and care. There is enough organizational evidence that shows that continuous experimentation and learning followed by consolidation can lead to major new capabilities in a short period of three to five years without major organizational trauma.

MANAGING THE ORGANIZATIONAL EVOLUTION

Let us consider the case of Madras Cements, a division of the Ramco Group in India. The Ramco Group is primarily involved in cement, textiles, and software development. Madras Cements was a profitable business with revenues of $138 million in 2001.

Ramasubramaniya Rajah, chairman of the board, and P. R. Venka-
trama Rajah, vice chairman, were convinced that business performance—both growth and profitability—would be dramatically
altered if they could streamline their social and technical processes.
A. V. Dharmakrishnan, senior finance vice president, in 2001 was
given the responsibility to be the chief architect of this transformation. He noticed an enormous amount of unproductive effort
within the organization that was begging for change. It was also
clear that the nature of competition in his business would change.
Customers would need better visibility to their suppliers and
would need supplies on a "just-in-time basis." Given the extreme
difficulties in the transport of cement in India due to the very poor
quality of the infrastructure—railroads and highways—he knew he
needed a system that would give him real-time alerts when bottle-
necks emerged. The new demands of external market conditions
and opportunities from internal inefficiencies called for a radical
change.

He also realized that the least painful approach to changing the
dominant logic of his managers was to start with the ICT architecture and change the business processes. He felt transparency, visibility to information, and shared information would dramatically
reduce the frequency with which management operated on gut
feelings, opinions, and intuition. Evidence-based management was
his goal. In addition to his overall financial responsibility for the
firm, he also took the additional responsibility for the IT organization of Madras Cements. He defined the IT vision for the company
as this: "To make information technology an integral part of business and ensure that it empowers people with appropriate information for decision making, thus enhancing the productivity of human
resources." He set out to change the legacy systems of his organization, which included a standard packaged ERP solution and a
portfolio of home-grown applications in various plants by adopting a component-based architecture, as discussed in Chapter 4.

At the start of this journey in 2001, Madras Cements lacked
real-time visibility to its business operations, and the information

reaching line managers was neither consistent nor standardized. As a result, decisions were made with information that was often inconsistent. Inevitably, the decision process gravitated to gut feelings of managers and the past performance history of the plants. Mr. Dharmakrishnan initiated migration to evidence-based management by gradually increasing the transparency in business operations at and to various levels in management. For example, the daily operational level target and performance on quality, productivity, and costs at each plant were made visible. It was visible to the plant and to corporate officers simultaneously. This first step was met with enormous opposition, both socially and from the IT group. The plant heads refused to monitor such detail because they believed it was the job of the line operators. Making data with this level of granularity available at all levels in the organization was very threatening. Everybody knew what the problems were. There was no place to hide. In this new transformation, the CEO forced these metrics to be presented in relative comparison to other plants. When the plant managers refused, divisional heads in the corporate office were assigned to conduct plant-level reviews based on measures of inefficiency (variance from plans and in comparison with other plants) from real-time reports.

The CEO altered the chairman's review meeting to focus attention on these real-time business process metrics. Managers at all levels got the message. The CEO and senior leaders pushed consistently and with urgency to make the entire chain of processes from order to delivery and cash transparent. Prior to this initiative, plants more than 500 miles from the corporate office would connect with senior management about once a month for a review. Now, this new environment transformed a loose federation of plants and facilities into a single large virtual unit with multiple plants over 1,000 miles apart that compared themselves with others and competed to excel. Benchmarking on process performance across plants was not a traditional quarterly or annual exercise. It was in real time!

As performance of any process deviated from the norms, the concerned process owners were asked to learn from other plants about how they met their performance goals.

This led to enormous, sustainable improvements in operations and significant increases in productivity. Transparency and rapid communications fostered shared learning and trading of best practices. Throughput increased by 10 tons per hour (4.5 percent increase), power consumption efficiency improved by 10 percent, efficiency of freight operations and procurement improved by 20 percent, and variations in cement bag weights across plants were substantially reduced. These changes resulted in a recurring $8.5 million increase in annual profits—an increase of 21 percent in 2001. We will present the broader business performance improvements from this transformation later.

Senior managers at Madras Cements also faced the daily frustration of making timely cement deliveries via road and rail transportation, given the poor quality of infrastructure in India. Prompt response to customers, on-time delivery, and quality at the best price are mandatory requirements to compete effectively in the highly competitive cement industry. Indeed, delays in delivery can result in the product hardening within the mixer!

ACHIEVING REAL-TIME VISIBILITY TO INVENTORY AND LOGISTICS

Achieving real-time visibility to inventory and logistics is a business necessity. Many companies in the United States and Europe deploy GPS technology to track the movement of goods, allowing this visibility. However, Madras Cements was not convinced it needed to make the multi-million-dollar investments required in 2003 for creating a GPS-based ICT architecture.

Madras Cements provided all truck drivers with cell phones that cost them about $30 each. The company designed business processes and respective protocols for sending and receiving short message service (SMS) text messages so that exact time and locations for each truck could be tracked through cell phone messages. This flexibility was made possible through a component-based ICT platform that provided live inventory information at the truck level. The system generated alerts and exceptions on delays proactively based on the pattern of these cell phone messages. Management was able to get visibility to performance at the individual truck and driver level to help improve their processes. The analyses of real-time data on the movement of cement, delivery performance, and utilization of various stock points led to enormous improvements in the company's performance, including elimination of several stock points and warehouses, with annual recurring savings exceeding $4 million. The solution was not high tech, but it was effective and at low cost.

As discussed earlier in this chapter, this transformation at Madras Cements was not only about migrating its ICT architecture to a component-based platform. The migration in the company's social architecture was more challenging and significant, as shown in Table 5.1. In this social migration, the company did not adopt the "bloodbath approach" of eliminating a chunk of its managers. The company focused on changing the mindsets of managers. Mr. Dharmakrishnan believed that the initial reluctance among managers to readily accept a transparent environment dissipated as initial experiments with real-time visibility of operations (using new metrics) made the entire team aware of the significant inefficiencies built into their management decision-making environment. Mr. Dharmakrishnan said of this phase of transformation: "The first few experiments exposed the quality of our decision making and showed how inefficient our decisions were." This broad-based realization helped him change the orientation and mindset of managers such that they were able to accept a new competitive reality and the corresponding managerial practices.

As the managerial environment changed, it encouraged managers to excel in their processes and to be the best relative to their counterparts in other plants or divisions. This mindset also facilitated rapid knowledge creation and sharing across various units. Their review meetings were transformed from an unplanned firefighting mode to a mode of proactive problem solving and identification of new opportunities. For example, prior to this transformation, plant managers from all six plants and the zonal marketing managers, equipped with their own PowerPoint presentations, would travel several hundred miles to the corporate office for monthly review meetings. A major part of these meetings was spent on either reconciling differences in data or debating "what constituted true data." Often, there were no checks on the data presented by managers. Instead, the data were passively accepted by others, which meant that decisions were made based on data that few actually believed in.

This review process was totally transformed. These meetings today are conducted from the corporate office through a common video dashboard accessed by plant and marketing heads from their respective locations. The video dashboard relays "live" real-time data from the common system, and discussion starts with exceptions and opportunities. Managers have been socialized to move away from static PowerPoint slides to reviews based on live real-time data so that any claims, promises, or points of view can be checked immediately. This shift from decisions based on gut feeling to decisions based on real-time data has been a significant change. This transformation has not been restricted to monthly review meetings. All senior managers in manufacturing and marketing created their own dashboards with the key metrics and exceptions they wished to track. They now conduct daily management in a way that helps them be more prepared for their review meetings. It is also not just the managers. All employees—from truck drivers and plant operators to plant foremen—have had to change their orientation to this new environment with full transparency in business metrics and performance. Managers needed to remove the wall of perception between the front office and back office in their migration to $N = 1$ and $R = G$.

Let us examine now, in Tables 5.1 to 5.3, the three comprehensive changes in social architecture, ICT architecture, and business results at Madras Cements over the period 2003 to 2006.

TABLE 5.1 MIGRATION IN SOCIAL ARCHITECTURE AT MADRAS CEMENTS

Before the Transformation Journey	Current Practices
Quarterly and yearly closings were massive efforts, with several finance and accounting professionals working for days.	There are real-time trial balances and book closures in only a few days based on real-time data.
There was a hierarchical organization structure with five levels and less transparency.	There is a move toward a flat organization structure with transparency and controlled real-time data access to all levels.
There was no real-time data on plant performance or sales; managerial decisions and monthly reviews were based on gut feelings and guesswork.	Managers decide, based on real-time data, which business process metrics to track.
Monthly review meetings were more argumentative and were prolonged for hours just to reach agreement on common numbers on performance between manufacturing and marketing. Reviews were based on PowerPoint presentations using data compiled by plant managers and regional sales and marketing heads. Managers could hide behind their data.	Monthly reviews are based on real-time dashboard information that captures the performance of the business processes in operation now! Managers face this new level of transparency.
A reactive approach to management was based on events from past data (a week or month old).	The approach to management is proactive and based on predefined real-time exception reports for each business process.
More than 80 percent of senior managers' time was spent on meetings reconciling data from various sources and reviews of past performance, leading to a firefighting approach to management.	Less than 30 percent of management time is spent on proactively attending to the exceptions prompted in the dashboard.

Before the Transformation Journey	Current Practices
There was high variance in customer delivery performance despite inventory in 16 warehouses across the country.	There is guaranteed 24-hour delivery across the country. Customers may also choose their customized routes.
The company's logistics partners and other vendors were assessed on aggregate performance measures for the month and quarter. These assessments were subjective and based on perceptions.	Vendor and partner assessments are based on real-time data on performance. For example, fleet vendors are assessed based on performance at the individual truck and driver level ($N = 1$).
Manufacturing plants operated in silos. Benchmarks on plant performance and resource consumption were based on gut feelings and aggregate data.	Plant assessment and adoption of best practices, process Innovation, and productivity are based on real-time data. Best practices and knowledge are diffused easily across their six plants.
The senior management viewed ICT as a black box and a cost sink. They treated the IT department almost the same way they treated their other utility vendors that ran their cafeteria or managed their office supplies. The IT department was evaluated primarily based on cost and efficiency.	Senior management understands the capacity for flexibility in their ICT platform. Projects are jointly managed by IT and the respective business units.

The changes in the social and the technical architectures of the firm led to many benefits. Customer satisfaction was at an all-time high. Productivity of plants and managers was at a new level—a level that even the CEO did not anticipate when he started the journey. The transformation was less onerous than expected because the transformation process started with strategic clarity. Key indicators of the changes in performance of the company are shown in Table 5.3.

The example of Madras Cements allows us to recognize the interactions between the social and the technical architecture and the role of business processes in mediating and influencing both. Why was this transformation at Madras Cements successful? It succeeded because senior management took the initiative and because

TABLE 5.2 MIGRATION IN TECHNICAL ARCHITECTURE AT MADRAS CEMENTS

Before the Transformation Journey	Current Practices
There were disparate legacy applications and data across plants with no or little integration.	A component-based platform, as discussed in Chapter 4, has allowed for integration of data across processes.
Silo applications were distributed across business functions with some patchwork to force integration at the time of financial closing. Neither the IT organization nor the top management executives were able to gauge the extent of the change possible to their business processes or the cost and impact of such changes.	A single platform now links all processes and data with a metadata framework. Managers can assess the impact of any proposed change on other related business processes.
Standard reports were presented by the package vendor, which seldom had data in the form managers wanted. As a result, these reports and the data were not used by business managers.	The reporting platform is customizable so that individual managers can define the data they want to see and also specify the parameter bounds for specific business process performance for real-time exception reporting. Managers use these reports intensely and modify them as needed to understand the evolving market and business conditions.
The IT applications were plant specific and internally focused on the automation of internal processes.	The ICT architecture has connected their core systems to their vendors and partners, including truck drivers with their cell phones, to bring real-time transparency to vendor performance, customer delivery, and logistics.

the transformation was driven from the business side. The company did not depend on an external IT vendor or an ERP package firm to *deliver the best processes* or practices to it. The company built its own process. The level of flexibility demanded from the customized dashboards and integration the company needed could not be achieved using a standard packaged ERP solution. Using a component-based ICT architecture instead, as discussed in Chapter 4, helped the company achieve the required changes in its busi-

TABLE 5.3 CHANGE IN BUSINESS RESULTS AT MADRAS CEMENTS

Business Metric	As of March 31, 2001	As of March 31, 2007	Industry Average in 2006*
Sales, $ million	$138	$351	$210
Profits (PBDIT†), $ million	$40	$125	$40
Capacity, million tons per year	5.75	6.0	3.0
Number of employees per million-ton capacity	304	281	840
Capacity utilization	46%	95%	95%
Cost of sales (net sales, PBDIT) as a percent of sales	71%	64%	81%

* The industry average numbers are from the *ICRA Report on the Cement Industry for 2006,* which in turn is based on statistics from the 23 major listed cement companies in India.

† Profit before depreciation, interest, and taxes.

ness processes. Mr. Dharmakrishnan believes that his competitors who run their businesses based on standard ERP products cannot recognize the level of flexibility in his platform. We should also note that this transformation at Madras Cements was not accomplished in one step. It was accomplished in incremental steps that were consistent over three years.

We started this chapter by focusing on the organizational legacies and the dominant logic of the firm. As businesses change, the dominant logic can become an impediment to identifying and exploiting the new opportunities. Changing the dominant logic or the organizational legacy is a prerequisite for continued competitiveness. Operationally, this task is about changing the underlying business processes with ease. Managers have had long and often unpleasant experiences with business process transformations. We believe that is a result of a significant lack of strategic clarity and undermanagement of the social side of the transformation. Madras Cements provides an example of the benefits of doing it right.

In the next chapter we will examine the links between managerial skills, mindsets, and authority and decision structures and the technical architecture of the firm.

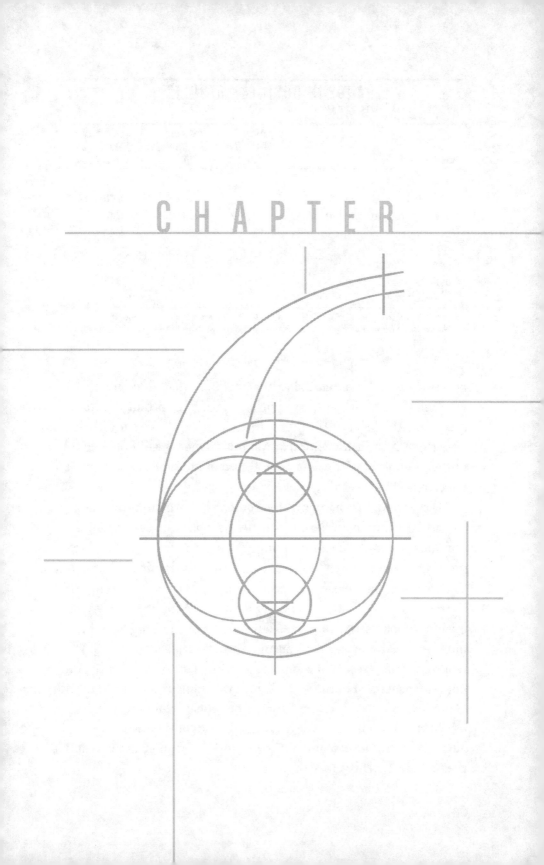

CHAPTER

6

n the last chapter, we examined the need for recognizing and managing organizational legacies—both social and technical. We provided a framework for managing the transition from an existing technical and social setting to one that is oriented toward an $N = 1$ and $R = G$ world. Unique, customized experiences by definition assume that

EFFICIENCY AND FLEXIBILITY: MANAGING THE TENSION

business processes are flexible and can accommodate continuous innovation. Variety, flexibility, adaptation, and continuous innovation of processes are critical. Similarly, $R = G$ suggests that we need processes that continually adapt to the demands of consumers as well as leverage the skill and the asset base of partners in their global networks. The need for flexibility, adaptation, resilience, and continuous innovation are embedded in the concept of $N = 1$ and $R = G$.

This does not mean that efficiency is unimportant in the $N = 1$ and $R = G$ world. For example, Google cannot assume that consumers will put up with downtime on their systems or that advertisers will be tolerant of poor billing practices. Starbucks cannot serve poor-quality coffee or keep its premises dirty. ING must do its risk analysis accurately to offer individual prices for individual consumers.

There is a need for quality and reliability, cost effectiveness, speed, and efficiency. Innovation and flexibility must coexist with efficiency and reliability.

In this chapter, we will examine tensions that are caused by the simultaneous demands for high levels of efficiency and flexibility to create value in an $N = 1$ and $R = G$ world. We will frame this need to focus on "apparent opposites" as a tension and not a trade-off. In most firms, managers used to the either-or view of the world take sides—efficiency versus innovation. We need to move to a both-and view. This challenge rests primarily on the capability of the internal business systems to support efficiency and innovation—fighting variability in some aspects of the business, as in the quality of coffee, while simultaneously supporting some variations in individual consumers' experiences in any of the thousands of stores around the world.

Competing in the global business environment demands that managers identify the appropriate opportunities for efficiency and innovation in a business. For example, $N = 1$ does not mean that individual consumers should have the opportunity to design the shape of their iPods or define their own rules for assessing risk in insurance. Success in innovating new business models for the $N = 1$ and $R = G$ environment, whether the business is in tires, shoes, or insurance, is all about finding the right mix of capacities for flexibility and efficiency. For example, in the case of Pomarfin shoes discussed in Chapter 1, the interfaces to measure the unique shape and size of individual customers' feet reflect flexibility. Pomarfin's manufacturing process uses computerized machines at low-cost locations such as Estonia to deepen capacity for efficiency and deliver personalized shoes at the best price. In the case of Apple, while its iPods and iTunes allow customers to uniquely cocreate experience, the quality of sound from the iPod or the music-downloading experience from the iTunes Web site needs to be consistent. Similar approaches to managing efficiency and flexibility can be identified in all our examples.

FLEXIBILITY-EFFICIENCY TENSION

The dominant logic and current business models shape the capacity for efficiency and flexibility in business processes. As we saw in Chapters 4 and 5, business processes are influenced by the ICT architecture. The reality is that most companies are unable to cope with the simultaneous needs of flexibility and efficiency. Most large firms are at different points in their transition from Phase 1 to Phase 3 depicted in Figure 4.3. A majority of them are in Phase 2 where most of their business processes are trapped in large enterprise systems. However, the technical architecture is not the only culprit. The capacity for agility in decision making through flexible business processes in large firms also rests on appropriate social architectures involving decision rights, skills, and capacities to accept change among managers, as we saw in the last chapter.

Business managers often recognize the need for flexibility and efficiency. Based on our work with more than 500 senior managers in large companies, we have been able to identify the nature and seriousness of the disconnects between the business processes desired by leaders and the reality that confronts them. Invariably, managers suggest that the ICT architecture and the speed of response have lagged behind their need and desire for change. For example, a major auto supplier in the United States was lured by the attractive costs overseas and moved rapidly to shift sourcing of components to China. While it appeared to be a simple and an easy business decision at first sight, the company soon realized that it was using its logistics partners to airlift parts from China. This logistics nightmare was wiping out the cost benefits the company had anticipated from outsourcing.

In fact, the company ended up with higher costs than it would have had from manufacturing those components in Michigan. The culprit in this case was both the social and ICT architecture within this large firm. The company's designers were used to submitting a number of last-minute changes to the company's suppliers. The designers were socialized to assume this flexibility. This practice of informal contacts with suppliers that allowed for an "iterative design" process was not built into the ICT architecture. Neither was this practice transparent to managers who made the decision to outsource. This practice of making last-minute changes to the design had worked previously because the suppliers were very close to the company physically and could adapt to these changes. The suppliers had also understood the need for this iterative process and had made adjustments to accommodate it.

However, outsourcing component manufacturing to China exposed the practice of an intimate connection between design and manufacturing groups within the business culture. Outsourcing to China required a clear process of handover of completed design instructions. This change altered not only the proximity but also the culture of joint socialization between the designers and suppliers. Chinese suppliers produced according to specifications. By the time the designers had submitted their Version 2.0 of the specifications, the Chinese suppliers had already processed Version 1.0 and had put the components in containers that were en route to Michigan.

Hence, the firm was left with no alternative but to accept additional manufacturing costs and the expensive airlifting of Version 2.0 components. The decision to leverage low-cost resources and capabilities from China was driven by business reality. But the company's ICT and social architectures were not ready with the right mix of capabilities for efficiency and flexibility. Systems and capabilities lagged strategy. The systems involved from design to supplier procurement were not transparent. It is not a surprise that the iterative process was totally overlooked in making the decision to outsource manufacturing. The offshore model demanded greater lead time and greater clarity. The handover process from design to manufacturing had to be clear and explicit. This also demanded that the design teams had to come to terms with their design processes and accept that they had to freeze their designs before they were sent to suppliers. The need for deciding the nature of the decision-making processes in the design teams had to be totally reevaluated because in an automobile, the components and sub-systems interact.

This tension between efficiency and flexibility is not limited to the business processes linked to leveraging global resources. For example, let us take the traditional television cable network firms that offer monthly packages at fixed prices. Here, the assumption is that all the customers are interested in a minimum package for monthly subscription. But this may not be true. Some customers may want to have the choice to watch more or less TV in a specific month. For example, customers who are on vacation for a month or whose children are busy with studies may not want to watch TV for a month. Why can't the cost of TV viewing be adjusted according to the preferences of individual consumers? In the current business model, it is a nuisance for customers to switch off the connection for a month and reconnect as and when they need it. Anyone who has tried to reconnect knows what a difficult task this is. Often, it can take a few days and an additional connection charge to get the service. As a consequence, customers are trapped, and, in most cases, they don't change their cable services even when they are on vacation for a month. Customers are certainly not happy with the experience, to say the least.

Let us consider a different model adopted by StarHub in Singapore and Parasat Cable TV in the Philippines. Here, the cable company offers prepaid cards and digital accounts on the Web with fixed amounts of television time and a digital device connected to the television to track usage. This means that individual customers can use the prepaid card to personalize the way they watch television. *They pay per use, not per month.* As a customer, I get to use my television time and pay for it when I want to! This is not a radical innovation. But it is certainly closer to $N = 1$. It is a different perspective on delivering service.

This approach makes new demands on the underlying business processes. The firm has to have in place processes for tracking and billing television viewing time on an event and customer basis. The concept of "prime time" may be redefined, as we can determine the prime time for individual customers based on their personal viewing habits. Further, real information may substitute for market survey and sampling–based deductions of effective and efficient pricing of advertisements. Needless to say, this approach to pricing raises new challenges for privacy and security. But customers can determine the level of monitoring they are willing to accept. Advertisers also will prefer this aggregation of real-time and customer-specific information over aggregate information based on third-party surveys. Television can look like Google for the advertisers. Regional cable services in Singapore, the Philippines, and China are experimenting with this model.

However, migration to this prepaid TV model for traditional cable companies in the United States is not trivial. Adopting this model will demand significant changes to business processes within firms to reflect a new level of flexibility and efficiency in their social and technical architecture. In the traditional business model of cable TV firms, business processes in customer order, billing, and collection were standardized based on a fixed number of choices. Efficiency was the dominant norm, and these processes were assessed based on speed and productivity in terms of transactions or collections. The new business model based on pay-per-use services demands microbilling and analytics to derive contextual insights from individual customer preferences, similar to the examples discussed in Chapter 3. More important, the demands on management attention to spot new trends and act on those may call for a new level of flexibility in these processes.

As the firm learns about customer preferences, its respective business processes will evolve over time. Hence the *ICT architecture* needs to be transformed and the *managers* need to be socialized for a new approach to decision making to reflect this need for flexibility. In the new business model, efficiency in business processes is necessary, but it is not a sufficient condition for success.

As regulatory walls break down and global competition intensifies to cocreate unique value for customers, even the well-protected telecom and cable markets in the United States are likely to change. A step toward the new business model may not be a choice. A recent announcement by Verizon to open its telecom network for customers to connect any device of their choice— be it a digital camera, a cell phone, a music player, or any wireless device—is unprecedented in the U.S. telecom market. Verizon plans to bill customers based on how they use the network—that is, the solution type and the number of bits. This business process is contrary to its traditional monthly subscription for connecting phones. Given such a proposal from wireless carriers, cable TV firms even in well-regulated environments may not have a choice but to rethink their business models from their customers' perspective.

COMPOSITION OF FLEXIBILITY AND EFFICIENCY

The examples of Parasat Cable TV and the auto firm discussed here highlight the need to balance efficiency and flexibility in the portfolio of business processes. In order to attain this balance, it is important to understand what constitutes efficiency and a flexibility and innovation orientation in a business process. We can better understand this question by investigating two types of business processes in the same business.

Let us consider the example of online Web advertising. The traditional business model of placing display advertisements as static banners in predefined sites requires an efficiency-oriented business process. As depicted in Table 6.1, business processes in this model need to be supported with standard templates for tracking customer requests per clicks for advertisements and mapping these requests to predefined rules for the pricing of the services and collection of the payments. The focus is on prompt service to customers based on the product offering, with a focus on standardized, fast, and reliable service to all customers. The incentives for employees need to be tuned to this quick delivery of service with minimal variance. The primary requirement from the IT architecture to support business processes in this business model is fairly simple. It is to provide clarity to customer transactions and capacity to track

TABLE 6.1 CHARACTERISTICS OF EFFICIENCY-ORIENTED BUSINESS PROCESSES

Social Architecture	Technical Architecture
Culture and training are based on process execution excellence.	Standard process templates and best-practices applications are used.
Incentives exist for operational excellence and variance reduction.	The focus is on variance reduction. The capacity exists to monitor variance in business processes.
There is clarity and certainty in business process metrics and outcomes.	
There is clarity in performance outcomes.	There are rigid controls for changes.
	The database and systems are transaction oriented.

and contain variance. Hence, there is a need for transparency in metrics on accounts receivables (collection efficiency), customer satisfaction with the service, and premium for specific advertising slots.

Let us consider a different business model in the same search domain—a service called SmartAds recently announced by Yahoo! In this model, Yahoo! will generate "on-the-fly" customized advertisements for marketers to reach individual buyers. The advertisements are personalized to individual customers ($N = 1$) using information on customer profile, availability of stock, and pricing information from retail outlets close to that customer's location. For example, a customer who has recently searched for flat-panel televisions may have seen an advertisement for various models of such TVs with prices available at the nearest Circuit City or Best Buy retail outlet. This model enables an $N = 1$ approach and is scalable. While a marketer may buy the space in an entire online edition of a daily journal, a female customer in New York interested in photography will see a different advertisement than a male customer in California interested in surfing. The marketers may be charged a premium depending on the accuracy they achieve in matching the customer profile, search history, and local availability of products. The business processes needed to support such a model have to be flexible.

The requirements for social and technical capabilities are beyond the requirements for supporting standardized transactions as in static advertisements that demand variance reduction. As depicted in Table 6.2, the technical architecture that supports these business processes needs to connect with multiple systems and devices with ease and get real-time updates on inventory and pricing data from the vendors of the products being advertised. Analytics, as discussed in Chapter 3, will play a critical role in sensing weak signals and spotting new trends in customer preferences. The technical architecture supporting these business processes needs to facilitate collaboration among marketers, Yahoo!, and retail outlets to create a unique experience for customers. The social architecture to support these processes should prepare managers to expect flexibility and change as a given. Managers should be allowed to experiment with new ways to personalize advertisements and constantly improve matching of advertisements to the individual needs of marketers and their customers. Here it is also about incentives for generating variance in their advertisement offering and not merely about containing variance as in the case of efficiency-oriented business processes.

TABLE 6.2 CHARACTERISTICS OF FLEXIBILITY-ORIENTED BUSINESS PROCESSES

Social Architecture	Technical Architecture
Culture and management are oriented for change and transparency.	The ability exists to connect with multiple devices within and in an extended enterprise including customers and vendors.
Managers have the capacity to learn and adapt.	Interconnections are accomplished easily with other systems from within the firm and vendors.
There is clarity in decision rights to facilitate fast change.	The data focus is beyond the transactions. The capacity exists to generate insights based on new trends and weak signals.
Incentives exist for experimentation.	The capability exists to facilitate collaboration across the firm and its partners and thus identify new opportunities for process innovation and customer value.

MANAGING THE MIGRATION

Point of Departure: A Series of Disconnects

The tension in managing efficiency and flexibility in firms exposes disconnects between the new demands on social and technical architectures (for $N = 1$ and $R = G$) and organizational legacies. A first step in this transformation, therefore, is to understand a series of business and ICT and social disconnects and make them explicit. This is almost a precondition to deciding how to migrate rapidly from organizational legacy systems to a system that is more in tune with the needs of an $N = 1$ and $R = G$ world. We need an understanding of the causes of the pain before we can fix it.

Line of Business and CIO Disconnect

It is critical to understand the fault line between business managers and their ICT organization, and how it can be bridged. We call this the *line of business and CIO disconnect*. CIOs are often constrained by legacy infrastructure (mostly in large firms). This legacy manifests itself in poor data quality, multiple home-grown applications, and critical business processes trapped in applications and systems supplied by vendors. Vendors, such as SAP, provide standard solutions. These solutions may not reflect the evolving needs of the businesses the CIO is expected to serve. This legacy problem explains why managers can find issues such as changing vendors or working within networks of vendors to be so challenging.

We can identify two critical questions that are basic to understanding the nature and causes of the disconnect between business needs and ICT capabilities:

1. How do senior managers approach ICT investments?

2. How deeply do business unit managers get involved in making ICT architecture and process design decisions?

FIGURE 6.1
The Implicit Business IT Disconnect

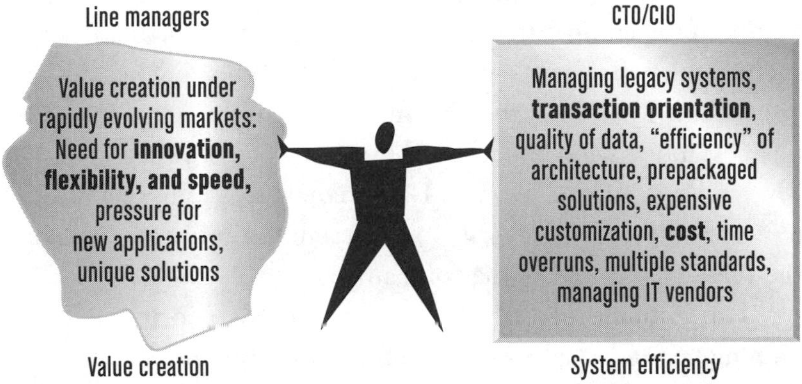

Line managers

Value creation under rapidly evolving markets: Need for **innovation, flexibility, and speed,** pressure for new applications, unique solutions

Value creation

CTO/CIO

Managing legacy systems, **transaction orientation**, quality of data, "efficiency" of architecture, prepackaged solutions, expensive customization, **cost**, time overruns, multiple standards, managing IT vendors

System efficiency

In many large firms, there is an implicit disconnect in the expectations and incentives set for business line and technology managers. As depicted in Figure 6.1, while line managers are expected to grow the business by swiftly spotting changing customer needs and by adapting processes to leverage global resources, the CIOs and their organizations are often assessed on efficiency metrics that are internal to the IT organization, such as spending on and consolidation of technology and data centers. As a result, CIOs often focus on the internal efficiency of their IT organization and invest in innovation only on an incremental basis. It is reported that more than 70 percent of IT budgets in large firms is spent on incremental maintenance of existing systems. This further complicates the ICT architecture in terms of patched legacy applications and vendor-specific products. It is not surprising that the CIO focus is on maintenance of existing systems and not business innovation, as we have discussed earlier.

The constant need to build a deep understanding of customers to create value drives line managers' focus on capacity for agility in decisions and flexibility in business processes. Often, line managers have a black-box view of ICT architecture and the challenges their CIOs face, given the legacy systems and the incentive structure within which they have to make decisions. The dialogue between the two can be difficult and a bit amusing. On one hand, the nature of the competitive dynamics faced by the line managers is such that they may not have full clarity to the evolving business requirement. Therefore, the information needs for supporting new business models and underlying business processes are often intuitive and not fully developed. Line managers also have a limited understanding of the capacity for inherent flexibility embedded in the ICT architecture of the company.

This combination of evolving business needs, poorly defined requirements, and a lack of appreciation for the limitations and capabilities of the ICT architecture can lead to unrealistic expectations. The CIO and her organization, on the other hand, are often saddled with a legacy infrastructure that includes aging home-grown application systems and/or large enterprise systems implemented with partners over many years with little visibility to the processes, large databases, and data quality issues. The tension depicted in Figure 6.1 is inevitable. Hence, it is common for the IT organizations and line managers to talk past each other. In many organizations, the role of the CIOs and ICT architecture is seen as a support function that delivers to the needs expressed by the line managers at the lowest cost. The story line from the business line managers' perspective is often "The CIO and the IT team are too technically oriented and do not address my business needs!" The counterperspective from the CIO and his team is often "The business managers have not specified exactly what they want!" These two teams are often expected to pull out a synchronization of ICT capabilities with business strategy in spite of the undercurrent of disconnects in incentives, orientations, time frames, and focus.

The exhortation in most firms is that the IT organizations and the business managers need to work in partnership to create true business value. We believe that this will not happen without a shared understanding and agenda between the business managers and the ICT organization. This calls for a *common framework and a business process governance structure* to facilitate dialogue within the organization to close the gap between ICT and the business managers. Appropriate incentives and expectations need to be in place. The disconnect sets expectation for the IT organization to deliver "more for less" year after year. This can lead to further impediments in the long run. For example, a senior partner in a major accounting firm revealed that in building compliance with Sarbanes-Oxley requirements in a large firm plagued with legacy systems and lack of transparency in controls, the firm was presented with two options. The first option was to invest significantly as a one-time investment to revamp the processes and get a new system with transparency in processes and controls. The second option was to incrementally invest in fixing the legacy systems with patches and customization. The latter option was a Band-Aid solution to a serious problem. Although it was clear that the incremental approach will eventually end up in higher costs, the firm chose the second option.

The tension illustrated in Figure 6.1 is also social. One such social issue is the lack of involvement of business managers in IT decisions from a "business solutions" perspective. In most cases, the business managers maintain a distance from IT decisions for two reasons. First, it is not their zone of comfort. As discussed in the opening chapter, although most of the products and business processes across industries are increasingly becoming digitized and thus creating the opportunities in an $N = 1$ and $R = G$ world, few senior managers are comfortable with the concepts of embedded software, enterprise systems, Web services, and wikis. Second, senior managers in many large firms believe that ICT services are utilities and can be delivered by any outside vendor once they have clarity to business problems.

While this is true for some parts of ICT services, as discussed in Chapter 2, this argument does not hold for the ICT applications and business analytics layers depicted in Figure 2.2. These parts of the ICT architecture enable firms to set proprietary rules and business process capabilities to differentiate their business models uniquely. While some of the applications software and analytic solutions may be outsourced to vendors for convenience, cost or speed, and value, internal leadership from the firm must own and manage the governance of the overall ICT architecture that enables business processes and provides a framework for executing the business model. But business managers often miss the importance of building and governing the business process architecture.

The problem starts right from the business schools where these senior business executives are groomed. Less than 15 percent of the top 10 business schools in the United States mandate a course on the role of information technology in enabling business processes and fueling business innovation and efficiency as part of their core MBA curriculum. In most cases, these MBA students, who are in line to become senior line managers or business unit heads in large firms, graduate without a deep understanding of the opportunities, challenges, and risks that the underlying ICT architecture represents. The fault is not one-sided. In some cases, the business schools also end up offering courses that are so totally focused on technology that MBA students do not find them relevant.

The ICT Vendor Disconnect

The incentives for large ICT vendors and the needs of large firms vary. Firms start with a focus on business solutions. While vendors may begin the engagement as solutions providers, they eventually end up selling their products or services. Our point here is not that vendors do not add value. IT vendors do inform their clients about the best practices followed in the industry and across industries. Our point is that *that is not enough*. Seldom do vendors realize that a CIO's needs in a large firm are no different from $N = 1$ and $R = G$. More than 70 percent of the $2 trillion plus of ICT needs is outsourced. Multiple vendors supply the CIO. In this sense, it is a clear $R = G$ environment. However, the CIO, in order to serve his firm well, must build a unique ICT architecture focused on the business needs of his firm. This is about specificity of needs and uniqueness of applications. The ICT vendors must see the CIO as $N = 1$ as well. Vendors cannot be delivering the same products and solutions they provide to other big and small manufacturers. Vendors are reluctant to recognize this emerging reality.

For example, let us consider the ServiceTech business unit of the $3 billion TVS Group in India. Its business model is about providing after-sales service support in India to various electronics products such as cell phones, laptops, and credit card readers of leading multinational brands such as Lenovo, Dell, Ericsson, and Nokia. In addition to its own retail outlets for service, TVS leverages its relationship with over 500 service partners across the country to provide service at the store, on site, or by phone. Naturally, many multinational brands find this network attractive as they expand their presence in the growing Indian market. But the needs and service contracts for each of these multinational corporations (MNCs) are unique. The business model of TVS ServiceTech, therefore, is closer to $N = 1$ and $R = G$ as it attempts to meet the unique needs of these MNCs by allowing them to leverage its network and service partners. It is clear that the business processes to support this model need to accommodate both efficiency and flexibility.

While many ICT vendors may offer a predesigned solution, the business model of TVS ServiceTech demanded flexibility to accommodate the needs of its MNC customers, such as Ericsson and Lenovo. TVS had to approach the selection and management of ICT vendors with care. It was also clear that while some ICT product vendors offered a reverse logistics solution, the capability to define MNC-specific business processes and interfaces that also hide customer-specific data from one another was a challenge. It was difficult to find an $N = 1$ solution from traditional vendors. Vendors were offering standard products with options for minor changes at the boundary. In addition, TVS needed powerful analytics for real-time insights on service quality, efficiency, and performance of all its service partners. TVS had to work with multiple ICT vendors to identify new ways to cocreate and configure products such that these needs could be met. In addition, TVS had to manage ICT vendor service contracts such that there was an incentive for the vendors to change business processes according to the unique needs that MNC customers imposed on TVS.

The conclusions are clear. Choosing, evaluating, and subsequently contracting with an ICT vendor are quite crucial activities. Often firms use the same approach to vendor management across vendors and in the different layers of the ICT stack as shown in Figure 2.2. An efficiency- and compliance-oriented approach to assess a vendor (based on reliability and timeliness) is relevant to the bottom two layers of ICT in Figure 2.2. However, the top two layers of business process applications and analytics call for a different approach. In these layers, vendor service levels should be negotiated based on both efficiency measures and new metrics that reflect the capacity for adaptation and flexibility. For example, the analytics and enterprise software systems vendors that represent the top two layers of the ICT stack should be compensated based not just on the functionality of the system but also on the improvements in the relevant business performance metrics. These contracts should be based on business and IT metrics. Solution providers should be viewed as risk-sharing partners in the anticipated business changes and should be rewarded with appropriate premiums. This can be a first step toward transforming ICT vendors from mere sellers of products or services to cocreators of value with the firm.

It can be argued that the IT vendors may be reluctant to accept such a risk-sharing offer. But emerging ICT architectures as discussed in Chapter 4 can enable firms and their IT vendors to engage in these risk-sharing partnerships. However, the first step toward such partnerships is to create visibility in business processes and the respective performance metrics. For example, a large auto company closed a deal worth nearly half a billion dollars, announcing partnerships with two major ICT vendors. The expectations from these ICT vendors were made explicit—to improve quality by 10 times and reduce cost and cycle time for providing ICT services to business by half. The intention was right. But the implementation was not.

After three years, various business units within the firm were not happy with the quality of services provided by this integrated partnership with the two major vendors. An evaluation of this disconnect showed that the performance expectations were primarily set in terms of ICT metrics such as cost, quality, and cycle time. Performance expectations were operational, such as productivity of programmers, postrelease defect rates in delivered applications, and time to deliver applications. While the goal was to improve the flexibility available to businesses, the performance metrics reflected efficiency in how the ICT group would develop applications. These metrics were *about the process of developing systems and not business solutions.* Even in these ICT system metrics, there was no agreement on the baseline measures. While the ICT vendors were claiming that they were delivering services at half the cost with significant improvement in quality and cycle time, the firm had no way to confirm this assertion without clarity in understanding about its baseline measures. In addition, senior managers in various business units were threatening to outsource services because they perceived that their primary business concerns were not being addressed. The two ICT vendors were not assessed based on any business processes performance measures, although they were solutions providers. This situation may not be unique to this large firm. It is common to find large and expensive ICT projects that lack clarity and transparency to the business impacts of investments.

A few firms that are focused on business model innovation are starting to change this tradition. They are learning to creatively leverage specific capabilities of global vendors. For example, the contract between Bharti Telecom in India (a \$4.2 billion firm) and IBM is unique in this respect. The contract between Bharti and IBM is on a revenue-sharing basis. The incentives for IBM—the vendor—are aligned with the growth in revenues for Bharti.

The quality parameters of the contract include penalty and bonus clauses based on Bharti's customer-focused performance. This is a unique engagement in the portfolio of IBM. IBM often presents this relationship as an example of the ideal relationship between ICT vendors and their customers—a cocreation of value, of sharing the risks and rewards of the business success of Bharti Telecom. If Bharti and IBM can change the traditional and established patterns of contracting, why can't you change the nature of your engagement with your ICT vendor? If you are an ICT vendor, why not change your approach to delivering value to your client?

BUSINESS PROCESS PORTFOLIO

The transformation of business processes for flexibility and efficiency requires that managers not only understand why technology and strategy must be connected but also deepen their understanding of the business process portfolio itself. How should you approach structuring the *business process portfolio*? It is clear from most of the examples we have discussed—whether tires, shoes, or banking—that accommodating variance and flexibility in business processes is a prerequisite for delivering unique customer experiences throughout the global supply chain. A firm's business process design must be flexible to enable the firm to arrive at solutions that meet the individual preferences of customers—and flexible at the back end to connect with vendors and partners on an as-needed basis. This ensures cocreating value for customers more efficiently. The critical dimensions managers must weigh in deciding whether a given business process should be redesigned are the direct role of that process in either the $N = 1$ or $R = G$ aspect of the business model, the level of change in the process rules over time, the degree of certainty in the outcome of the process, and the nature of data being accessed by the process.

In Table 6.3, we present an approach to classifying these business processes along various dimensions. Consider, for example, the business process focused on orders from customers. This process is quite critical for ensuring a unique experience, as it interfaces directly with consumers. Therefore, it is rated high for its relevance to $N = 1$. Similarly, we should assume that any process that impacts the customer interface and delivery will be high priority in supporting $N = 1$. Processes focused on delivery will also affect all the vendors involved. This will impact $R = G$. Further, as not all consumers desire the same level of personalization or involvement, systems have to be flexible. Rigid predesigned software package applications may be inappropriate.

These dimensions for classifying business processes are not exhaustive. Managers must identify the dimensions that make sense for their specific businesses and classify them accordingly. Clarity to the nature of business processes will help better fit the appropriate social orientation and technical architecture to execute the business model effectively. Such classification of business processes as illustrated in Table 6.3 may not be static. The portfolio of business processes needs to be governed dynamically in relation to market needs. This governance may require new capabilities and changes in the current roles of line managers and CIOs.

TABLE 6.3 BUSINESS PROCESS PORTFOLIO

	Direct Link to Customers, $N = 1$	Direct Link to Vendors, $R = G$	Rate of Change	Certainty in Process Outcomes	Nature of Data
Customer order					
Internal finance					
Payroll in HR					
Training in HR					
Procurement					

REVISITING THE ROLES OF
LINE MANAGERS, CIOS, AND CTOS

The tensions between flexibility, efficiency, and the need to focus on flexible business processes force a new convergence of the roles of the business managers, CIOs, and chief technology officers (CTOs). Their roles used to be distinct, and often they could work in organizational silos. Today, the focus on scanning for new technologies that can be relevant to the businesses of the company CTO must be combined with incorporating the technologies in the ICT capabilities. For example, consumers want to access the firm, say, a financial institution, using a multitude of devices—PCs, cell phones, ATMs, and the firm's branch offices. This accessibility is critical in creating a personalized experience. The question for CTOs is, how will the modalities of connectivity evolve? For the CIOs, how do we ensure that our ICT architecture can accept these modalities?

Let us consider, for example, the Health Insurance Plan (HIP) of New York. It caters to over 4 million members and has a revenue base of $4.5 billion. Pedro Villalba, its CTO, has a team that constantly surveys emerging technologies for unique value propositions for the business. For example, the team spotted early on an opportunity to combine wireless technology and embedded intelligence to design a personal device for some of its customers (patients). The goal was to track a list of vital statistics, such as weight and blood glucose levels. Constant monitoring of these body parameters with trend analysis and analytics that provided appropriate triggers for doctors to call in patients for a physical visit not only improved the health of the patients but also provided personalized care at lower cost. The patients who needed only routine monitoring of vital statistics were not hospitalized. Further, it also avoided patient visits on a weekly basis for a checkup, which saved time for both patients and doctors. This is an example of experimenting with the emerging technologies to create intelligent products and processes to deliver unique value in an $N = 1$ environment. This is a clear case of convergence of the traditional roles of the CTO, the CIO, and line managers.

BUSINESS PROCESS GOVERNANCE COUNCIL

Managing disconnects among the line managers, CTOs, and CIOs, the vendors, and the firm and coping with emerging demands for flexibility and efficiency requires that firms create a framework for managing the quality of their business processes. An important first step is to develop clarity in the definition of the business processes, accountability for business processes, and decision rights. As we move closer to the $N = 1$ and $R = G$ business models, business processes must be capable of continuous evolution. This demand manifests itself in different ways in established businesses such as GM or Cargill and new and emerging global businesses such as Infosys or ICICI. In the case of traditional firms, such as GM, the challenge begins with the need to consolidate diverse business processes trapped in multiple applications and products, often with no access to the initial designers of the system. For example, at Cargill the initial task was to identify multiple versions of the same business processes across geographies and business units resulting from the company's legacy of acquisitions of businesses in the past. This then led to the standardization of processes.

The same challenge and need for business process governance manifests itself differently in the case of emerging and fast-growing global businesses such as Infosys or ICICI. While these firms do not start with the baggage of legacy processes, their rapid growth in multiple geographies and changing scope of operations present a challenge. Unmanaged, rapid growth can lead to rapid localization of business processes. In the absence of formal governance mechanisms, this trajectory can soon lead them to the same problems faced by GM and Cargill—a legacy of processes replete with redundancy and inconsistency. *No firm today can ignore business process governance.*

We suggest that firms create a business process governance council that will include the senior line managers, human resources officers, the CIO, and the CTO. The council will be charged with managing the evolution of business capabilities embedded in business processes and in the skills of managers. This council should be charged with connecting the evolving demands on the business, the changes to the business models used by the firm, and the flexibility and efficiency in business processes needed to support business unit managers. Needless to say, the council members need to continually balance the social and technical capabilities with business needs. For example, when Infosys established such a council to govern its global business processes across functions and business units, it called for a shift from a functional organizational structure to one built on process clusters. For example, Infosys views sales and marketing as one business process cluster, whereas finance and procurement is viewed as another cluster. Businesses will of course need to develop their own process clusters to determine their process portfolio.

While the CTO and the CIO can develop the technical architecture, the human resources group has a more onerous task: developing new skills rapidly in the organization. It is important to note that the role of this council can rapidly turn into an exercise in prioritizing and allocating new IT investments. However, the primary role of this council is not ICT or training budget management. Rather, the council must focus on the evolving needs of the business starting from the elements in Figure 6.2. This should be followed by prioritizing and mapping the respective ICT and HR investments to make these business process changes. On a periodic basis, this council should also be informed by the CTO and her team on experimentation with new technologies in the business processes, as in the case of the Health Insurance Plan of New York. The focus must be on the synchronization of business, human resource, and ICT strategies such that new capabilities are built to anticipate and cocreate unique value with customers.

FIGURE 6.2
An Approach to Building Capabilities for Efficiency and Flexibility

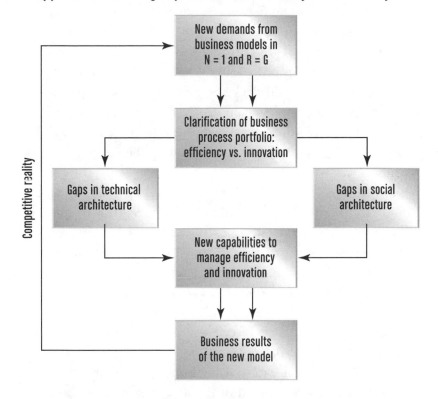

ELASTICITY OF BUSINESS PROCESSES

While the business processes need to be flexible and efficient, we need to be sensitive to the elasticity of business processes. *Elasticity* can be defined as the extent to which processes can be stretched to accommodate strategically dissimilar businesses. This is quite an important consideration in diversified business firms. The portfolio of businesses may have dissimilar strategic requirements. Can a single ICT architecture and social architecture accommodate a wide variety of strategic imperatives? The portfolio in a diversified firm can span a wide spectrum, as was the case in the Dow Corning Corporation.

Dow Corning had businesses ranging from engineered materials (uniquely $N = 1$) cocreated with customers who required significant technical and engineering services to bulk purchases of sealants and silicone fluids that were sold on price.

In the late 1990s, Dow Corning was in crisis. In the midst of Chapter 11 bankruptcy proceedings (based on product liability issues with a product that never constituted more than 1 percent of the company's sales), the company experienced flat revenues and declining margins in its dominant product lines. There was no global integration of its systems and no visibility to the requirements of customers, globally.

The company had over 7,000 stock-keeping units (SKUs) ranging from bulk chemicals sold in container loads to tubes of sealing caulk. Because the silicones business had been historically a high-tech business, the sales teams consisted of experts with deep knowledge of their products and customer-specific applications. They loved to provide consulting services, bundled with products at premium prices. That was their dominant logic.

The financial situation forced senior managers to reexamine this dominant logic. Is one business model appropriate to manage the wide variety of businesses within the company? Should we impose one cost structure on all of them? Can one set of business processes be appropriate for multiple businesses in a diversified firm? To bring clarity to its business models, Dow Corning created task forces. These task forces were given the freedom to start with a clean sheet of paper and examine their businesses. This analysis by the internal task forces exposed the fault lines in the dominant logic. The company had two *distinctly different types of businesses*.

One set of businesses required a close relationship with customers. Solutions were cocreated. Many solutions were unique for a specific application. For example, a special rubber compound was needed for a new mobile phone being designed by a global telecommunications customer. It needed to be light and had to withstand the customer's "drop test." The sales volume initially was low and the market demand uncertain. The customer shared the initial investment. There was risk sharing and pricing specific to that engagement. The rubber compound was cocreated, and emerging intellectual property was jointly owned. On the other extreme, some products were sold in bulk and the specifications were standard. The customer did not need hand-holding (technical support and other services)—in fact, the customer resented it and the obligatory expense associated with it. So in 2002, Dow Corning separated the businesses into two models, each with its own distinct brand (although Dow Corning Corporation owns both registered trademarks): one representing customized solutions and products (more than 7,000 SKUs) and the other representing large-volume specialty chemicals (initially, only 250 SKUs). A separate brand identity for the large-volume business was established, and thus the *Xiameter brand* became distinct from the *Dow Corning brand*. The company set clear criteria for determining which customers could be serviced by Xiameter. The questions were these:

1. Do you buy in large volume?

2. Can you plan your material needs two to four weeks in advance?

3. Can you operate with no customer or technical support?

Dow Corning separated its business into two models to serve customers as appropriate. That is, the company gave customers a choice in how they wanted to purchase products or solutions based on their specific needs. Customers can purchase from the Dow Corning brand and/or from the Xiameter brand (if they qualify). The underlying logic for the business model separation is shown in Table 6.4.

TRANSITIONING THE BUSINESS PROCESSES

Dow Corning's ICT architecture transformation preceded the recognition that the business processes were not elastic enough to

TABLE 6.4 BUSINESS PROCESS REQUIREMENTS

Xiameter Brand	Dow Corning Brand
Sales are based on price and lead time; however, reliable supply is very important.	Customers are looking for new and unique solutions from Dow Corning.
Given the lead time, products are made to order, virtually eliminating all inventories for the Xiameter brand.	Specific variants of a product may be customized for each customer.
Customers buy products.	Consulting services are valued separately from materials and may be bundled or unbundled with the product price, depending on the customer requirements. Products and services may be charged separately or together.
Capacity utilization is optimized by selling full batches of material or selling it in truckloads.	
The customers in this business are large-volume buyers and not solution seekers.	Products are delivered in all quantities based on customer requirements.
Customers are mature and are buying the products as commodities.	Customer engagement often involves joint development of products with exclusive licensing for customers.
The business model is to build the scale and large volume in sales.	
Company uses a transaction-based Web site.	Pricing of products and services is based on the specific value added.
Products are sold in large volume through market-based pricing.	Expert services are available to customers globally, leveraging live help centers around the world and Dow Corning distributor networks.
Customers enter their own orders online, and then they track and manage their own orders electronically, requiring minimal personal support from the firm.	
The sales teams in this business model are more like traders.	Dowcorning.com was designed to collaborate and connect with customers.
Systems and processes are designed to optimize inventory and production capacity.	Transactions are made on the company's service-based Web site, which offers extensive technical information, a collaborative environment, and the ability to order.
	Prices are value-based (services may be bundled or unbundled with product prices).
	Extensive customer service is available to address unique customer needs.
	Sales team members are customer service professionals with access to a global network of product specialists.
	Systems and processes are designed to optimize customer service.

accommodate this wide variety of businesses. Prior to 1996, a large number of legacy systems existed around the globe. The customer order, inventory, and supply chain systems were regional with de-coupled batch integration. The regional systems for North America and Europe worked, but with the rapidly expanding market in Asia, a third regional system required yet another level of complexity in global integration. The company spent four years building a global order execution system before concluding that an enterprise resource planning (ERP) software package was the only long-term, sustainable platform for a global business. The company implemented a global business process platform using SAP.

Dow Corning had one consulting partner to implement the new IT system worldwide and to ensure its compatibility with the global business processes. Dow Corning was one of the first companies to implement one version of the SAP enterprisewide solution across the world to cover all business units. The company also standardized the lower levels of the ICT stack shown in Chapter 2, Figure 2.2. IBM personal computers were selected, but only two specific models (for desktop and laptop)! Servers were Solaris Unix. In essence, the company created a standardized ICT backbone that supports both business models. However, each business model has a distinct brand, a distinct personality, and therefore a distinct Web site. The separation is real.

The Dow Corning brand offers options to customers, and thus it requires flexibility. To deliver on that brand promise, the company rewrote the rules of engagement. Dow Corning offers customers flexibility in terms of order size and turnaround ($N = 1$). Technical information centers around the globe provide customers and prospective customers with technical information virtually 24 hours a day. The company created a central knowledge base for its experts and distributed it globally ($R = G$). This allows the company to learn about new opportunities, based on its customer engagement worldwide. For example, a technical expert in Seattle could suggest a solution for a customer in Taiwan. The access to its global knowledge base helps to mitigate risks. Flexibility was built into the customer order processes to enable bundling or un-bundling of services with product purchases.

On the other hand, Xiameter rules are much more straightfor-ward based on the experience that its consumers desire. The cus-tomers know the products and do not want to be bothered with a lot of consulting help. It is designed to provide the essential service—providing quality product on time—at market-driven prices. It is self-service in its orientation. Automation is also criti-cal for Xiameter. Customers place orders, and the materials are scheduled and produced without human intervention. Customers receive automated e-mails confirming that their orders have been received; once the orders have been shipped, the invoices are deliv-ered electronically. All this is made possible through SAP.

More important was the separation of the social architecture to reflect the distinct nature of the two types of businesses. The company formed a separate team for Xiameter and established a distinct space for that team. A small sales team was trained to be more like commodities traders, focusing on prices and volumes. Incentives were realigned.

While the customer-facing infrastructure was distinct for these businesses, the same plants that serve Dow Corning businesses also serve Xiameter. The core processes that control manufactur-ing, logistics, and inventory levels had to focus on efficiencies.

CONCLUSION

The tension between flexibility and efficiency cannot be avoided. It is in the very nature of the $N = 1$ and $R = G$ world. Business processes—the glue between the ICT architecture and the social architecture—are at the heart of managing this tension. For build-ing a portfolio of business processes, managers must come to terms with disconnects that may exist between business units and the ICT organization, as well as with the incentives of vendors and the firm. Creating new approaches to the governance of the business processes can facilitate migration to the requirements of an $N = 1$

and $R = G$ world. Finally, we demonstrated that there are limits to the elasticity of business processes and that top managers in diversified firms need to recognize them. The implication is that one system does not fit all businesses.

In the next chapter, we will take the requirements of the ICT and social architecture transformation to an $N = 1$ and $R = G$ world and ask, how do we mobilize talent for this transformation?

CHAPTER

The strategy for innovation described in this book clearly requires new skills. $R = G$ suggests that no firm can develop all the products and services it needs to provide personalized experiences for each customer. Nor can any firm develop all the managerial capabilities it needs to transform the organization. In Chapters 5 and 6, we discussed

DYNAMIC RECONFIGURATION OF TALENT

the issues related to escaping organizational legacies and building new capabilities for managing innovation. We illustrated how firms should prepare to manage constant tensions between flexibility, efficiency, and reliability. This transformation is not just about changing the mindsets or dominant logic of managers; it is also about focusing on new levels of transparency and visibility in how the firm is managed.

We have to change the way we manage—how we continually match opportunities with resources. The focus must be on the skills of individuals and their attitudes to learning, as well as on the competence of teams and the ability to continually configure task-based teams with the best talent from around the world. For example, uniquely identifying the behavior and needs of a single individual from a customer base of millions—in Amazon.com, ING insurance, and the diabetes care program at ICICI—

requires analytics. We will argue that this holds true for the search for talent as well. A firm must treat its employees and vendors as unique individuals (or a collection of individuals) just as it treats its customers. Dynamic configuration of talent resources to meet the needs of specific tasks becomes a source of advantage. The key message is that for the transformation to be effective, managers must focus on mobilizing talent rapidly from both within and outside the firm. This flies in the face of formal hierarchies and silo-based behavior and thinking. In this chapter, we will outline an approach to mobilizing talent—within and outside the firm—that can build this new foundation for the transformation.

MOBILIZING TALENT, NOT OUTSOURCING

Unfortunately, outsourcing of jobs—be it manufacturing to China or services to India—has received an inordinate level of attention both among managers and in the press. The initial impetus for outsourcing was primarily cost arbitrage—meaning that firms can access comparable skills in India for a fraction of the costs of those skills in the United States or Europe. This probably was the motivation for the first round of outsourcing to Indian vendors of basic and low-tech work, such as maintenance and testing of software applications and checking for bugs during the Y2K scare.

But firms have moved along. Western firms have become quite sophisticated in their understanding of emerging markets. They have developed their own operations for software development and services such as customer support through call centers. Furthermore, all major firms, such as GE, Microsoft, Siemens, Philips, Cisco, Intel, Texas Instruments, and Motorola, have significant R&D facilities in China and India.

For example, Honeywell, the aerospace and automation controls firm, is rapidly expanding its R&D operations in India. Over the last few years, its unit in Bangalore, India, has been working on identifying new products and markets for Honeywell globally. A decade of involvement in India has enabled Honeywell to expand its operations from leveraging low-cost engineers for specific tasks such as embedded software development to assembling a full-fledged R&D center. Its R&D unit in India now carries the complete responsibility for new products from concept to market. The business rationale for this unit is also shifting from cost savings to new product and business development.

A similar trend is seen in other large MNCs such as Cisco, Oracle, SAP, GE, and Philips. For example, the Philips Innovation Campus in India is Philips's largest R&D center outside Holland. "Almost every global new product with software in it from Philips has a contribution from the Bangalore center," says Bob Hockstra, ex-CEO of the Philips India center. A research study from Stanford reports that multinational corporation R&D centers in China are not just providing technical product support, product localization, and product development for the local market. They are also developing products for the global market.

Many MNCs, including Honeywell, recognize that the Indian market provides unique opportunities for developing products and services for "India-like markets." Honeywell's R&D center in India is working on devices that reduce electricity loss in the grid. It is also developing an "intelligent thermostat" with embedded software that allows individual consumers to define their budget for energy consumption for a day or a month. They can personalize the way they want to consume energy ($N = 1$). The intelligent thermostat shuts off or controls electricity to specific appliances such as refrigerators, washers, or dryers according to the priorities set by the consumer. Managers at Honeywell believe that these products would have a significant opportunity in other markets, such as China or Africa.

This is not limited to the electronics and software industries. A number of global pharmaceutical firms, such as Allergan, Dupont, Eisai, and AstraZeneca, have significantly increased their R&D investments in India. The pharmaceutical industry is also undergoing a transformation with the availability of a rich talent pool and attractive markets in countries such as China and India and increasingly Eastern Europe. The dominance of Taiwan and other Asian countries in semiconductor manufacturing is well known.

While global firms are focusing on emerging markets such as India and China for growth and talent, some local firms are also outgrowing their national markets and building global operations. Indian and Chinese firms, such as the Tata Group, Infosys, Reliance, ICICI, Mahindra or Huwei, Haier, and Lenovo, are global firms in their own right. Globalization is creating a new dynamic. While established MNCs like IBM are focusing on India and China, new MNCs such as the Tata Group, ICICI, and Infosys are focusing on developed markets of the West. The search for talent is not just about Western firms going to cheaper Asian locations. It is about all firms, from the West and from emerging markets, searching for the talent that they need anywhere in the world.

Further, Indian firms have outgrown their original approach to a total cost arbitrage–based business model. Consider the software services industry. Figure 7.1 shows the chronological evolution of the change of Indian firms—from cost advantage to quality and innovation advantages. Needless to say, there is a significant variation in where a specific firm may be located in its evolution. However, it is safe to say that most of the key players and the new and emerging start-ups are in the innovation stage—be it process innovation (as in the use of TQM methodology for software development or business process services at Wipro) or the development of unique analytical skills as described in Chapter 3.

It is increasingly clear to global managers that outsourcing is not about "exporting jobs"; it is about "importing competitiveness." Firms compete. Motorola competes with Nokia and Samsung. GE competes with Siemens. IBM competes with Accenture, Infosys, and TCS. This is not about countries but about the competitiveness of firms. It is no surprise that global firms have recognized this need to access skills from around the world to compete effectively and provide superior service to customers. This recognition is forcing firms to build project teams that are multi-

FIGURE 7.1

The Evolution of IT Services from India

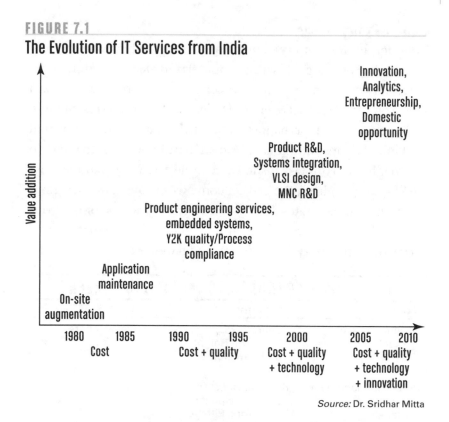

Source: Dr. Sridhar Mitta

geographic and multicultural. The focus is not just on cost. Cost is a consideration, but equally important is the quality, innovativeness of the solution, and speed. The patterns of work and the composition of the teams vary considerably as the nature of projects and access to talent required varies.

In the following paragraphs, we give examples of firms, such as IBM (established U.S.-based MNC) and TCS (emerging India-based MNC), configuring their resources for specific projects. You will notice that the pattern of resource configuration depends on the nature of the project and where the firms can find the appropriate skills. The patterns continually change. The relationships across geographies, business units, and vendors are not predetermined or static. The phenomenon is best described as a dynamic configuration of talent based on the specificity of needs. Consider the following examples.

Center Point Energy

Consider the Texas utility Center Point Energy, which wants to create a "smart power grid" with computerized electric meters, software, and sensors that can improve service and provide personalized advice on how to conserve energy to its customers. IBM is building the system to make this happen. The IBM team is scattered around the United States and India. The distribution of talent that had to be brought in to this task is shown in Table 7.1. You will notice that the 90-plus people on the project come from 15 locations, primarily in the United States and two locations in India. Contrast this with an IBM project for which most of the project team is located in one site—that is, the traditional model of work.

TABLE 7.1   IBM'S APPROACH TO MOBILIZING TALENT

Skills	Locations	Number of People
Weather modeling and data analysis	Austin, Texas; Yorktown Heights and Hawthorne, New York	8 researchers
Project management and financial modeling	Based in Houston and participants from New York, Pittsburgh, San Francisco, Los Angeles, and Chicago	50 people
Knowledge of local laws and public policy	Washington, Austin, New York, and Philadelphia	8 regulatory specialists
Knowledge of grid technology and quality oversight	New York and Miami	20 engineering managers
Design of software and programming	Bangalore, Pune, India	6 software developers

Source: Steve Lohr, "At IBM, A Smarter Way to Outsource," *New York Times,* July 5, 2007.

Scuderia Ferrari

The Fiat-owned Scuderia Ferrari is the Formula One racing car that is nearly custom-developed every year. Ferrari has selected Tata Consultancy Services (TCS) from India as a technology partner in the development of the next version of the racing car. TCS is providing information technology solutions and engineering services. It was the company's excellence in domain expertise and its capacity to execute projects on time that made TCS a winner in Ferrari's search for global partners. The TCS engagement with Ferrari involves both the broader 2000 luxury car division and the customized Formula One division, which makes only four custom-built cars in a year.

Ferrari is leveraging TCS's resources in multiple domains, including enterprise IT, vehicle electronics, and aerodynamics. The team composition with its skills and location is depicted in Table 7.2. The team size of over 70 is spread almost equally between Ferrari and TCS. The nature of this engagement between TCS and Ferrari calls for an intense collaboration between both teams. This collaborative nature of the project requires on-site presence of the TCS team in Maranello, Italy, where the Ferrari Grand Prix team is based. More that 90 percent of the TCS team in this project are on site in Maranello, Italy, working closely with the Ferrari design team. Ferrari's mission is to build the best cars that win races. Its drivers come from different countries, and the car may also be made with global resources.

TABLE 7.2 FERRARI'S APPROACH TO MOBILIZING TALENT: TCS-FERRARI ENGAGEMENT

Skills	Locations	Number of People
Vehicle electronics	Maranello, Italy	18 from Ferrari, 5 from TCS
Aerodynamics	Maranello, Italy	8 from Ferarri
Software design	Maranello, Italy	3 from Ferrari, 20 from TCS
Software testing	Maranello, Italy	8 from TCS

British Telecom

The composition and physical location of teams in a global project execution also evolves. For example, in contrast to the Ferrari engagement, consider the TCS engagement with British Telecom (BT) to upgrade the entire telecom network of BT to an Internet

Protocol–based data network called the *twenty-first-century net-work*. This engagement necessitated a full understanding of the legacy BT telecom network with a mix of old technologies, such as circuit switches, and new equipment.

TCS worked with BT to develop a plan for the migration of the entire network. The initial design solution team involved approximately 20 solutions designers each from BT and TCS. The plan included detailed steps on design, testing, and deployment of the various nodes in the network. As the project evolved, the increasing clarity to the task and the underlying activities allowed TCS to leverage cost advantages in India. TCS has shifted a major chunk of services linked to systems integration, design, and testing to India. It has set up an exclusive lab for BT in Chennai, India, with 10 solutions designers and 115 testing and development experts. The composition of this TCS engagement is presented in Table 7.3. This model of offshore resource leverage has required detailed documentation of tasks such as software development and testing and an explicit understanding of the network migration processes.

TABLE 7.3 BRITISH TELECOM'S APPROACH TO MOBILIZING TALENT: TCS-BRITISH TELECOM ENGAGEMENT

Skills	Locations	Number of People
Telecom network design solutions specialists	London, United Kingdom	20 from BT
Telecom network design solutions specialists	London, United Kingdom	22 from TCS
Telecom software design specialists	Chennai, India	20 from TCS
Telecom software developers	Chennai, India	70 from TCS
Telecom software testers	Chennai India	45 from TCS

At a superficial level, this configuration of resources looks like "business as usual." What is new here is that these configurations are constantly changing, even within a firm and within a project as it evolves:

1. Many of these tasks and/or projects are implemented in multiple locations and around the world.

2. Expertise is geographically distributed (as in the IBM example) and can be distributed between firms (as in the TCS-Ferrari and TCS-BT examples).

3. The composition of teams is task specific, and the nature of tasks evolves over time from new and complex activities to routine. (This was the case in the BT-TCS example, in which the task related to the migration of the network started with a complex task codeveloped with BT first and implemented on site in the United Kingdom till the process was well understood. It then moved to India.)

4. There are no fixed patterns in the migration of jobs. It is not just the movement of jobs from the United States or other locations to India. The configurations of teams differ based on the tasks and the availability of appropriate talent for specific projects.

5. The common theme is about talent arbitrage, not just cost arbitrage.

The change in the patterns of work and composition of teams in global firms need not be limited to complex software-intensive development projects. This transformation of how work is done cuts across business functions and industries.

In Chapter 3, we discussed the challenges faced by Wyndham Worldwide in the hospitality industry when it needed to recruit 20 marketing analysts in a short time. The company leveraged talent in analytics from Marketics (now a part of WNS Global Services) in Bangalore. As a result of their early exposure to global resources in the software domain, technology firms may have an advantage in leading others in adapting innovative patterns of work.

For example, let us consider the collaboration between Lenovo (the Chinese MNC in the personal computer business) and Ogilvy & Mather (O&M), the advertising wing of the media group WPP. Lenovo and O&M have moved their marketing services to a global hub in Bangalore. A team of around 85 employees (20 representing Lenovo and 65 representing O&M) in this marketing hub in India is connected to the marketing staff of Lenovo and O&M in 60 countries around the globe. This experiment challenges the traditional belief that branding and advertising activities are best addressed at each local market and location. These activities were always considered country and/or culture specific. The Lenovo experiment shows that branding and advertising activities can be disaggregated and that not all elements need to be culture specific. In fact, some of the culture-specific activities may be better executed from a central hub in a remote location based on the collective knowledge and access to talent. Further, this approach may reduce the redundancy and wastage of creative effort.

This concept of a central hub for marketing and branding activities emerged as Lenovo was faced with redundancy in processes and activities across the global operations that it inherited from IBM. The key skills in a typical branding and advertising campaign involve strategic planners, client relationship managers, and the creative team that brings new ideas. In the case of Lenovo, these skills were distributed and duplicated globally (a legacy of its acquisition of the PC business from IBM).

The company consequently centralized these activities in its hub in Bangalore and established discipline in workflows and business processes through appropriate systems. A request for creative work from Paris thus is forwarded to the group in India working on the European market. Once completed, the work is submitted to Paris or London for a local creative director to review and send back for improvements, if needed. All the work activities in the hub related to every project are tracked (including the time spent in creative activities). Employees at this central hub are encouraged to build their knowledge base on the global markets they are working on. Senior executives of Lenovo and O&M periodically visit this central hub to facilitate in building this knowledge. Account executives from the hub are also expected to travel across geographies and bring in their collective learning on various markets and activities to the hub.

The Indian hub of Lenovo supports nearly 25 languages. Lenovo is the first multinational firm to host its global marketing hub in India. While it is too soon to claim success, immediate returns from this experiment are impressive. Rush jobs from multiple locations in Europe are turned around within four hours. The hub has executed more than 400 global assignments in the first four months of operation. There has been no rejection of recommendations by the local creative directors in their global markets.

The idea of a central hub is not limited to marketing services at Lenovo. It is an extension of its practice of operating global hubs for product family or global design activities. For example, Lenovo has a desktop hub in China and a notebook hub in Tokyo. Its design hub for all its products is based in its design headquarters in Raleigh, North Carolina. Lenovo is not a unique case. This trend is also seen in other industries.

The conclusions from the foregoing trends are clear: The search for talent has gone well beyond cost arbitrage. Lowering cost is still a concern, but it is coupled with the need for better quality, innovation, and speed. Therefore, firms will engage in pulling together teams of people based on their skills, attitudes, and experiences to work on specific projects. What we see here is the breakdown of the traditional hierarchical systems in which business, functional, and geographic groups "owned" people. Talent used to be trapped in boxes in the organizational charts. In contrast, we are moving to a system of project management in which projects are *temporary organizational systems*. The transition is critical to recognize. The message is this: "I, as a skilled associate, do not belong to the India or the U.S. operations, even though

I may live in one of those countries and be managed administratively by the country manager. I belong to a global practice group, and I can be called upon to work on specific projects based on my unique skills and experiences." Thus each employee starts to belong to multiple systems:

1. A member of a business functional unit (for example, financial markets business group and/or human resources function)

2. A member of a country team (for example, U.S., Chinese, or Indian operations)

3. A member of a project team of the moment (for example, Indian programmers in IBM's Texas Center Point Energy utility project)

4. A member of a vendor's firm who works as a member of the team of the ABC firm (for example, the TCS team in the Ferrari race car electronics project)

The majority of the employees may not have this somewhat ambiguous and shifting organizational affiliation. However, for the highly skilled and the most coveted people, this will increasingly be the reality. What is the underlying logic here?

DYNAMIC RECONFIGURATION OF TALENT

As we have seen throughout the book, firms have to learn to dynamically reconfigure human resources—for example, which vendors will serve a particular request for shirts for JCPenney as in Li & Fung. Similarly, each particular call from a customer in Aviva, as we saw in Chapter 3, gets routed to a specific call center agent— based on the characteristics of the customer, the complexity of the call, and the skills of the call center agent. For example, a complex call from an important customer can get routed to an agent in Australia. The next call may be answered from India. This process is best described as *dynamic, real-time reconfiguration of resources* (say, call center agents in this case). This is the same as Li & Fung's routing specific orders for shirts to a different configuration of vendors based on skills, availability of capacity, urgency, and so on. What we are witnessing is the development of similar capabilities at a more granular level—the capacity to assemble unique talent from both within and outside the firm for executing specific tasks.

What is the implication? The days of mass production—making one item in a repetitive, linear supply chain or the assembly line—may be over. Be they automotive, tires, shoes, or insurance firms, they do not create value by selling a product that is mass produced. They create a unique experience to one customer at a time by surrounding, if necessary, the physical product with services.

The value proposition is not the tire but the personalized usage of tire; not health insurance based on demographics but a health management system based on a personalized risk profile and continuous monitoring of the progress of an illness. As a result, the work of managers changes dramatically. It is no longer just managing an assembly line efficiently but responding to continually evolving opportunities. The core platform for value has shifted from product and service to solution and experience for the customer. Managerial work, as a result, is continuously changing. Unlike mass production, each request from a customer can be different.

Consider Dell. I can order a desktop without a monitor. For that order, Dell will not activate the supplier of monitors. But the next order may include a monitor. The activation of the supply base depends on the specific order received. Extending this argument, at a granular level, each cocreation opportunity (and a customer interaction) can be viewed as a specific project involving a unique configuration of resources. Software vendors from India face this problem. Their entire business consists of a series of projects to which they assign specific individuals. Each project may demand specific business domain knowledge and software skills. They continually reconfigure resources. TCS's engagements with Ferrari and British Telecom are two such examples. As illustrated in the Lenovo example, the emerging nature of managerial work—managing a series of micro- and macroprojects within the firm—suggests that a dynamic configuration of talent cannot take place unless we pay specific attention to the following:

> Managers need to know where the talent is within the organization and where it can be accessed easily from the outside.

> Managers need to help project team members cope with stresses caused by time pressures, ambiguous power and authority relationships, and cross-cultural and interpersonal interactions. The reconfigured systems need to be fluid. It is like building a *Velcro organization* in which teams can come together and disengage without effort.

> Managers need to create the capacity to reduce "frictional losses" in the dynamic configuration of resources—the difficulties in getting teams to work together effectively without delays and loss of creativity. This is about *continuous improvement and innovation*.

WHERE IS THE TALENT? THE GLOBAL SEARCH

In a global firm, it is hard to know where the talent is. Talent is, by definition, nonhierarchical. Expertise in mathematical modeling of risk in global supply chains may have no relationship to the hierarchical position of a person. Further, the ability to effectively work in a cross-cultural team may not be very transparent.

So the first step in developing an understanding of how to mobilize task-specific teams is building a process for transparent and objective assessment of the skills, attitudes, and experiences of all people. Managers must be able to, in real time, access the human resource database and assemble the names, locations, and availability of people with specific skills. The system must be able to respond to questions such as "Show me all who have specific skills in designing noise abatement systems in a car." The search may take a few steps such as skills in automotive design, noise management, interior noise, materials and noise, and so on. Managers must recognize that these teams may have people from multiple locations and multiple levels in the hierarchy. A young engineer from China may be a unique domain expert. He may be working in a team of several senior scientists and engineers. IBM recognizes this. It is building a knowledge management system to track its global talent. For example, this system allows an IBM manager in Brazil to easily track and form a team of 15 software testing experts from across the globe for the right price.

For this level of transparency to be built into the system, every employee must be clearly screened for skills, attitudes, and experiences in projects. Several firms have built unique services to accomplish this. For example, HireRight, a California firm, evaluates all new recruits to ensure that they have no criminal records, are not on drugs, and do possess the qualifications they claim to have. This background check is done through a search of public databases such as court and police records and university records, as well as through a search of work experience verification, including interviewing (with the candidate's permission) the candidate and her previous employers. There is a dose of human interpretation of the data collected. This check is accomplished prior to recruitment efforts to ensure that the data that are put into a record are authentic. A variation of this work is done by human resource groups within the firm. We recognize that background checks of the type just described are not unique or new. But this type of evaluation provides the baseline for creating a transparent talent management system. HireRight just happens to be a firm that has built this expertise into a growing business worldwide.

THE RUSH FOR TALENT

Firms recognize that there is competition for talent. Building and accessing a talent pool requires four distinct tasks:

1. Increase the number of skilled people.

2. Challenge the industry norms about the way work is done so that people with lower levels of skills can be trained to do the work effectively.

3. Create an excitement around your firm and your skill needs.

4. Disaggregate work and deskill it so that people with little formal education can do it.

We see all these strategies being employed by leading-edge firms. For example, ICICI could not wait for universities in India to generate talent to support its growing number of branches and the expansion of its product portfolio. In a partnership with NIIT, the largest computer skills training institute in the country, ICICI rolled out a certificate program to tap college graduates across multiple disciplines ranging from science and mathematics to liberal arts. ICICI provided the content for the courses. NIIT provided the training methodologies. The vast network of thousands of NIIT-affiliated training centers across the country was used to deliver the program. The graduates could go to any bank of their choice. ICICI created a large pool of well-trained people, and, needless to say, it made job offers to the top performers in these programs. ICICI has grown in number from 18,000 to 38,000 in the last two years.

Managers faced with severe talent shortages are reexamining accepted beliefs in matching skills with jobs. For example, TCS, Infosys, and other software firms in India face a severe talent shortage due to the vigorous growth in the Indian software industry. These firms have recruited a number of science and commerce graduates (as opposed to engineering graduates) for the testing of software applications. Since software testing is a sequence of well-defined tasks with specified inputs and outputs, managers at these firms determined that they did not need to employ software engineers to test the systems. The cost of a science or commerce graduate is about one-third that of a software engineer. The quality of software testing is also better in many cases. Prior to this experiment, the traditional belief was that only engineers could be good at testing software. Infosys and other software firms are finding that some of the top testers can be groomed into software developers with appropriate training in the latest development methods.

IBM, Infosys, and TCS are experimenting with new ideas to leverage raw talent in India to counter significant increases in wages for software professionals. The challenge is to convert young graduates with no experience to industry-ready assets that can be deployed in multinational projects.

IBM is creating an ecosystem of universities and institutes through funding and cocreation of courses. Furthermore, it is building a virtual network of students and faculty to work on challenges posed by real-world projects. A recent contest involved a case study of a business system that should be ported to an IBM middleware platform. IBM received an overwhelming response. More than 60,000 students and 5,000 faculty members participated in the contest from all over India.

The search for talent may also force firms to rethink their policies and their approach to talent acquisition. For example, Hyderabad-based Satyam Computers, one of the large software export vendors in India, is experimenting in leveraging resources from Indian villages. For the leading Indian software firms that recruit tens of thousands every year, the recruitment process is complex. They typically receive nearly a million applications in response to their job postings, and even the initial screening of applications can be very expensive. Satyam opted to experiment with resources in an Indian village a few hundred miles from Hyderabad to improve the efficiency of its recruitment process. The company defined the résumé-screening process at the lowest level of granularity and explicitly set the rules for each task. For example, looking for key words such as "Java" or ".net" and finding the number of years of experience or last salary from a résumé are defined as specific tasks. Satyam hired a number of high school graduates to identify these key words from digital résumés and create a consistent database of applicants for Satyam managers to query on an as-needed basis. The manpower cost of such a center in the village was less than $1 per day. Following this, Satyam is also experimenting with doing some traditional accounting business processes in the villages.

It is clear from the above that firms are trying multiple approaches to increase the available talent pool. There are several other well-known examples of large technology firms such as Cisco, Nokia, and Oracle leveraging talent in India beyond software. For example, Nokia manufactures cell phones in Chennai. Oracle, Intel, and Cisco have committed billions of dollars to leverage talent for research and development. This is just a start to managing talent. Once the person is hired, firms need to make sure that there is a systematic assessment of the skill levels and domain expertise of that person. Meritrack is a start-up in India that has developed methods for providing a testing service for the quantitative and reasoning skills of people. Furthermore, it can also provide a self-administered test on skills in a specific domain—say, equity research.

Meritrack develops these tests based on inputs from world experts on a domain such as equity research. Individual employees take both these tests to enable management to know the employees' specific skills—both in general terms (for example, good in analytical skills) and in terms of the domain of expertise (for example, equity research). Meritrack screens over 100,000 people per month for a large number of well-known firms such as ICICI and Microsoft. Meritrack is growing at 80 percent per year.

But these inputs are not enough. Managers need to know the capacity of specific individuals to work under pressure, across time zones, remotely, and across cultures. Therefore, past experiences in projects are a critical input to the system. Evalueserve, an Indian research outsourcing firm, has developed a system for improving the performance of individuals as team members. For example, most of the company's work is in short-duration projects—say, market research for a specific product in Spain. This may involve telephone interviews and desk research. Evalueserve may assign a team of six people for a week. At the end of the week, all members of the team get a 360-degree appraisal. Each individual may get as much as 30 separate feedback sessions per year, providing a continuous stream of data that that person can use for self-improvement. This certainly improves a person's ability to collaborate and work effectively as a member of a team. It also provides adequate feedback on a person's strengths and weaknesses as a team member. Other firms, such as Perot Systems and 24/7 Customer, also do the same. In many cases, call center operators get daily feedback on their performance. The process must not be limited to just the call center operators or junior managers. It must be for the whole organization.

Furthermore, the system must tell managers, at any point in time, how busy each employee is and on what projects. This allows managers to make real-time reallocation decisions. For example, if an ideal team member is dedicated 100 percent of the time to other projects, managers have to choose the second best or change priorities on the fly. This may be more difficult than it appears, as moving a person from projects in progress is neither desirable nor practical.

The management of the firm can achieve more flexibility to reassign people in work teams and assignments if it builds a transparent human resources system as shown in Figure 7.2.

Such a system allows managers to access the available pool of talent within the organization. A similar process may be required to enable them to access talent from outside vendors. The vendors may have a prequalified set of employees who may be selectively accessed. This ideal state cannot often be reached in some locations due to privacy laws. Which aspects of a person's profile can be made available to others within the organization and how that information can be used will continue to remain controversial. However, most of the information that is required can be made available with the explicit knowledge of the individuals concerned.

FIGURE 7.2

Steps in Building a Transparent Talent Management System

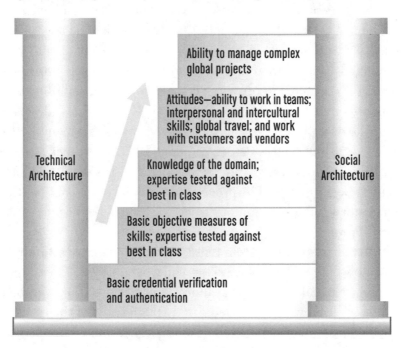

This approach to creating a transparent talent management system suggests that *the basic unit of analysis of an organization or its basic building block is an individual.* It is each individual's skills and capabilities that are configured to make the system deliver in an $N = 1$ and $R = G$ world of value creation. The business processes that underlie such a system allow for access, transparency, and ability to continually configure talent resources into project teams as well as measure their performance.

BUILDING A VELCRO ORGANIZATION

Real-time dynamic reconfiguration of people resources presents a problem: All of us are socialized to think of organizational life in a certain way—the role of the hierarchy, power, and authority for resource allocation and decision making, relationships within organizational silos (for example, a business unit or a function or geography), and role clarity. If one is a scientist in a lab or a young MBA in the planning unit, there is an illusion of role clarity (do research and work on strategic plan documents). The new approach to identifying and selectively organizing people based on their skills, attitudes, and experiences poses a new challenge for the individual.

Let us look at the problem through the eyes of the young female MBA from Michigan, who was hired for her analytical skills. She can, in our talent management system, be asked to be part of a China team. She can say to herself, "Yes, I am part of the strategic planning unit, and I report administratively to the director of strategy. However, I am from China, and I worked for five years in Beijing in the Department of Energy. I know the country, the energy bureaucracy in China, and its approach to foreign firms. I was part of a team that managed these relationships for two of my five years there. I understand why the project manager in charge of entering China wants me in her team. However, I am not doing what I was recruited for—analysis. I am not sure who my boss is. I am equally concerned about who will evaluate my performance and how. I am spending less time with my colleagues in the strategic planning group. I am traveling a lot. I am working with business development and the energy business group a lot. Is this good for me?"

We hear this a lot from young managers not accustomed to the real-time reconfiguration of resources approach. Our young manager in planning is getting a real exposure to business development and is learning a great deal about the company. She is also contributing significantly to the project. But stresses and strains are common in such teams. Individuals have a right to know where they stand at a given time and to know the prospects for progress in their careers. A transparent system of performance evaluation—skills, attitudes, behaviors, and performance—is a prerequisite. Training for specific opportunities, as well as training of a person, is crucial. *Furthermore, individual employees must know what new challenges they can expect over a period of five years. Making this transparent to the employees makes it easier to reduce these tensions.*

While the project scope and deliverables can be clear, power and influence, performance measurement, and career management can be sources of tension. In a traditional hierarchical organization, a person's talent may be only partially used (as in strategic analysis), but it can offer role clarity. In a talent management system, this ambiguity in power relationships, career progression, and performance evaluation must be dealt with head on. Furthermore, global project teams can introduce another element of stress. Long work hours, multiple time zones, pressures working with a group where face-to-face contact can be minimal, and the bases for collaboration can add to the stress. Recognizing these stresses on individuals can be critical for making these teams work.

We have to start with the assumption that we are moving away from clear and fully defined organizational homes for people— represented at any given time by the hierarchical organization (the organizational chart)—to a *Velcro organization* in which individuals come together temporarily to perform a task in a role related to that task and that particular task can change next week. The rise of the Velcro employee is where the global supply chain for talent is headed. We are moving to a state in which people come together and disengage seamlessly, as in Velcro connections. This is different from the current notion of organizational change. So as the organization structure evolves, organizations will have to be understood on three levels:

1. *Formal hierarchical structure:* This level is the anatomy of the organization. The bone structure is fixed. Yes, there will be the hierarchy to which people belong. For most people, "I am part of China and I am a project manager in Business Unit X" will still be a reality. It may not tell that employee what he will be doing at any given time. But this illusion of certainty is a must. Moreover, for 80 percent of the organization, this is all that they need to know.

2. *Business processes and analytics:* This level is the circulatory system of the organization. The business processes and analytics allow an organization to adapt, be flexible, and stay in tune with the continuous change in the business landscape. These processes allow managers to reconfigure resources in real time.

3. *Personal attitudes and skills:* These allow managers to cope with the stresses inherent in the dynamic reconfiguration of resources—in this case, talent in the organization—to projects big and small.

As is obvious to the reader, the relative importance of formal hierarchies and organizational arrangements is likely to decrease in an $N = 1$ and $R = G$ world. However, the importance of business processes and the skills and interpersonal competence of the individual managers will become significantly more important. Individuals will have to live in a constantly evolving work environment, be capable of working in multiple teams and becoming productive in short order, and have a high level of self-awareness. Managers may not have a choice in migrating to this new world-of-work order. But migrating without a strategic direction can enormously increase the risks to the organization, including the flight of top talent. This is a new management challenge.

CONTINUOUS IMPROVEMENT IN PERFORMANCE

While we can wonder how difficult it can be for individuals to adjust to this new approach to a Velcro organization, we must remind ourselves that this is not a difficult environment for those who are growing up in an environment of multitasking, Facebook, blogs, and wikis. Young men and women are accustomed to this "role of the moment" in their lives. We have to make it a part of their reality in the large organization. We have to reduce the frictional losses involved in building cross-cultural teams and making them effective. We have to enhance the capacity for collaboration. Companies that have to depend on cross-cultural collaboration and project teams of the moment, such as Indian software firms, are pioneering new approaches to this organizational form.

Let us consider the engagement between TCS and Aviva, a global insurance group. As part of its global strategy, Aviva opted to leverage the expertise of TCS in developing new IT applications to provide other IT services. This engagement evolved into multiple projects implemented at the offshore delivery center of TCS in India. TCS developed a relationship portal called the Partner Interaction Management System to enhance the quality of collaboration and minimize frictional loss. It was an interactive knowledge management system to aid in managing people, business processes, and other artifacts to facilitate smooth collaboration.

The primary objective was to seamlessly integrate global members of the project teams across Aviva in the United Kingdom and TCS in India. The graphical user interface was made similar in look and feel to the Aviva intranet screens. It was accessible to all members of the project teams across TCS and Aviva. A role-based security was maintained to guard access to sensitive information.

All project artifacts, including requirements documents, design documents, development methodology, test plans, minutes of review meetings, client visit details, and information about project members on the two sides, were available on the portal. The system also allowed for contextual alerts to be sent to project members based on specific changes in a project, such as the addition of new members or changes to relevant documents or project goals. The access to various knowledge artifacts in this system made it easier for new members joining the projects on either side to quickly learn the context and begin to contribute. In addition to the technical artifacts, this portal also provided information to bridge the cultural gap between the two groups of project members in TCS and Aviva. For example, this section contained information on Indian culture, ethics, and work environment.

The goal of these efforts is to continuously improve the performance of the project teams by reducing frictional losses. The teams must be put together in real time and must start functioning effectively in real time. Elaborate team-building efforts and wasted time are signs of inefficiency.

A NEW VIEW OF MANAGERIAL WORK

The critical tasks of mobilizing talented people on a global basis and building effective work teams from them demand a new approach to understanding managerial work. The $N = 1$ and $R = G$ world demands that the work of the firm be divided into a large number of micro- and macroprojects.

Microprojects involve specific, simple tasks that can be accomplished in a short period of time and often remotely. Mapping the key words in a résumé as in the case of Satyam is an example. *Macroprojects* are broader, more complex, more open-ended, and involve talent from multiple locations. The design of aerodynamic features in Ferrari cars is an example. The macroprojects may be further divided into microprojects.

Unlike an assembly line, where products can be produced according to a predetermined forecast, the new approach to value creation focuses on demands based on what consumers need at any given time. Instead of the firm's producing according to a forecast and trying to sell what it has produced, in this model, the firm produces only what consumers want at a given time. Value is cocreated, one consumer and one experience at a time. This influences every aspect of management—not just manufacturing and logistics. For example, advertising in the digital age is not just TV-based broadcasting to a large audience, as has been the case in the past; today it is focused on and tailored to one individual, in that person's specific context in time, as in the way Google functions.

The execution of strategy, in this model, is accomplished through a series of micro- and macroprojects. This requires managers to focus on a continuous reconfiguration of resources as opposed to a stable configuration of an assembly line and manufacturing to forecast. Reconfiguration of resources, as we saw in the various examples—IBM, TCS, and others—must start with recognition that the talent required to execute any one of these microprojects is distributed across multiple locations and often across multiple geographies.

Furthermore, the teams have to be task specific. Expertise is often hierarchy agnostic. Someone with a bigger salary and title does not necessarily know more about a specific domain. Expertise, especially in new areas of work, may reside in younger people. For example, understanding of marketing and advertising in the digital age may be greater in a younger member of the team who is more in tune with and participates in social Web sites such as MySpace, Facebook, and Couchsurfing.com. Individuality, personalization, autonomy, and other aspects of the emerging culture are not theoretical constructs to this generation. Many of the senior marketing managers at 50 (with a few exceptions) may not have a visceral understanding of these developments.

Breaking the tyranny of the hierarchy in the configuration of teams is critical. We suggest a simple experiment. Take 20 project teams, at random, in your firm and analyze their membership. Assess the percentage of these teams that consist of people from the multiple hierarchical levels that exist in the organization. This is a simple way to understand the dominant logic within the firm and how far the firm has to travel to become nonhierarchical. We find in many cases that the membership in these teams may have very little to do with who really does the work. Those who do the work typically tend to be at lower levels in the hierarchy—a good measure of the informal and formal systems within the firm.

Finally, we have to access talent from around the world, both from within the firm and selectively from the outside. This dynamic reconfiguration of talent from around the world as new projects arise also requires management to act in real time. Li & Fung must react to the fabricators of shirts from among the 9,500 factories in Asia without delay if it is to keep the pipeline to JCPenney stores adequately stocked. When Li & Fung receives an order

for the same type of shirt, it may fill the order using different factories based on the utilization of capacity, quality delivered, and cost.
Not only must the company respond rapidly, but it must also dynamically optimize whatever resources are available at that moment.
The same is true of pulling together a team of people to execute a
project.

Unlike factories producing a shirt, for which specifications can
be laid down to minimize frictional losses from multiple vendors'
working together—be it in scheduling or quality of work—bringing
people together in teams involves intercultural and interpersonal
tensions. For people to work in teams effectively, individuals must
be trained to deal with the tensions inherent in ambiguous power
and authority relationships, differences in cultural backgrounds,
and the newness of tasks. The focus is not just on individuals and
their expertise but also on their capacity to work in multiple teams.
Continuous feedback and support help individual contributors become self-aware of their weaknesses and strengths. These are critical for reducing the frictional losses in teams.

The new managerial work is focused on the development of
new knowledge to address evolving problems. The focus is on continuous improvement and innovation. This calls for new metrics
for evaluating the performance of individuals and teams. How well
did they address the problem? What resources were used? How
replicable is the approach? How creative was the solution? Did it
get the consumers to have a unique cocreated experience? How
well did individuals perform? What new skills do they have to develop? What support do they need? These are questions at the
heart of a dynamic and continually evolving organization.

Continuous change and evolution, the ability to focus on new
projects and become part of new teams, and the ability to disaggregate tasks and reintegrate them are all part of the new reality.
However, without a broadly conceived, clearly articulated, and
widely understood agenda in the organization, continuous change
can be very disruptive. People need to have common and constant

"pivots"—values and beliefs—that allow for continuous change to be seen as positive and necessary. A shared point of view is critical.

The commitment to cocreating personalized experiences for consumers ($N = 1$) as a philosophy and as an article of faith in how to create wealth is a starting point for employees and vendors to understand the need for continuous configuration of resources— $R = G$. Furthermore, such a system is unlikely to evolve without well-developed business processes that are explicit and flexible, as we saw in Chapters 2 and 4. Focusing on $N = 1$ with millions of consumers also demands that the firm have well-developed analytics. Finally, formal organizational structures must give way to a focus on individuals and their skills, behaviors, and attitudes. The appropriate units of analysis and work are individuals and their abilities, not hierarchical structures. The need to function at the $N = 1$ level, not surprisingly, focuses managerial attention on individuals. It follows that employees should be treated as $N = 1$ to gain the consumer focus of $N = 1$. This is the opportunity and the challenge for managers.

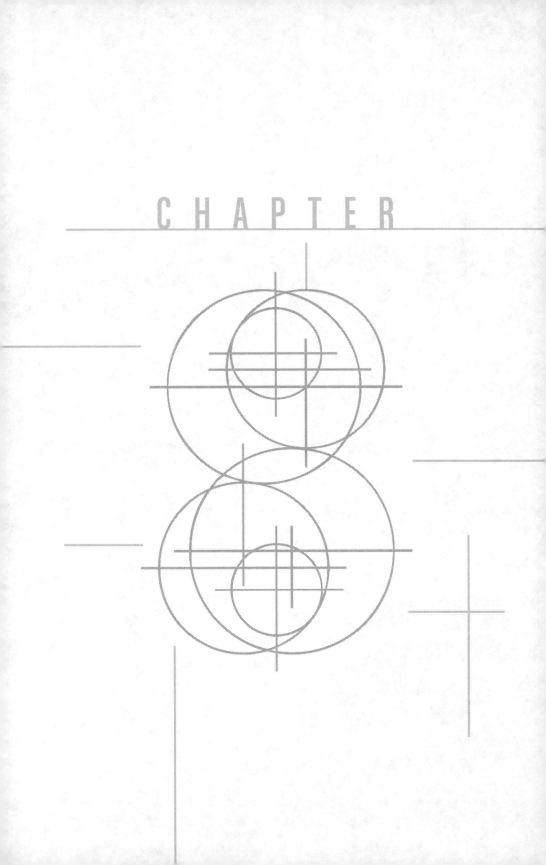

CHAPTER

8

There is a fundamental shift in the *focus, the sources, and the processes of innovation and value creation.* Forced by digitization, connectivity, and open and free access to information and social networks, an informed and active consumer base is emerging. Consumers are willing to engage and cocreate their own personalized experiences, as we have seen in the

AN AGENDA FOR MANAGERS: FOCUS ON THE ESSENCE OF INNOVATION

many case studies in this book. These case studies, primarily used as illustrations, represent but a small fraction of the transformation underway.

For example, it is not just Nike and Pomarfin that allow consumers to design their own shoes. Add to that list VANS, Tupli, and Stevemadden.com. Customized design of shoes by the consumers started with high-priced athletic footwear and moved to fashion footwear. Now shoes priced in the range of $40 to $170 are sold with this business model. The overall business environment is rapidly gravitating to $N = 1$—that is, the emerging business model for value creation described in this book.

In order to execute $N = 1$ business models, firms will require a new approach to accessing and using resources.

The resource base will expand *beyond a firm to an ecosystem of firms and individuals*. This ecosystem could be either local or global. The transformation of the business environment toward the $N = 1$ and $R = G$ model of value creation provides an unprecedented opportunity for innovation.

This transformation does not leave any industry untouched. We have provided examples from a wide variety of industries shaping this transformation, including high tech (for example, Google, Apple, Yahoo!, Netflix, and Cisco), rust belt (for example, tires and cement), manufacturing (for example, HP, Lenovo, and auto manufacturers), and services (for example, ICICI, UPS, and TCS). And as we saw in Chapter 1, the transformation will also challenge the traditional distinctions between B2B and B2C organizations, product versus process innovations, manufacturing versus service businesses, and hardware versus software firms. This change will envelop firms from developed markets such as North America, Europe, and Japan as well as from emerging markets such as India and China. Increasingly, as our examples point out, there will be collaboration to develop analytics and other resources between well-established firms in the West and emerging, specialist micro-multinationals in India, China, and other countries. Privileged access to talent, not ownership of talent, will be the defining characteristic of this transformation. However, for most firms, escaping their legacy systems and transforming their organizations toward an $N = 1$ and $R = G$ world of innovation and value creation will not be trivial or easy.

THE NEW HOUSE OF INNOVATION

The core thesis of this book can be captured in the New House of Innovation (Figure 8.1) that we briefly outlined in the Introduction. This visual illustrates the essential connections between the various architectural elements that create an entrepreneurial and innovative culture in a firm. The pillars are the inexorable trend toward $N = 1$ and $R = G$. But connecting the demands of $N = 1$ and

FIGURE 8.1
The New House of Innovation

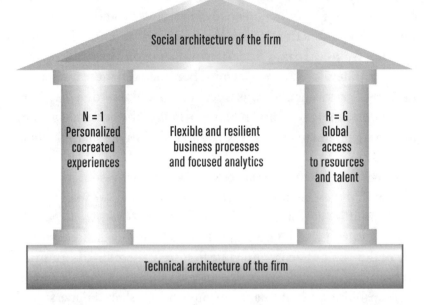

$R = G$ are the business processes and analytics. Similarly, as we have demonstrated, this transformation to an innovative culture cannot take place without a realignment of both the technical and the social architectures of the firm. The connecting link between the social and the technical architectures is the business process, which is supported by focused analytics.

It is important to understand that the New House of Innovation is an *integrated package*. We cannot cherry-pick bits and pieces of the house. For example, we cannot create an innovation culture without a clear and unambiguous commitment from managers to the basic drivers of innovation: $N = 1$ and $R = G$. This clarity and commitment will inform how the firm will move forward. The conceptual and administrative changes in how companies are managed will follow from this commitment.

For example, managers must reorient business functions to deliver the *efficiency and flexibility* demanded in this new world of value creation. $N = 1$ will demand new levels of transparency and insights into the needs, skills, and behaviors of individual consumers such that the firm can be supportive of cocreated personalized experiences. Furthermore, *consumers evolve*. Their expectations and skills evolve. This trend will influence a continuous evolution of the nature of several functions within the firm, such as marketing, sales, human resources management, manufacturing and services, and support. Therefore, managers must become adept at real-time actions that are event and consumer specific. This will necessitate continuous improvements and innovations in the underlying technical systems and managerial skills and attitudes that deliver value. It will also intensify the search for resources and talent ($R = G$).

The need for and the capacity to reconfigure resources will be critical as well. The move toward an $N = 1$ and $R = G$ world is not an event; it is an evolution. Therefore, *this transformation must be seen as a journey*. No journey can start without a clear understanding of the point of departure. The first step, therefore, is for firms to build a common perspective on their current business model and capabilities. Senior managers must have a shared understanding of their starting points through a candid discussion and reflection of the current state of business processes, systems, and people. We believe that the future sources of competitive advantage will rest on how systematically firms shape these capabilities to the demands of $N = 1$ and $R = G$.

THE NEW SOURCES OF COMPETITIVE ADVANTAGE

We believe that the traditional sources of competitive advantage, such as access to capital, physical location, and raw materials or technology, will become table stakes. These factors are diminishing in their importance as sources of competitive advantage. Access to these factors is becoming easier. As we move to an $N = 1$ and $R = G$ world of value creation, we believe that competitive advantage will depend on a firm's approach to business processes that can seamlessly connect consumers and resources and manage simultaneously the needs for efficiency and flexibility. Firms will compete in providing a unique quality of experience in their products and services to each customer. It will be a race to provide a unique customer experience at the lowest cost. The need for enabling unique and contextual experience from each customer ($N = 1$) will shape the demand for rapid reconfiguration of resources, ideas, and talent globally ($R = G$).

The capabilities for dynamic reconfiguration of global resources are embedded in the business process architecture and analytical capabilities built into the system. *Business processes* are the core links between *business strategy* and *action* through which the products and services are delivered and experiences are created for customers. For example, customer support business processes are critical for Aviva and JPMorgan to create a unique and contextual experience for individual customers by routing customers' calls to the right agents in India, the Philippines, or Europe based on the specific needs of the calls and customers' individual profiles. A business process, like the circulatory system, *is often organizationally invisible but crucial*. Focus on innovation will reverse the attitudes of senior managers toward business processes. It must get top managers' attention. Transparency in business processes and the capacity for flexibility and efficiency in business process architecture will emerge as one of the sources of competitive advantage as firms transform to compete in an $N = 1$ and $R = G$ world of business.

This new world of business also demands *real-time contextual insights* for management action. For example, for Yahoo! to dynamically match the right advertisements for each customer or for UPS or the Department of Defense to transform their trucks, planes, and ships to floating warehouses and meet specific customer needs, they need transparency in their processes and performance at the level of every customer, every supplier, and every employee (for example, every truck driver, as in the case of UPS). Similarly, Amazon.com, Netflix, and ICICI require analytics to understand the economics of servicing each customer. Hence, business process capabilities are necessary but not sufficient. Business process architecture should be aided with powerful analytics for firms to get a visceral understanding of each customer, supplier, partner, and employee. This allows the firms to manage the risk from new opportunities and deliver unique value to customers.

As digitization permeates every aspect of business, every business is, in effect, an e-business. Every business process is enabled by the underlying ICT architecture. It is meaningless to expect capacities for flexibility and efficiency in business processes when they rest on an aging legacy system designed with rigid technology platforms. For example, ING could not implement a new business model that can tailor insurance policies for specific customers and underwrite the same policy in minutes if its business functions were supported by nonintegrated legacy systems. ING needed a new ICT platform to build the capability.

Hence, senior managers need to pay attention to the quality and capabilities of the ICT architecture. While the hardware and connectivity part of this architecture can be delegated to the IT departments and vendors, CEOs and line managers cannot delegate strategic decisions on the business applications, analytic capabilities, and data warehousing. It is the business applications and the analytics engine that form the backbone of the business process architecture. In order to compete effectively, firms need to build forward-looking ICT platforms as specified in Chapter 4. It is the combination of such ICT platforms and business process capabilities aided by analytics that delivers contextual insights and cuts short management latency for action. Hence, this combination will emerge as key capabilities required to compete as firms transform into the $N = 1$ and $R = G$ model of business.

THE MIGRATION TO A NEW APPROACH TO MANAGEMENT

The business transformation to $N = 1$ and $R = G$ will necessitate new approaches to managing. Managers need to cope with new tensions in managing seemingly opposing capabilities such as flexibility and efficiency in their business. Google and Yahoo! may present unique advertisements based on the search and demographic profile of each customer (flexibility). But the contents of these advertisements need to be reliable (efficiency). Personalized shoes delivered by Pomarfin cannot be of bad-quality leather. In a traditional sense, flexibility is not associated with scale while efficiency in business processes is. The new demands of $N = 1$ and $R = G$ are for scale with flexibility and customer-specific processes with efficiency. The shift to this seemingly contrasting combination of capabilities will require changes in the social architecture of the firm—that is, managerial mindsets, skills, behaviors, and decision structures. Hence, this transformation will involve migrating management practices to build new skills, attitudes, and behaviors.

This migration should be planned. Managers can develop a methodical approach to this transformation. We have presented one such approach here. The first step in this process is for managers to collectively build clarity to their point of departure. This can be achieved by an audit of existing beliefs and capabilities in the organization. For example, gaining clarity to the current dominant logic in the firm is a good start. Managers should also take stock of their business process portfolios and the respective application systems and databases that support the business process architecture and analytical capabilities. This will provide a complete picture of the existing social and technical architectures of the organization.

$N = 1$ AND $R = G$:
A REALITY BY 2015/2020

We have argued that $N = 1$ and $R = G$ will be the basis for innovation and value creation. This trend is happening faster than anyone expected. We believe that by 2015 to 2020, in a very short period of 7 to 12 years, this transformation will not be big news. It will increasingly be the norm in many industries. What gives us this confidence? Consider the following:

> At a very conservative estimate, more than 5 billion people will be connected through cell phone networks and the Internet.

> The rapid progress of social networks and the access people have to information will create the ability for all of us to exercise our individuality. MySpace, Facebook, and YouTube are becoming part of the global culture. More than 100 million people already use MySpace, and over 50 million use Facebook. YouTube, which is about two years old, is already influencing presidential debates in the United States.

> Everyone will get access to infrastructure. For example, Amazon.com already allows its infrastructure to be used by others, such as buyers and sellers on eBay. The Amazon.com Web Services offerings allow any small business or individual to leverage capacity in Amazon.com's global infrastructure. Some examples of these virtual services are payment and procurement solutions. The elastic disk service offered by Amazon.com over the Internet allows consumers to use the capacity they need. They do not have to buy disks in fixed sizes.

> Powerful analytics and large database management capabilities including virtualization of computing (a technique that simulates computing resources) will add to the propensity to cocreate. It will be easier, cheaper, and accessible.

> Most important, the generation of active consumers in 2015 is 12 to 15 years old today. They are growing up in a new environment in which they are used to individuality and self-expression. Managers can experience the differences in eagerness to collaborate and cocreate across the two groups of employees on either side of 35 years in age in their teams. The capacity to collaborate is the highest among those between 22 and 30 years of age.

We can crystallize these changes into three key trends that will determine how consumers will relate to institutions such as firms and to each other. In addition, these trends will influence how firms will evolve in their collaboration with one another. The three critical trends are these:

1. Convergence in ubiquitous connectivity in voice, data, and video through cell phones, PCs, and the Internet

2. Ubiquitous access to computing at continually decreasing costs through advances in new technologies and innovations in delivery models

3. Rapid and vibrant experimentation in new platforms for collaboration that span both personal (social) and professional lives

We believe that these trends are shaping a new ecosystem for firms and individuals to connect with ease and cocreate new experiences through access to global resources. These trends can be visualized as shown in Figure 8.2. This construct was developed for us by our friend and ex-student Praveen Suthrum, president of Nextservices, Inc. Praveen belongs to the younger generation, which is current with the evolving new business models. (See Table 8.1 at the end of this chapter for an overview of the firms that cluster around the outer points of this construct.)

On the connectivity axis in the figure, increasingly traditional telecom voice carriers and device providers, Internet service providers (data), and traditional cable TV (video content enablers) are converging to offer ubiquitous connectivity at low cost. iPhones and BlackBerries have redefined the concept and reach of smart phones. These devices deliver audio, data, and video contents that are personalized.

Furthermore, access to connectivity and content through voice, data, and video is increasing in quality and decreasing in price. This means that billions of people will be connected not just to voice communications but to data and increasingly to video.

FIGURE 8.2

Three Key Trends That Will Determine How Consumers Will Relate to Institutions Such as Firms and to One Another

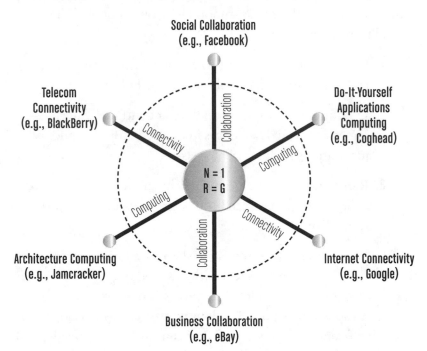

This convergence will allow for these billions to be part of the connected web for the first time in human history.

More recently there has been a push toward open standards and systems in this convergence. For example, firms such as Verizon and Google are proposing an open platform for network connectivity that will allow multiple devices to connect. There is also an attempt to make access to devices free. For example, Google is trying to force an open-source mobile device platform using the new high-speed wireless connectivity. In summary, access to connectivity to personalized content through a device of the individual consumer's choice is becoming an expected reality.

Similarly, on the computing axis in Figure 8.2, we are witnessing the convergence of products and services by traditional computing firms to simple and easy-to-use application building blocks that are inexpensive. Hence, computing is becoming totally accessible. For example, we already discussed Amazon.com's pioneering role in allowing small and medium firms and individuals to rent capacity for storage and software in Amazon.com's infrastructure through a hosted model. Another example is Coghead, a software firm in California that provides a radically new way for small firms and individuals to develop and deliver customized Web applications at a fraction of the cost of regular packaged implementations. Coghead's "Do-It-Yourself (D-I-Y)" framework allows users to build customized applications within hours or days as opposed to months and years in traditional frameworks. Users pay a small monthly fee on a *pay-per-use* basis as opposed to making huge upfront investments. Coghead already has over 25,000 customers.

The models from Amazon.com, Coghead, and other firms are making access to infrastructure less difficult. Such pay-per-use approaches to computing and storage capacity as in Amazon.com, Jamcracker, and Zoho are just the start. There is a trend here in shifting infrastructure expenses from high fixed costs to low variable costs on an as-needed basis. More important, this convergence of computing allows individuals with minimum skills to get on with their own portfolio of operations with a large plethora of do-it-yourself (DIY) tools.

The third trend is about the emerging collaboration platforms. Social networks are transcending personal communities to business applications, as shown along the collaboration axis in the figure. The distinction between "private" and "public" is vanishing very fast. The distinction between collaboration in a personal and business context is also blurring. For example, wikis and blogs are being increasingly used inside large firms to democratize access to information and knowledge and improve cycle time. Platforms by Google and Facebook are as critical to advertising and brand building as they are to creating individual networks of personal friends.

Overlaying these trends are the megaplatforms for individual access created by large firms such as Google, Yahoo!, Microsoft, and Amazon.com. These firms have invested billions of dollars in creating their unique platforms to connect with individuals and firms. As shown in Figure 8.2 and Table 8.1, a large number of firms along the three axes are experimenting with new models for collaboration and personalized access to information. The table represents a small sample of companies driving collaboration. For the Web-savvy reader, the placement of some of these companies might appear conflicting; this is bound to happen in an environment that is rapidly converging. Firms are developing their own platforms (for example, Salesforce) or are riding on existing megaplatforms (for example, the 10,000 applications built by third-party developers on Facebook).

This evolving ecosystem, as depicted in the figure, has several managerial implications for enabling $N = 1$ and $R = G$. First, this ecosystem does not make a distinction between the rich and the poor—someone in Cape Town, Saigon, or Pune will have as much access as someone in Tokyo, New York, or Helsinki. Second, access to computing is becoming easy and affordable, and it requires no lumpy up-front investment. More important, DIY tools make it accessible to all—even the less sophisticated. Finally, social networks, driven by the previous two trends in the convergence of connectivity and computing, will dominate how we live, work, and transact business. $N = 1$ and $R = G$ are at the heart of this ecosystem driven by the convergence of connectivity, computing, and collaboration. These trends have implications beyond high-tech firms such as Google, Yahoo!, or Coghead. The capabilities created in this ecosystem will make it easier for more firms like Bridgestone, Goodyear, ICICI, and TutorVista to connect with their customers and cocreate value through access to global resources in their respective business domains. These trends both feed the move toward $N = 1$ and $R = G$ and are energized by it. This has become a "virtuous cycle."

AN APPROACH FOR THE
JOURNEY TO N = 1 AND R = G

Given these trends, what should be the agenda for senior managers? First, senior managers must start with a point of view about the future, which they then need to share widely within their firms. We believe that a five- to seven-year time horizon is appropriate. The trend is obvious. We are not suggesting that by 2015 all industries will have transformed. We are suggesting that there is a compelling reason to start experimenting now. Those who delay the process will be left behind or forced to catch up with their more thoughtful competitors. Catching up is always a risky process.

Once there is clarity and agreement on the collective capabilities at the point of their departure, managers need to develop a vision of their future: the nature of their interpretation of the $N = 1$ and $R = G$ world in their industry. Each firm will have to define the steps that it has to take to move the organization in that direction. It is obvious that each firm, even within an industry, will have a different migration path. The migration path will depend on the nature of the current state as well as the capacity for change. Some can move faster than others. The specifications of a shared and desired destination will help managers identify the new capabilities and skills that need to be built.

The migration from the point of departure to the future cannot be accomplished in a single step. The entire migration process must be broken down into small feasible steps, as illustrated in Figure 8.3.

Having a clear goal does not imply a one-step transformation. In fact, that is not possible. The competitive landscape will evolve and will be subject to multiple social and technological turns and twists. The only certainty is $N = 1$ and $R = G$, not the manifestations of this core reality. Therefore, it is prudent to take small, measured steps by building specific milestones. These milestones allow an organization to evolve rapidly, each one carefully designed to build new capabilities in the organization.

FIGURE 8.3
Fold the Future In

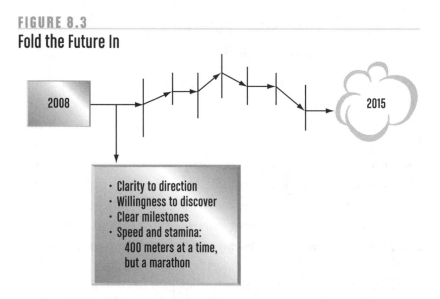

Furthermore, the migration pattern must be directionally focused. No organization needs to know all the steps ahead of it when it embarks on this journey because the whole journey is about *learning by doing, taking small steps,* and *consolidating gains as we go along.*

The key message to managers is simple: *Fold the future in.* Do not extrapolate the past or the current state of affairs in your industry. What you know and how you work will not get us to the future.

The approach to migration we suggest depends on the following premises of large-scale transformation:

1. All transformation starts with a distinct and clear point of view about the future. Value creation will depend on $N = 1$ and $R = G$ in the future.

2. There must be a clear articulation of the current capabilities of the organization and clarity about the point of departure.

3. It must be recognized that the managerial processes and capabilities that got us to where we are cannot get us to where we want to go.

4. Migration must be broken down into smaller milestones and critical doable steps. The criteria must be that these steps are directionally right, doable, and able to add new and desired capabilities.

5. It must be recognized that we cannot know all the details of the total journey. We have to discover as we learn by doing. The first step may inform the second, and so on.

6. We have to have the sense of urgency (the speed of a 400-meter runner) and the stamina to stay the course (the persistence of a marathoner). Transformation is about both speed and stamina.

7. We can develop detailed metrics to measure the progress for each one of the steps or milestones.

8. A long-term focus with short-term actions is the essence of organizational transformation.

9. This process recognizes that managers have to "perform" during the transformation. Blocking and tackling is necessary, but their focus on where we are going is equally important.

10. Capability building is an arduous process in a large firm. It cannot be done by broad pronouncements. Rather, it requires careful articulation of specific steps.

11. Capability building must focus on both the technical and the social infrastructures at the same time.

12. Finally, there are bound to be time lags between efforts and results. Dealing with these lags and recognizing that the journey will have missteps are key to making long-term sustainable changes.

The journey requires imagination, a passion for value creation, and the ability to convert concepts into detailed steps. This is the new leadership challenge: recognizing both the here and now and the future. Look at the firm as an engine that must generate profits now and at the same time renew itself to create the capacity for sustainable value creation. It requires leaders to imagine the future of their firms and at the same time act responsibly and now.

The emerging business transformation we have described is based on trends that cannot be reversed. Consumer activism, ubiquitous connectivity, convergence of technologies and industries, globalization of markets, and global search for and access to resources—these are trends that are not within the control of any one firm. These trends lead, inevitably, to a world we describe as $N = 1$ and $R = G$. Our suggestion is simple: *Embrace the inevitable.* Make the trends work for you.

The role of leadership in organizations will be crucial in this transformation. We need leaders who can imagine and inspire and who can shape the world as it can be. The opportunities for value creation are so many that the prize is worth the effort. The journey can be exhilarating. You have the opportunity to shape the next round of globalization and build a more empowered society.

TABLE 8.1 NEW MODELS FOR COLLABORATION AND PERSONALIZED ACCESS TO INFORMATION: FIRMS THAT CLUSTER ALONG EACH DIMENSION IN FIGURE 8.2

SOCIAL COLLABORATION

Company	Business type	Description
Facebook	Social networking	Popular social networking platform (Microsoft invested $250 million, valuing it at $15 billion)
Neighborhoods	Social networking	eBay's community networking Web site focused on specific products (e.g., iPhones)
Orkut	Social networking	Google-owned popular social networking Web site; successful in India and Brazil
MySpace	Social networking	News Corp.–owned popular social networking Web site, which started with an initial focus on music bands
Ning	Social networking	Online platform to let users create their own social communities
Friendster	Social networking	Popular 50 million user-base social networking Web site
Hi5	Social networking	Popular social networking Web site, particularly in Central America
OpenSocial	Social networking	Google's interoperable platform that allows easy development of social networking applications
Second Life	Social networking	Internet-based virtual world that allows users to live a "second" life
Habbo Hotel	Social networking	Web site that targets teenagers; receives 6 million unique visitors every month
Bebo	Social networking	Largest social networking site in the U.K., Ireland, and New Zealand
Slide	Social networking	Largest developer of third-party applications for Facebook
Flock	Social networking	Recently launched social Web browser
Twitter	Social networking	Lets friends keep track of users through short instant messages
Club Penguin	Social networking	Disney-owned social networking Web site targeted at children
Tagged	Social networking	Popular social networking Web site that allows users to showcase their personalities and talents

SOCIAL COLLABORATION *(cont.)*		
Company	**Business type**	**Description**
Digg	Social bookmarking	Allows communities to bookmark Web sites and ranks popularity
StumbleUpon	Social bookmarking	eBay-owned company that lets users bookmark and share Web sites as they stumble upon them
Del.icio.us	Social bookmarking	Popular social bookmarking service for storing, sharing, and identifying bookmarked Web sites
Wikipedia	Content sharing	Largest and fastest-growing openly editable encyclopedia with 9.25 million articles
Wikia	Content sharing	Content-sharing Web site that helps create and support wiki-based communities
Knol	Content sharing	Google product for knowledge sharing
Meebo	Chat	Platform that supports multiple Internet messaging services via its Web site
Blogger	Blogging	Google's blog publishing software
Wordpress	Blogging	Blog publishing software developed on an open source platform
Tabblo	Photo community	HP-owned photo community site that lets users share photos and words
Flickr	Photo community	Yahoo!-owned photo-sharing platform, one of the first examples of Web 2.0
Shaadi.com	Community networking	Web-based matrimonial service targeted at the Indian community
Hulu	Video	NBC-owned on-demand video online service
YouTube	Video sharing	Google-owned (purchased for $1.65 billion) site that lets users upload, view, and share video clips
Joost	Internet-based video entertainment	Started by Skype founders, Web site allowing TV show distribution via peer-to-peer networking
Vimeo	Video sharing	Password-protected video sharing
Metacafe	Video sharing	Online video entertainment company that pays creators for content based on ranking
Dabble	Video search	Human-powered video search service

BUSINESS COLLABORATION		
Company	Business type	Description
Salesforce.com	CRM	Web-based collaboration software that has become a platform for various third-party business applications
Basecamp	Project management	Project management collaboration software
SugarCRM	CRM	Web-based collaboration software previously built on an open source platform
LinkedIn	Business networking	Popular business networking Web site with 17 million users
Plaxo	Business networking	Online address book service
Zimbra	Collaboration	Yahoo!-owned and open source–based e-mail and calendar collaboration software
WebEx	Collaboration	Cisco-owned on-demand Web collaboration software popular for video and Web conferencing
OpenCourseWare	Collaboration	MIT's online initiative to publish course materials freely on the Web
eBay	Auction	Largest online auction platform, allowing businesses and people to sell goods online
PayPal	e-Commerce	eBay-owned software allowing payments and money transfers via the Internet
Technorati	Search	Search engine for blogs
YouSendIt	Collaboration	Site allowing sharing files of large sizes via the Web
Adify	Advertising	Online marketplace for highly targeted advertisements
AdWords	Advertising	Google's popular advertising solution
JotSpot	Collaboration	Google-owned structured wiki solution for businesses
Vitrue	Video	Technology platform for video content from businesses
Slashdot	News	User-submitted news site with technology/science bent
SharePoint	Collaboration	Microsoft's Web-based collaboration and document management platform
SAP	Collaboration	Large-scale enterprise resource planning software

BUSINESS COLLABORATION *(cont.)*		
Company	Business type	Description
Oracle Collaboration Suite	Collaboration	Enterprisewide collaboration
Fast Search & Transfer	Search	Norway-based site operating in the enterprise search space (Microsoft purchased Fast for $1.2 billion in January 2008)
Amazon.com	Collaboration	World's largest bookstore and a platform for retail and business applications
BEA AcquaLogic	Software platform	Service-oriented architecture platform to manage diverse business processes

DO-IT-YOURSELF APPLICATIONS COMPUTING		
Amazon DevPay	Accounting	Simple-to-use billing and account management for Web services built on Amazon's platform and using its billing infrastructure
Zillow	Real estate	Popular Google Maps mash-up providing free real estate information such as value estimates of homes
Clearspring	Internet platform	Internet platform that allows distribution, tracking, and exchange of dynamic Web-based applications (a.k.a. widgets)
Netvibes	Aggregation	Site that integrates several Web-based applications such as e-mail, news, weather, stock, and other widgets (similar to iGoogle)
Kayak	Travel	Travel Web site that consolidates deals (airline tickets, hotel rooms, and rental cars) from other travel Web sites
Jamcracker	Internet platform	Platform aggregating and distributing on-demand Web-based services from a variety of software vendors, system integrators, and ISVs
Yugma	Web meetings	Platform providing free Web conferencing
Mogulus	Video broadcasting	Web-based video streaming platform, particularly for Web TV channel providers

DO-IT-YOURSELF APPLICATIONS COMPUTING *(cont.)*

Company	Business type	Description
Ustream	Video broadcasting	Dead-simple Web-based video streaming platform
Spotrunner	Advertising	Web site enabling local businesses to select customizable TV ads, TV channels, and regions for high-quality TV advertisements
Zoho	Web-based office productivity suite	Web-based word processor service providing spreadsheets, pre-sentations, Web conferencing, and the like
Lulu	Publishing	Web-based self-publishing service that helps from start to sale of books, e books, music, images, and so forth
Yahoo Pipes	Aggregation	Yahoo!'s Web application for building applications that aggregate and manipulate feeds from different Web pages
SuccessFactors	HR	Web-based performance management software
Quickbase	Workflow platform	Intuit's software-as-a-service platform to manage projects, sales, training, HR, IT, and so forth.
Rearden Commerce	Web-based personal assistant	Personal assistant for travel, shopping, restaurant booking, and other needs
Coghead	Platform to build Web applications	Visual method for tech-savvy business people to drag-drop and build Web applications
Audacity	Audio editor	Free Web-based audio editor for recording and modifying sounds
Juice Receiver (iPodder)	Custom online audio player	Platform that allows users to create custom online audio anytime
Screencast.com	Screencasting	Hosting solution to share multi-media content online
DabbleDB	Web-based data platform	Platform to build, share, view, and search multiple databases online

ARCHITECTURE COMPUTING

Company	Business type	Description
Amazon EC2	Computing	Amazon's Elastic Compute Cloud is a Web service that provides flexible computing power
Amazon S3	Storage	Simple Storage Service providing unlimited online storage space for minor cost

ARCHITECTURE COMPUTING *(cont.)*		
Company	**Business type**	**Description**
Amazon SimpleDB	Storage	Web service to run queries on structured online and in real-time (works in tandem with EC2 and S3)
VMware	Virtualization	Platform for solutions that allow creation of multiple instances of software and servers, thus making the physical need of such resources redundant
Virtual Iron	Virtualization	Platform providing server consolidation and virtual infrastructure management solutions
Redhat	Linux platform	Automation platform constituting all aspects of the IT environment needed to run applications anywhere, including virtualization
EMC	Storage	Fortune 500 company software for information management and storage for large enterprises
SanDisk	Storage	Flash disk storage leader enabling mobility of storage (e.g., V-Mate is a media storage device)
Dash GPS	GPS	First Internet-enabled GPS device
Blackwave	Internet video	Provider of systems for storing and delivering video content online; targets content distribution networks, aggregators, and media companies
TELECOM CONNECTIVITY		
AdMob	Advertising	Mobile advertising marketplace, claiming to be the world's largest
LiMo	Platform	Linux for Mobile platform to build mobile applications
NTT DoCoMo	Mobile operator	Japan's top mobile provider of services such as i-mode (mobile Internet service) and Osaifu Keitai (mobile wallet)
T-Mobile	Mobile operator	Subsidiary of Deutsche Telekom that also provides Internet hotspots at Starbucks
Vodafone	Mobile operator	U.K.-based mobile provider, the world's largest mobile provider
AT&T, Verizon, Sprint	Mobile operators	U.S.-based mobile operators
Qualcomm, Broadcom	Communication	Communication chip companies

TELECOM CONNECTIVITY *(cont.)*

Company	Business type	Description
Mobio	Mobile applications	Downloadable mobile applications, including one to locate cheap gas
BlackBerry, Nokia, Motorola, Siemens, Ericsson, iPhone	Mobile devices	Mobile device manufacturers and telecom suppliers
Skype	IP telephony	eBay-owned platform enabling voice, data, and video communication via the Internet
Vonage	IP telephony	Popular voice-over-IP (VoIP) solution
Gizmo SIPphone	IP telephony	Provider of low-cost calling to users of Yahoo!, Google Talk, Windows Live, and SIP networks
SoonR	Mobile connectivity	Connector of mobile phones to remote PCs, organizers, and Skype
Google Android	SDK for mobile devices	Google-managed provider of software kit for developers to build mobile applications (expected to shake the mobile phone industry with its applications)
Tiny Pictures	Mobile media	Provider of software to enable creation and distribution of camera-phone output

INTERNET CONNECTIVITY

Company	Business type	Description
Hong Kong Broadband, US Internet, AT&T, LocustWorld, Earthlink, Verizon, MetroFi, Aiirnet, IBM, Fon, Verizon, Northrop Grumman, Tropos Network, Clearwire, Sprint Nextel, BSNL, Google, Intel	Wireless broadband providers	Several broadband Internet providers involved in providing wide area wireless connectivity in different cities. (Google is bidding for a slice of the wireless spectrum in the United States.)

NOTES

Introduction

5 "The intellectual underpinnings . . .": C. K. Prahalad and Venkat Ramaswamy, *The Future of Competition: Co-creating Unique Value with Customers,* Harvard Business School Publishing, Boston, 2004.

5 "This was the substance of the book . . .": C. K. Prahalad, *The Fortune at the Bottom of the Pyramid: Eradicating Poverty through Profits,* Wharton School Publishing, Upper Saddle River, N.J., 2006. See also Allen L. Hammond, William J. Kramer, Robert S. Katz, Julia T. Tran, and Courtland Walker, *The Next 4 Billion: Market Size and Business Strategy at the Base of the Pyramid,* World Resources Institute (WRI), Washington, D.C., and International Finance Corporation (IFC), World Bank, Washington, D.C., 2007.

Chapter 1

12 "Now consider an alternative . . .": More details on the Web site www.TutorVista.com.

13 "Initial results show . . .": Steve Lohr, "Hello, India? I Need Help with My Math," *New York Times,* October 31, 2007.

22 "We will use the acronym DART . . .": C. K. Prahalad and Venkat Ramaswamy, *The Future of Competition: Co-creating Unique Value with Customers,* Harvard Business School Press, Boston, 2004.

22 "This initiative . . .": Ian Cowie, "Norwich Union: Pay as You Drive," *Telegraph UK,* December 22, 2007. See also www.norwichunion.com.

23 "The disk drives are made by Toshiba . . .": Reg Linden, Kenneth L. Kraemer, and Jason Dedrick, "Who Captures Value in a Global Innovation System? The Case of Apple's iPod," Personal Computing Industry Center (PCIC) Working Paper, Paul Merage School of Business, University of California, Irvine, June 2007.

24 "In order to serve that one consumer better . . .": Brad Stone, "Sold on eBay, Shipped by Amazon.com," *New York Times*, April 27, 2007.

26 "Low cost (mass production) and differentiation (variety) . . .": Michael E. Porter, *Competitive Strategy: Techniques for Analyzing Industries and Competitors*, Free Press, New York, 1980 (new edition: Free Press, 2004).

28 "The focus on the poor as active consumers . . .": C. K. Prahalad, *The Fortune at the Bottom of the Pyramid: Eradicating Poverty through Profits*, Wharton School Publishing, Upper Saddle River, N.J., 2006.

28–29 "OnStar, the telematics network of General Motors . . .": Peter Koudal, Hau L. Lee, Barchi Peleg, Paresh Rajwat, and Seungjin Whang, *OnStar: Connecting to Customers through Telematics*, Stanford Graduate School of Business Case Study GS38, 2004.

30 "Consumers are increasingly . . .": C. K. Prahalad and Venkat Ramaswamy, "Co-opting Customer Competence," *Harvard Business Review*, January 2000.

31 "They offer advice . . .": Ibid.

40 "For example, MySpace reports . . .": "Social Graph-iti: There's Less to Facebook and Other Social Networks than Meets the Eye," *Economist*, October 18, 2007.

40 "Value for this new generation . . .": C. K. Prahalad and M. S. Krishnan, "The New Meaning of Quality in the Information Age," *Harvard Business Review*, September 1, 1999.

Chapter 2

60 "The transformation of ICICI . . .": www.icicibank.com.

65 "The ICICI trading platform . . .": Discussion with ICICI Bank senior executives, www.icicibank.com.

74 "In a typical large firm . . .": Paul Travis, "Breaking the 80-20 Rule of IT Budgets," *Informationweek*, February 21, 2005.

78 "The popular argument . . .": Nicholas G. Carr, *Does IT Matter? Information Technology and the Corrosion of Competitive Advantage*, Harvard Business School Press, Boston, 2004.

79 "A business process is most broadly defined . . .": Daniel Morris and Joel Brandon, *Reengineering Your Business*, McGraw-Hill, New York, 1993.

79 "A collection of related, structured activities . . .": www.gao.gov/policy/itguide/glossary.htm.

79 "A business process is a recipe . . .": en.wikipedia.org/wiki/Business_process.

79 "A business process is the complete and dynamically coordinated set . . .": Howard Smith and Peter Fingar, *Business Process Management: The Third Wave*, Meghan-Kiffer Press, Tampa, 2003.

79 "A process is a structured, measured set of activities . . .": Thomas H. Davenport, *Process Innovation: Reengineering Work through Information Technology*, Harvard Business School Press, Boston, 1993.

79 "Business process implies . . .": http://www.peterkeen.com/recent/books/extracts/emgbp001.htm#what_is_bp. See also Peter G. W. Keen and Ellen M. Knapp, *Every Manager's Guide to Business Processes: A Glossary of Key Terms & Concepts for Today's Business Leader* (paperback), Harvard Business School Press, Boston, 1995.

Chapter 3

81 "For example, recognizing that SMS (text) messaging . . .": The use of SMS messaging to settle payments and make remittances is spreading rapidly in the Philippines and China. See, for example, the market potential for this solution in China as noted in Chris Ip and Ana Yip, "Upwardly Mobile China's SMS Network Could Help Unleash a Shopping Revolution in Rural China," *McKinsey Quarterly*, March 31, 2007.

85 "Microsoft recently announced . . .": Steve Lohr, "Microsoft to Buy Health Information Search Engine," *New York Times*, February 27, 2007.

87 "The company has a healthy growth rate . . .": SAS Schneider Electric Case Study on Supply Solutions (http://www.sas.com/success).

88 "We want to know the global purchases . . .": *Schneider Electric Streamlines SRM with SAS*, SAS Institute Case Study, *CRMToday* (crm2day.com) (http://www.crm2day.com/library/EpukEAAyppTmylTHqO.php).

91 "The performance goals of each agent . . .": Conversation with Manish Jain, Head of Corporate Communications, Perot Systems India. See also Ross School of Business University of Michigan Case Study, "Perot Systems: Business Process Capabilities for Global Resource Leverage," unpublished University of Michigan case study, March 2008.

91 "Perot Systems has also extended into a new business service . . .": www.perotsystems.com.

94 "This information has enabled the company . . .": Conversation with

Raj P. Kondur, CEO of Nirvana Business Solutions (NirvanaBPO), April 2006.

94 "Similarly, consider the collaboration . . .": *Mathematics, Statistics and Sales Chat—A Web Retailer Case Study*, 24/7 Customer White Paper, October 2006.

95 "Dave Barnes, senior vice president and CIO at UPS . . .": Corey Dade, "Moving Ahead," *Wall Street Journal*, July 24, 2006.

101 "The engagement between Wyndham Worldwide . . .": Marketics has been recently acquired by WNS Global Services.

103 "It is reported that a couple of them . . .": Katie Hafner, "Netflix Prize Still Awaits a Movie Seer," *New York Times*, June 4, 2007.

107 "For example, K. V. Kamath . . .": "Gambling on Customers," *McKinsey Quarterly*, July 2003.

107 "Just as CEOs cannot totally delegate . . .": Leo Puri, "The CEO as CIO: An Interview with K. V. Kamath of ICICI," *McKinsey Quarterly*, March 2007.

Chapter 4

114 "This could cost hundreds of millions of dollars . . .": www.crm forum.com.

118 "The backlash against Facebook . . .": Kevin Allison, "Facebook Set for a Delicate Balancing Act," *Financial Times*, December 28, 2007.

120 "For example, Massachusetts-based Eastern Mountain Sports . . .": Jeffrey Neville, "EMS: Adventures in X-treme Web 2.0," *CIO Magazine*, January 1, 2007.

122 "The goal is to get global business process templates right . . .": Conversation with vice president for SAP practice at Tata Consultancy Services Limited (TCS), February 2007.

131 "We have to move to Phase 3 . . .": Peter Herzum and Oliver Sims, *Business Component Factory: A Comprehensive Overview of Component-Based Development for the Enterprise*, Wiley, New York, 1999.

138 "The Ramco Virtual Works . . .": www.ramco.com.

139 "The 3D Visual Enterprise . . .": www.unisys.com.

139 "ITC is a successful, $3.5 billion Indian conglomerate . . .": www.itc portal.com.

139 "It enabled these farmers to check market prices . . .": Mundi is a rural intermediate marketplace in India for agriculture products.

139 "A detailed description of the ITC case . . .": C. K. Prahalad, *The Fortune at the Bottom of the Pyramid: Eradicating Poverty through Profits*, Wharton School Publishing, Upper Saddle River, N.J., 2006. Also see

Ross School of Business, University of Michigan, Case Study, *ITC-E Choupal*, 2003.

141 "After a considerable due diligence . . .": The authors worked as consultants to Ramco Systems during the development of this framework.

141 "The system was large . . .": A *function point* is defined as a unit of software functionality. A system with 100,000 function points is a large-scale deployment. The best-in-class error rate for such a deployment is about 2 to 3 percent. The Virtual Works deployment, because of its architecture, had much fewer errors in comparison to the average.

142 "Age Miedema, chief operating officer at ING . . .": Jill Colford, Unisys case study on ING, www.unisys.com/products/enterprise__servers/in sights/articles/articles.htm?insightsID=111219, and interview with UNISYS team, June 2007.

143 "ING assessed various alternatives . . .": *A New Platform and Core Business Component-based Platform for Nationale-Nederlanden*, in a Unisys case study, 2006.

143 "Now brokers can quote . . .": Kimberly Harris-Ferrante, *ING Group Invests in IT Architecture to Boost Business Success*, Gartner Report, Stamford, Conn., January 2006.

143 "The latency to handle a broker"s request . . .": *A New Platform and Core Business Component-based Platform for Nationale-Nederlanden*, in a Unisys case study, 2006.

Chapter 5

148 "We call this the dominant logic of the firm": C. K. Prahalad and R. A. Bettis, "The Dominant Logic; A New Linkage between Diversity and Performance:Summary," *Strategic Management Journal*, vol. 7, no. 6, November–December 1986, pp. 485–502.

151 "While their social legitimacy . . .": This controversy has been brewing for over seven years. See, for example, *Trade & Environment Database*, case studies, No. 649, January 2002; Matt Moffet, "Brazil Issues AIDS Drug Ultimatum: Generic Production to Begin if Abbott Won't Lower Price," *Wall Street Journal*, June 27, 2005; and counterpoint to these perspectives from the various publications of *Mediciens sans Frontieras* (MSF).

155 "It is estimated that more than 70 percent . . .": Paul Travis, "Breaking the 80-20 Rule of IT Budgets," *Informationweek*, February 21, 2005.

159 "As reported in a recent article . . .": Erin White, "Theory & Practice: Rethinking the Quality-Improvement Program," *Wall Street Journal*, September 19, 2005.

161 "While efficiency is a powerful valence . . .": C. K. Prahalad and M. S. Krishnan, "The Dynamic Synchronization of Strategy and Information Technology," *MIT Sloan Management Review*, vol. 43, no. 4, Summer 2002, p. 24.

164 "There is enough organizational evidence . . .": Karl E. Weick, *Sensemaking in Organizations (Foundations of Organizational Science)*, Sage Publications, Thousand Oaks, Calif., 1995.

165 "He defined the IT vision for the company . . .": From Madras Cements internal presentations.

Chapter 6

177 "Invariably, managers suggest . . .": C. K. Prahalad and M. S. Krishnan, "The Dynamic Synchronization of Strategy and Information Technology," *MIT Sloan Management Review*, vol. 43, no. 4, Summer 2002, p. 24.

179 "Let us consider a different model . . .": Sunstar, "Parasat Readying Own Prepaid Cards," www. Sunstar.com, January 11, 2006.

181 "A recent announcement by Verizon . . .": Laura M. Holson, "Verizon Plans Wider Options for Cellphone Users," *New York Times*, November 28, 2007.

182 "Let us consider a different business model . . .": Louise Story, "Online Customized Ads Move a Step Closer," *New York Times*, July 2, 2007.

185 "It is reported . . .": Paul Travis, "Breaking the 80-20 Rule of IT Budgets," *Informationweek*, February 21, 2005.

186–187 "This calls for a *common framework* . . .": M. S. Krishnan, N. Dayasindhu, and J. Sivashankar, "Moving beyond Alignment: IT Grabs the Baton," *Optimize*, vol. 6, no. 4, April 2007.

191 "For example, the contract . . .": "The Outsourcing Gambit," *Economic Times*, India, September 14, 2007.

193 "This process is quite critical . . .": C. K. Prahalad and M. S. Krishnan, "The New Meaning of Quality in the Information Age," *Harvard Business Review*, September 1999.

Chapter 7

206 "Over the last few years . . .": Mitu Jayashankar, "Innovation Flows from East to West," *Economic Times*, July 12, 2007.

207 "For example, the Philips Innovation Campus . . .": "MNC R&D Centers Mushroom in India," *Express Computer*, June 9, 2003.

207 "They are also developing products . . .": Xiaohong (Iris) Quan, "Multinational Research and Development Labs in China: Local and Global

Innovation," research project, Stanford Program on Regions of Innovation and Entrepreneurship, Stanford University, Stanford, Calif., 2005.

207 "A number of global pharmaceutical firms . . .": P. B. Jayakumar, "MNCs Still Bullish on India R&D," *Business Standard*, August 27, 2007.

208 "However, it is safe to say . . .": Wipro and TQM references, Steve Hamm, "Taking a Page from Toyota's Playbook," *BusinessWeek*, August 22, 2005.

208 "It is increasingly clear to global managers . . .": C. K. Prahalad, "The Art of Outsourcing," op-ed, *Wall Street Journal*, June 8, 2005.

214 "For example, let us consider the collaboration . . .": "Why Lenovo Got Bangalored," *Economic Times*, September 15, 2007.

228 "TCS developed a relationship portal . . .": Microsoft Office Systems, *Extranet Web Portal Streamlines Communications Between Aviva and TCS*, Customer Solutions Case Study, 2004.

Chapter 8

235 "For example, it is not just Nike and Pomarfin . . .": Elizabeth Olson, "If the Shoe Fits, Wear It. If Not, Design One That Does," *New York Times*, December 2, 2007.

245 "Coghead, a software firm in California . . .": See www.Coghead.com.

INDEX

ABOUT THE AUTHORS

C. K. Prahalad is the international bestselling coauthor of *The Future of Competition* and *Competing for the Future* and author of *The Fortune at the Bottom of the Pyramid*. He is the Paul and Ruth McCracken Distinguished University Professor of Strategy, Ross School of Business, University of Michigan. Prahalad was named "The World's Most Influential Management Thinker" in 2007 by the *Times* of London and "the most influential thinker on business strategy today" by *BusinessWeek*.

M. S. Krishnan is a Hallman Fellow & Professor of Business Information and Technology, Ross School of Business, University of Michigan. Krishnan was named as one of the 21 voices of Quality for the 21st century by the American Society of Quality and as a Power Thinker on Business Technology by *Informationweek* and *Optimize* in 2004.

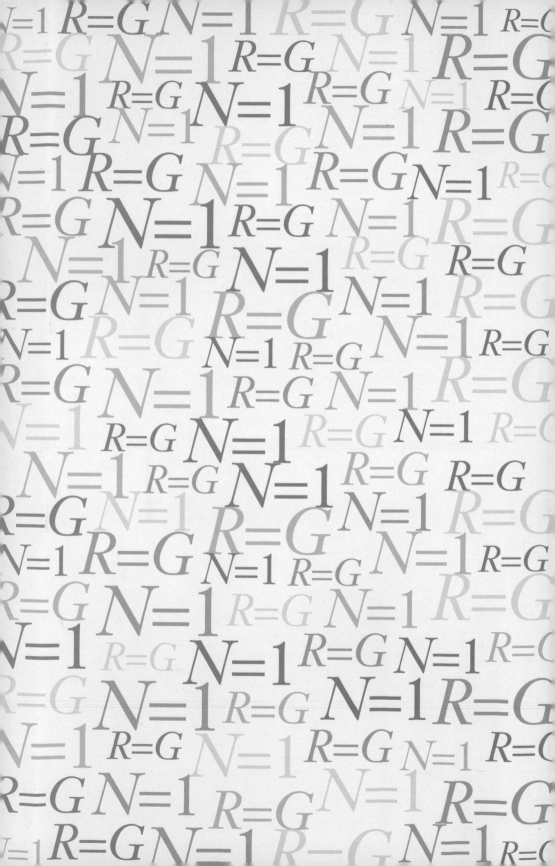